COLLEGE AND CAREER READY

Helping All Students Succeed Beyond High School

David T. Conley

JOSSEY-BASS
A Wiley Imprint
www.josseybass.com

Published by Jossey-Bass
A Wiley Imprint
989 Market Street, San Francisco, CA 94103-1741—www.josseybass.com

Readers should be aware that Internet Web sites offered as citations and/or sources for further information may have changed or disappeared between the time this was written and when it is read.

Jossey-Bass books and products are available through most bookstores. To contact Jossey-Bass directly call our Customer Care Department within the U.S. at 800-956-7739, outside the U.S. at 317-572-3986, or fax 317-572-4002.

Jossey-Bass also publishes its books in a variety of electronic formats. Some content that appears in print may not be available in electronic books.

Library of Congress Cataloging-in-Publication Data

Conley, David T., 1948-
    College and career ready: helping all students succeed beyond high school /
    David T. Conley.—1st ed.
        p.   cm.
    Includes index.
    ISBN 978-0-470-25791-3 (cloth)
        1. Universities and colleges.   2. Education, Higher—United States—Evaluation.
3. College graduates—Employment.   4. School-to-work transition.   I. Title.
    LB2822.82.C667 2010
    371.2'270973—dc22

                                                            2009037350

Printed in the United States of America
FIRST EDITION
HB Printing   10 9 8 7 6 5 4

Contents

Part One: Redefining College and Career Readiness

To Herb Kohl, my inspiration to become a writer; to Dave and Vera Mae Fredrickson, my mentors and role models; and to John and Jaye Zola, who challenge us all to be better educators.

Preface

I am the first in my family to go to college. My maternal grandparents came from southern Italy at the turn of the twentieth century and settled in Toledo, Ohio, where my grandfather became a house painter and my grandmother raised nine children. My paternal grandparents were born and raised in central Ohio and lived much of their adult lives in Toledo as well. My grandfather was a machinist for the railroad, my grandmother a housewife. I am not certain of the level of formal education my grandparents attained (this was not a topic discussed in my family), but I'm pretty sure no one finished high school.

My own parents did complete high school but were unable to go on to college. My mother was midway in birth order through the nine children in her family and was needed to help raise the younger children. My father, who graduated at the height of the Great Depression, took on a series of blue-collar jobs and then went into the army shortly before December 7, 1941. After the war, when they married and began their baby boom family, my parents both worked steadily but did not cultivate careers. My father, using his army experience as a starting point, was lucky to get a job after the war as a warehouseman, a position that was followed by a succession of positions that required little or no formal training or certification. After my brother and I began school, my mother got her real estate license and began selling tract homes in the rapidly growing Santa Clara Valley in California, now known more commonly as Silicon Valley.

We were able to live a comfortable life in a succession of what appeared to me at the time to be nice middle-class neighborhoods, in part because such neighborhoods were still possibilities for a family with one solid blue-collar income and a supplementary secondary income. The differences between my family and those of my friends, many of whose fathers worked at the newly opened IBM plant down the valley, were never readily apparent. As far as I knew, I was just another middle-class kid. My parents' occupations and education levels did not mark me in any discernable way.

My brother and I attended reasonably good schools, many of which were brand new when we attended them due to the influx of baby boom children. Partly because I am a good test taker, I was always placed in the highest groups at each grade level in these schools, which always seemed to have well-defined tracks. School came easily to me, and it never seemed very difficult to do well in class.

Although the warning signs were clearly there in middle school, it wasn't until high school that trouble began in earnest. My freshman year saw the beginning of a series of bad decisions and choices on my part and by those around me. I ran with a crowd a bit older and quite a bit rowdier than I had in elementary school. In my ability-tracked high school, I was placed initially into the top track, while my friends all ended up in the middle or bottom track. Needless to say, this was distressing to a young person who was most interested in hanging out with friends.

My solution, after getting kicked out of a few classes for correcting teachers, interjecting my version of clever remarks and observations, and generally exhibiting what was listed on my record as "defiant behavior," was to march into my counselor's office and demand that I be placed in a lower academic track. Mind you, I was initiating this, not the school. My counselor, a mild-mannered man and by all indications a good person and citizen (he served on the local city council), barely missed a beat in agreeing with me and then reworking my schedule, with copious input on my part, to get me into classes with most of my friends. In his defense, he did give me the obligatory speech about being able to perform at a higher level if I would only work up to my potential, which, he said, was very high, but that whole line of reasoning meant little to me. I had no idea what my potential was, let alone what I would have to do to work up to it.

To say I was crushingly bored in the middle-level track would be an understatement, but I amused myself by helping my friends, many of whom were a grade ahead and had already flunked the class in question at least once. It wasn't until a chance encounter during lunch in the second term of my sophomore year, when progress reports had been issued to all students, that an event took place that caused me to question myself and the whole situation into which I had gotten. My social group prided itself in doing as poorly as possible in school, and as each person showed up at lunch with his progress report (yes, all guys), he announced the number of Fs he had received. Each announcement was made with a combination of pride, amusement, and defiance.

I remember one young man enthusiastically exclaiming that he had five Fs. His bravado elicited a rejoinder by someone in the group who suggested this might be the result of his not being very bright (I'm rephrasing the exact language used to express this sentiment). The young man replied somewhat indignantly, "Hey, I could get all A's if I wanted to; I'm just not working up to my potential." Well, that sounded very familiar to me, so I asked him, "Who told you that?" "My counselor," he replied.

And then I knew the terrible secret. The counselors must be telling everyone that they could do well if they only worked up to their potential. This sent a chill down my spine. Could I do better, or was my assortment of Cs, Ds, and Fs a reflection of the fact that I really wasn't so bright after all? Being the quintessential Type A personality underneath it all and extremely competitive even when no one was really competing with me, I resolved to get straight As the next term just to see if I could do it.

I wouldn't be writing this if I hadn't been able to do so, but that's not the end of the story and not really the point. Getting good grades in the middle academic track is not a tremendous accomplishment and not enough to prepare a student for college who would be first in his family to go beyond high school. My parents certainly supported and valued education, but they were not at all clear about what specifically I should be doing to prepare for life beyond high school or, for that matter, what they should be doing to help me. College would be a good thing, they both agreed, and I was always encouraged to consider it.

But what did that mean? In the crowd I ran with, no one was preparing to go to college (in fact, almost no one in my crowd went beyond high school). Counselors were people to see only if you wanted something, say, to get lunch period changed to, you guessed it, hang out with friends. The administration considered me vexing and would have liked to have gotten rid of me (and tried to do so a couple of times). My teachers were all very well intentioned, and I think they did the best they could, but none of them seemed to have a handle on what I should do beyond completing their classes successfully—and not giving them too hard a time in the process. I wish I could say I had that one teacher who took the time to set me straight and inspire me to reach my potential, but I didn't. I did have a Spanish teacher who had, he said, been a Formula 1 race car driver, and he had lots of good tales to tell (unfortunately all in English), but that's another story altogether.

I did get the word that there was this thing called the SAT and that you needed to sign up to take it, and that it was given on a *Saturday*, if you could believe it, at *8 o'clock in the morning*. So I signed up, and that was about it. I had no preparation whatsoever, and apparently I forgot to set my alarm clock on the night before the test was to be given. My mother was gone for that weekend, so it fell on my father to be in charge of the kids. Waking me up for the SATs was apparently not on his list of responsibilities, so I slept until 7:55, when I just happened to look over at the clock through drowsy eyes. It didn't take me long to realize I wasn't going to be able to get dressed and drive to the test site in five minutes, so I rolled over and went back to sleep. That was the last we heard about the SAT.

This small logistical error ended up being much more important when, during my senior year, I considered, however briefly, my post–high school options, of which there were few that I found attractive. Not wanting to make a career of my part-time job at a local gas station or to enter the military at that time, I saw community college as basically my only other choice. In my case, "choice" meant doing nothing before showing up the first day of fall classes to register. Enrolling in what was left of the courses, I managed somehow to end up in the Associate of Arts baccalaureate transfer program, a stroke of luck for which I have no direct explanation or attribution. The transfer program gave me some much-needed structure because I had fewer chances to continue making bad decisions. I had only to complete a designated set of requirements and would be eligible for admission to the state's four-year universities. In California, this included the University of California at Berkeley. Was it possible that someone with my rather meager academic credentials and lack of foresight would be able to be admitted and graduate four years later, after a total of six years in postsecondary education, from one of the top universities in the nation? As it turned out, the answer was yes.

I will be forever grateful to Clark Kerr, the author of California's Master Plan for Higher Education. That plan, which envisioned a multitiered postsecondary system, allowed students the opportunity to truly reach their full potential by being able to have a second chance that led to higher education. It gave me the opportunity to make up for the many missteps I had made throughout high school (I have chronicled only a few of them here). California policymakers at the time believed that a college-educated citizenry paid dividends to the community, state, and nation, and I hope I have been able to repay the faith of those visionaries in some small way throughout my postbaccalaureate career.

I am one of the few from my high school who somehow navigated the high school-to-college transition, however poorly and inefficiently. My concern, and the reason to some degree that I conduct the research I do and that I wrote this book, is that many, many young people are still allowed to make the same mistakes I did. An ever-increasing number will not have the second chance I had. Those who do often find it much more difficult now to make a successful transition to postsecondary education and complete a college program of study.

These young people will be affected much more than my grandparents, parents, or even my cohort by not being able to achieve their full educational potential. The world they are entering is far less forgiving of someone without high levels of formal education, certificates, and degrees, not just experience. It is incumbent on those of us who are able to do so to change the system so that secondary students cannot make bad decisions and have every opportunity to achieve their potential, whether or not they fully understand what that potential is.

Acknowledgments

This book contains findings accumulated over a long period of time and to which many people have contributed, directly or indirectly. My research in the area of college readiness began in earnest in 1994 with the adoption by the Oregon Board of Higher Education of the Proficiency-based Admission Standards System (PASS), which I directed and was one of the first systems designed to admit students to college based on demonstrated proficiency rather than grades from required high school courses. Many great people were part of the success of PASS, including Shirley Clark, Christine Tell, Mark Endsley, Rick Dills, Bob Olsen, Lynda Rose, Anne Stephens, Robert Roberts, Cecelia Hagen, and Bob Brownbridge.

The work done on PASS led eventually to the Standards for Success project, sponsored by the Association of American Universities and the Pew Charitable Trusts, which produced one of the first and most comprehensive sets of college readiness standards in the United States. Of the multitude of people who contributed to the success of that project, several stand out, among them Terri Ward, April Smith, Amy Radochonski, Shauna Handrahan, Ron Latanision, Kathy Bailey Mathae, Andrea Venezia, Mike Kirst, and Rich Brown.

Standards for Success led to the foundation of the Center for Educational Policy Research (CEPR) and then the Educational Policy Improvement Center (EPIC).

These centers have been blessed with a profusion of talented people, to all of whom I owe a debt of gratitude. I mention here only a few of the original group that worked on some of the initial research studies: Katharine Gallagher, Holly Langan, Kirsten Aspengren, Odile Stout, Gretchen Bredeson, Tim Meredith, and Tris O'Shaughnessy.

I want to acknowledge individually one colleague, no longer with us, who helped and inspired me in many ways over the past decade. Mike Riley was a true educational leader and visionary. He sought me out early in the Standards for Success project when he was a superintendent of the Bellevue, Washington, schools, long before the standards had received prominent attention. From that point on, we began a collaboration that continued until his passing and helped influence my thinking on the issue of college readiness. He was a wonderful collaborator and a true friend, and I miss him almost daily.

To this book in particular, several people have contributed in a variety of ways. Mary Martinez-Wenzl, along with a number of colleagues including Kathryn Rooney, assembled the school profiles featured in Chapter Five. They, along with Adrienne van der Valk, identified some of the examples that I use to help illustrate the key principles contained in Chapter Four. Lindsay Bradley helped proof the manuscript and, more important, helped keep me on track, focused, and productive. Andrea Venezia and Sheri Ranis read early versions of the manuscript and provided helpful feedback and suggestions. Support for the original paper in which the four dimensions of college readiness described in Chapter One were first presented and for the research on the schools described in Chapters Four and Five was provided by the Bill & Melinda Gates Foundation.

As with my other Jossey-Bass book, I am in debt to my editor, Lesley Iura, who works with a light touch and communicates a great deal in a few words. She and her team have been patient and supportive as I have struggled to complete what became an evolving piece of work. I also want to extend special thanks to the three external reviewers contracted by Jossey-Bass to review the draft manuscript. I hope they will be able to see the many changes I have implemented in response to the multiple issues they raised and suggestions they made.

Finally, let me be sure to acknowledge the one person without whom I would not have been able to accomplish any of this. Thanks, Judy.

About the Author

David T. Conley is professor of educational policy and leadership and founder and director of the Center for Educational Policy Research (CEPR), both at the University of Oregon, and founder and chief executive officer of the Educational Policy Improvement Center (EPIC) in Eugene, Oregon. These centers conduct research on a range of topics related to college readiness and other key policy issues through grants and contracts with a range of national organizations, states, school districts, and school networks. This line of inquiry focuses on what it takes for students to succeed in postsecondary education. His preceding book, *College Knowledge: What It Really Takes for Students to Succeed and What We Can Do to Get Them Ready*, outlines how high schools can help students succeed in entry-level university courses. He received his B.A. from the University of California, Berkeley, and master's and doctoral degrees from the University of Colorado, Boulder. Before joining the University of Oregon faculty, he spent twenty years in public education as a teacher, building level and central office administrator, and state education department executive.

Introduction

College and career readiness for all students seems to be an idea whose time has come. At the federal level, in state legislatures and school districts, and in an increasing number of high schools, the focus of improvement is on preparing more students to pursue learning beyond high school, generally in a postsecondary education environment. Although the idea that high schools should prepare students for college and careers is hardly novel, what *is* new is the notion that essentially all students should be capable of pursuing formal learning opportunities beyond high school. This is a radical departure from the comprehensive high school model that was designed to funnel students into tracks that led to very different futures and potential careers—some that required additional education and many others that did not.

SHOULD AND CAN TODAY'S HIGH SCHOOLS PREPARE ALL STUDENTS FOR COLLEGE AND CAREERS?

Should all students be prepared to go to a four-year or two-year college? This straightforward yet potentially volatile question yields strong emotional reactions from high school educators, parents, and business leaders throughout the

1

country. Although no one wants to be accused of closing off opportunities to young people, many educators observe that their students do not seem interested in doing the work necessary to be ready for postsecondary studies. Perhaps it makes more sense to help these students prepare for productive lives in endeavors that may not necessarily require education beyond a high school diploma.

The dilemma that this point of view highlights is that a choice is being made about a student's life and future. We expect students to make conscious choices whether to pursue college eligibility early in high school, essentially at age fourteen or fifteen. Those who do not choose courses wisely in their freshman and sophomore years find it difficult, even impossible, to be eligible for many colleges. Students make these choices with little guidance from adults and even less awareness of the long-term consequences of these choices. The real underlying issue is whether a decision of this nature should be left solely or primarily to students in the first place and whether the adults really know enough about student potential and capabilities to make such choices for them.

This does not necessarily mean all students should be compelled to pursue a single educational pathway, although a strong case can be made for a set of common core expectations for all students. The question is whether high school programs can be designed in a way that no matter what decision a student makes, the result will be that the student is eligible to pursue a two- or four-year program of postsecondary study and will be likely to succeed in such a program.

Throughout most of the twentieth century, the American high school was carefully and systematically designed to offer students a range of equally valuable choices (the more idealistic spin) or to track students into distinctly different futures (the more cynical spin). The fundamental assumption of the comprehensive high school model, the backbone of the twentieth-century American secondary school, is that students have different interests and abilities and that high schools should offer a range of programs in response to these differences. Students then make intelligent choices guided by an enlightened sense of self-interest and an understanding of who they are and what they want to become.

Unfortunately, the model never quite worked this way, or, more precisely, it worked this way for only a select subset of secondary students. Many young people were just as likely to build their schedules and make their class choices based on what time lunch was served or which classes their friends were taking as they were to use the opportunity to explore interests or pursue carefully considered goals.

A more serious flaw with the model was the tendency for entire groups of students within high schools to be assigned to particular programs. This led to self-fulfilling expectations about the capabilities and interests of these different groups of students. These groupings over time came to comprise students of the same race and ethnicity, income, or gender. Once assigned to a program of study, it was the rare student who could cross the lines to a different program, particularly when crossing the line meant joining a program composed of students with different demographic characteristics. Sometimes this occurred as a result of overt tracking, but just as often, the tracks emerged based on other factors, such as the availability of "singleton" courses that then drove all students needing that course to be grouped into several other courses together as well.

This system worked in the sense that few viewed it as seriously flawed, largely because the economy and society accommodated the output of these tracked high schools reasonably well. Young people had sufficient opportunity, and even those who left high school with minimal academic skills could look forward to some limited upward social mobility without additional formal education.

Today that dream is disappearing, with little likelihood of returning. The economic and political forces behind this change are familiar to all. The implications of a global knowledge economy appear almost constantly in the media and in daily dealings, for example. Evidence of the transformation of the U.S. economy is everywhere to be seen. Not everyone is happy with these changes, but few deny they are occurring or that they are significant.

The problem is that today's high school diploma qualifies students only for jobs that do not require what we like to think of as a high school education. This is testament to how low public expectations for the diploma have fallen and how bifurcated the job market has become. No one seems to assume that a high school graduate is particularly well educated. The hope is that the graduate can read and write at a rudimentary level or, lacking those skills, will at least show up for work on time, follow directions, and not take drugs.

The jobs open to those with a diploma are only marginally better than those available to individuals without one. In fact, many employers view the diploma more as a measure of social compliance than academic skills: the student followed the rules well enough to stay in school and graduate, which is very desirable from an employer's point of view, particularly for low-level jobs. But it is not a resounding endorsement of the skills of such an applicant.

While many, perhaps most, high school graduates certainly exceed these minimal expectations, many do not. More important, we have no real way to know the minimal level of skill that all diploma recipients have attained. State exit exams offer some clues, but many are given at the tenth grade and measure middle school–level academic content. In those cases, we know that high school graduates are capable at least of eighth-grade work. It's no surprise that a high school diploma is not a particularly good measure of college and career readiness.

COLLEGE READY AND WORK READY: ONE AND THE SAME?

One of the great debates taking shape nationally, in states, and even within high schools is not only the degree to which college readiness and work readiness are similar, but also the specific ways they are the same or different. This distinction was embedded into U.S. high schools during the early twentieth century when vocational education programs were introduced on a wide scale. Students needed to make a choice whether to pursue an academic or vocational future. In fact, large urban districts had high schools that were devoted entirely to vocational programs and drew students from across a city to receive highly specialized training in well-equipped settings.

In the intervening century, the U.S. economy has transformed from manufacturing to service and knowledge work. In addition, the range of jobs and industries has mushroomed. It is no longer possible to teach students a specific set of technical skills that prepares them for a wide range of jobs. Increasingly, that responsibility has fallen to the nation's community colleges and employer-sponsored on-the-job training programs.

The question then becomes: Is there a broader, more foundational set of knowledge and skills that spans school and work, and, if so, can this be taught to all students? For those advocating higher expectations for all students, an affirmative answer to this question would be convenient, because it would be possible to devise one set of standards and assessments for all students and one program of study for all.

In fact, a great deal of evidence does point in the direction that students can and should develop a core set of skills and knowledge and that this set of skills will transfer well across a range of postsecondary and workforce settings. These are sometimes described as soft skills and include attributes such as the ability to work independently and as a member of a team, follow directions, formulate and solve problems, learn continuously, analyze information, have personal goals, take responsibility for one's actions, demonstrate leadership as appropriate, take initiative and direct one's own actions within an organizational context, and have a perspective on one's place within an organization and in society.

To these soft skills are added academic competencies and capabilities that include the ability to communicate in writing; listen well; read technical documents; use mathematical understandings to interpret data and formulate and solve problems; develop understandings of scientific concepts, principles, rules, laws, and methods to develop greater understandings of the natural world and apply those understandings in a variety of ways; comprehend social systems and historical frameworks in order to provide perspective on activities undertaken in today's society; speak a second language and understand better the culture associated with that language as a result of learning the language; and develop aesthetic sensitivities, appreciation, and skills in order to engage in artistic pursuits and integrations of aesthetic elements into other areas.

The challenge educators face when trying to unify the two concepts is that they must sort out what is distinctive and what is common between the two concepts of college and work readiness. A helpful first step in addressing this challenge is to think in terms of *postsecondary readiness*, not college admission, and in terms of *career readiness* in place of work preparedness. These two distinctions are not merely semantic in nature. Thinking about postsecondary readiness opens the door to the myriad certificate programs at community colleges and a range of formal training programs that are offered after high school. Students will still need high skill levels to participate in these programs, along with a set of work habits and self-knowledge not much different from what is required of a student bound for a baccalaureate program.

Similarly, focusing on career readiness in place of work preparedness opens the door to setting standards for all students at a level that would enable them to proceed on a career pathway, not just be trained to get a job. Career readiness skills are at a level that would enable the student to qualify for and be capable of eventually moving beyond an entry-level position within a career cluster. It encompasses the ability to select an occupation that does in fact have a career pathway associated with it rather than simply taking the first job that comes along. For most career pathways, the requisite knowledge and skill requirements are highly compatible with the soft skills and core content knowledge referred to above.

In short, it is possible to conceive of a high school program that prepares all students for postsecondary learning opportunities and career pathways and not require students to make a choice between pursuing additional learning and not doing so. However, it can be devilishly difficult to create and put into practice a program of study that fully reflects this model. The foundation of U.S. high schools, as noted, is based on students' choosing between educational programs that lead to different futures or having the choice made for them by adults. Creating a true core program that embraces a common set of high expectations tied to academic performance will be difficult indeed for many high schools.

THE NEW CHALLENGE

Given the tremendous variance in the academic skills of high school graduates, it is no surprise that many struggle academically when they seek to advance their education beyond high school. Some are lucky enough to have completed a technical program that has trained them for an occupation, but they will not be able to advance very far along a career pathway in their field without the capacity to continue learning and acquiring skills. And they will not be well equipped to change occupations should economic conditions require them to do so. As adults, they will struggle with any type of training that requires reading, writing, mathematics, or thinking skills such as complex problem solving, analysis, interpretation, reasoning, and, in many cases, persistence.

Some who enter the workforce immediately after graduation may try to resume their education at a later date, only to confront the reality that they must begin by taking multiple remedial courses before they can progress toward their goal, be it a technical certificate or a bachelor's degree. In addition to lacking core academic knowledge, they may find that they do not know how to learn: they lack the ability to focus; organize their thoughts; process anything more complex than simple, unambiguous problems; structure their time to study; and persevere when faced with a difficult academic task.

The new reality is that students need a program that integrates high academic challenge with the exploration of a range of career options and opportunities. All students need to reach high levels of achievement and have opportunities to apply the knowledge and skills they are learning and mastering in relevant real-world settings. The challenge is to design high schools in ways that ensure that their instructional programs are doing one thing exceedingly well: focusing on a core set of knowledge and skills and then ensuring that all students have the opportunity to master the core at a level sufficient to enable them to continue learning beyond high school.

Selecting the core knowledge and skills is a critical first step because it requires that the faculty in the school agree on what is important for all students to know and be able to do. This common frame of reference then serves as the space within which high-quality, challenging programs are developed and implemented for all students. Such programs should be highly engaging and appealing, allowing students to apply learning in real-world contexts and to learn through a variety of interactive modes. The core learnings need not be abstract in a traditionally academic way, but they must be carefully calibrated to develop key knowledge and skills. They cannot be diluted for some groups of students under the guise of making them relevant or applied.

Change of this nature will be difficult for schools accustomed to following the comprehensive high school model. As many educational reformers and critics have noted, school change of any sort is complex, and high schools have proven to be the level of education most resistant to change. One problem is that high schools tend to accumulate geological layers of policies and practices. Each new policy or program is laid down on the previous ones, like successive strata, with little ever being taken away. These overburdened institutions have a great deal of difficulty adapting or changing their practices without experiencing great stresses and strains on the fault lines that run through them.

The movement to high schools with strong core programs that result in the vast majority of students being successfully prepared for life beyond high school will be positively tectonic in nature, sweeping away many previous programs and practices—a situation that will challenge the adults in the school to agree on and teach to a common core, deepen their own content knowledge, and adapt instructional methods so that more students can succeed. Why, then, should they undertake actions that might not be in their own best short-term interests? A partial answer is that they must understand the importance of the change, have a vision of what needs to be changed, be shown how they will be successful in any new model, and have access to the tools they will need to be successful.

An additional challenge to making this sort of transition in the purpose of high school is that the educational system is not designed to support any radical redistribution of resources, skills, priorities, practices, and programs. Local school boards and central office administrators do not want angry parents complaining that their son or daughter doesn't have access to a prized program or class. The idea of open enrollment for all courses is disagreeable to some parents, who see this as diminishing the accomplishments of their own children in some way. In schools with large concentrations of students from low-income families, it may be the community itself that calls for more job training and is suspicious of more college or career preparation opportunities. High schools will need a plan to communicate how a retooling oriented toward college and career helps local students more than simple job training does.

Policymakers send mixed messages regarding the standards that high schools should meet. A few states have been successful in implementing a set of graduation requirements that include some sort of higher credit requirements and a reasonably high exit exam score and then sticking to it long enough for high schools to attempt to prepare students to achieve the required level. But most states have gyrated from one set of standards, exit exam, or graduation requirement, and cut score to another, while simultaneously altering implementation time lines and consequences. All of this policy churn tends to reinforce the position of those educators and others who argue that this too shall pass. Passive-aggressive resistance is perhaps more difficult to combat than out-and-out defiance or anger over a new program or requirement. Sustained policy direction is necessary to support a new direction and new core expectations for high schools.

Postsecondary institutions, for their part, provide little help when high schools seek to raise expectations for their graduates. Entrance requirements themselves are relatively rudimentary at all but the most selective universities and colleges. At almost all the rest, students can be admitted through multiple methods, including some that allow them to bypass completely information on high school courses taken and grades received. The fact that many of these students end up in remedial education is not necessarily viewed as a problem that either the high school or college needs to address. It is now the student's responsibility.

Employers might be expected to hold the line for high standards, but most do not even examine students' high school transcripts. Organizations that do gauge applicant knowledge level often use their own basic skills tests, and they rely on testing thousands of candidates to identify a handful to whom they then offer employment. Few high school educators, or students for that matter, get the message that employers require high skill levels from applicants for entry-level positions because, in practice, employers rarely do, or they simply skim the pool for the few who do meet their requirements.

Given this lack of reinforcement by a range of institutions for the value of a high school diploma, how can high schools alone enforce new, clearer, higher standards and expectations? Is there some magic formula high school administrators and educators have been overlooking? Is there a silver bullet that will magically transform high school education so that all students are adequately prepared for a twenty-first-century society and economy?

The answer, unfortunately and predictably, is no. This dilemma is not resolved simply, neatly, and amicably. However, high school educators and administrators can take specific actions, many of which are explored in the chapters in this book. The starting point on this journey is a common understanding of what it means to be ready for college and careers if this is going to be the new functional goal for a high school education.

WHAT WE MEAN BY "READY FOR COLLEGE AND CAREERS"

In this book I talk of college and career readiness in tandem. But it's worth examining what I mean by each in a bit more detail. College readiness—in particular, in the context of the U.S. educational system—can mean many different things to many different people. What, then, is a fair standard to which high schools should or could be held when we say we want all students prepared for college? Perhaps the best way to interpret what this means is as follows: *High schools should be considered successful in proportion to the degree to which they prepare their students to continue to learn beyond high school.* By "learn," I mean the ability to engage in formal learning in any of a wide range of settings: university and college classrooms, community college two-year certificate programs, apprenticeships that require formal classroom instruction as one component, and military training that is technical in nature and necessitates the ability to process information through a variety of modes developed academically, such as reading, writing, and mathematics.

This definition encompasses a range of possible futures for students and, potentially, a range of possible means by which high schools might prepare students for these futures. But at the heart of this definition is the concept that students must possess a key set of skills, many of them commonly and perhaps erroneously associated more with college readiness and success than some of the other options open to students after high school.

I have detailed the type of knowledge and skill more fully in a previous book, *College Knowledge*, and I present in this book in Chapter Eight an example of a set of college readiness standards developed and adopted by a state. Furthermore, work at the national level to develop and implement common core standards for college and career readiness is ongoing and serves as a useful reference point. I also provide examples in subsequent chapters of how schools organize themselves to ensure that a wide range of students is being challenged and expected to develop these core academic skills and capabilities through many innovative and motivating programs and strategies. We do know a great deal about what students should be able to do to continue their learning beyond high school, and we have many successful models to which we can turn for insight and guidance.

Returning to the topic of what it means to be ready for learning beyond high school, some people, and many media outlets, take this to be ready to go to Harvard or some equally selective institution. Similarly, when defining the ability to afford college, costs are presented for the most expensive tier of postsecondary institutions. From the very beginning, we have a skewed sense of what it takes to go to college—one that does not represent the complexity and variance present in the forty-two hundred two-year and four-year postsecondary institutions in the country.

Similarly, media, parents, and even some educators tend to judge a high school's success in preparing students for college by the number of graduates who gain admission to one of the most selective institutions in the nation. Unfortunately for high schools, getting students admitted to these colleges and universities is so competitive that their admissions processes are as much art and craft as science. A student's admissions folio may be reviewed two, three, or up to seven times under close scrutiny by admissions professionals. Running this gauntlet successfully is as much or more a function of what the university is looking for to round out its incoming freshman class as it is a judgment on the high school's ability to prepare students for college. High schools cannot reasonably be expected to prepare students for this idiosyncratic process, which is designed as much to weigh a student's character as to gauge academic potential.

Interestingly, even these institutions choose on occasion to admit some students who are not adequately prepared in some subject areas. Although these cases are rare, they do exist. These colleges and universities know they are able to devote significant resources to ensuring that all the students they admit receive the help and support they need to succeed. That support can include special tutoring, close monitoring, academic labs, writing centers, designated advisors who check on student progress regularly, assignment to study groups and support groups, and carefully designed entry-level courses that provide scaffolded support to students initially to ensure they are able to succeed. Even students who are well prepared on paper often take advantage of these services at the most selective institutions, much to these students' advantage.

Large state universities represent a second tier of college preparation. Although their requirements may be superficially similar to the more selective institutions, they differ in several important respects. First, they pay much less attention to each individual's credentials beyond reviewing the course titles present on their transcripts, calculating grade point averages derived from course grades, and considering admissions test scores. Second, they tend to accept a much higher proportion of applicants. Notable exceptions to this generalization can be found at state flagship research universities, but even here, admission rates for in-state students are generally significantly higher than at the most selective private universities.

Third, public universities have a number of trap doors available to them that allow them to admit students on the margins or for whom some legitimate reason exists to grant an exception. Part of this is motivated by the desire not to exclude any potentially successful student, and part is dictated by the reality of needing to fill the freshman class each year, regardless of the composition of the applicant pool. This is not to say that state universities admit unprepared students necessarily, only that they draw from a pool consisting of students with a much wider degree of variance in their preparation than do colleges and universities in the more selective tiers. High school grade inflation, well documented by transcript studies conducted by ACT and others, has resulted in most entering students achieving high school grade-point averages that exceed 3.0 on a four-point scale. Yesterday's C is today's B, and, as a result, it is much more difficult to know which students are actually prepared for college based on grades alone.

Fourth, although many of these institutions make a show of not admitting students who are in need of remediation, all have some significant provisions to address the remedial needs of newly admitted students. In essence, they are prepared to admit students they have reason to believe are unprepared to succeed in at least some areas of study. Institutions that claim not to offer remedial courses often require students to take such classes at a local community college, and they may restrict the access these students have to certain credit-bearing courses at the institution until they complete remedial requirements.

What is more common, however, is to admit a student with the requirement that a remedial course be taken before beginning studies in a particular area, generally composition or mathematics, and then allow the student to determine when to take the remedial course. The result is that some students wait, sometimes for several years, before completing the remedial requirement and moving along to the credit-bearing course. In other cases, it may be possible to avoid the subject area where remediation is required altogether, particularly at institutions where a bachelor's degree can be earned without meeting significant mathematics requirements.

In fact, state colleges and universities do not really determine if entering students are fully prepared to succeed in entry-level college courses. Instead, they rely on probabilities for success in first-year courses gleaned from studies of the correlations between high school courses taken, grades received, scores earned on admissions tests, and grades in those freshman general education courses. These measures certainly are valid to the degree to which they explain a proportion of the variance associated with potential success. They also leave much unexplained. Into this gap fall many students who seem on paper to be ready for college but cannot pass placement tests or struggle mightily in entry-level college courses, often doing poorly enough that they change institutions in an attempt to find one that is consistent not only with their interests but with their level of academic preparation and performance. This movement among postsecondary institutions, particularly by lower-division undergraduates, is labeled "churning" by scholars and policy analysts who study this phenomenon.

The next tier in the U.S. postsecondary system consists of the community colleges, which are distinguished and defined by their open enrollment policies. They are often known as second-chance institutions—places where students can recover from mistakes they made and opportunities they missed in high school. Community colleges in the United States are somewhat unique in the world in that they offer programs of preparation for both the baccalaureate degree (through a two-year associate degree transfer program designed to meet general education requirements) and for technical certificate programs designed to lead directly to employment in a variety of fields. These certificates can vary from cosmetology to nursing, from automotive technician to computer-assisted design, from security guard to accountant. Many have no prerequisites, but some are very demanding regarding the academic preparation necessary to be admitted to them and are, in fact, quite selective. Community colleges are generally charged with being responsive to regional economic conditions and opportunities and providing services and programs geared to local needs and priorities.

The downside of this openness is the variance in readiness found among students choosing to attend community colleges. While many, perhaps most, of these students are potentially quite capable academically, for a variety of reasons they failed to master many of the rudimentary academic knowledge and skills necessary for postsecondary participation, or they faced other life challenges that precluded consideration of postsecondary education immediately out of high school. The community college often takes on a triage role, trying to sort among students who seem capable of being ready to move on to four-year programs and those ready for certificate programs from those who require significant support and development before being ready for any academic studies whatsoever.

The needs of American high school students for remediation after high school have become a matter of increasing interest and concern among policy-makers, although few legislatures have done much about it yet. To do so would threaten the cherished open enrollment policies of community colleges, which themselves tend to resist any initiative that might establish minimal knowledge and skill expectations for entering students. While most community colleges do make extensive use of placement tests and restrict access to particular programs, the open enrollment ethos is a cornerstone element of the community college mission and identity.

The unintended consequence of this entirely laudable commitment to accept all comers is that many high school students labor under the impression that they need to do little in high school yet can still show up at the community college and essentially make up for not taking high school seriously. This is a major miscalculation because community colleges do restrict access, based on a student's academic qualifications, to many of the programs leading to a four-year college degree and to a range of highly prized certificates.

The other related problem for students with this strategy is that they end up placing into remedial courses that largely repeat content taught initially in high school (or earlier) and for which the students receive no credit but for which they must pay tuition. This extends their time to completing the program and often leads to disillusionment, frustration, and discontinuation by students who recognize the distance they have to go to develop their academic skills to levels required to continue in many high-demand postsecondary programs.

Beyond the formal postsecondary sectors described here lies a range of other environments in which students can acquire key knowledge and skills necessary for success beyond high school. These include proprietary programs (for-profit technical institutes and others); apprenticeship training programs in the trades, often sponsored by unions or business associations; military training, which increasingly means technical and occupational skill development; and other opportunities, including starting a business or traveling for personal growth during a gap year as a means to find out which career path to pursue. These diverse options offer opportunities to young adults for whom enrollment in traditional postsecondary education is not necessarily the best choice at this time in their lives. Although these choices help ensure that students have multiple opportunities to pursue when they are ready to do so, none can be accomplished successfully without a core set of academic skills, dispositions, and knowledge.

What, then, does it mean to be "ready for college" in the American educational system? At one level, it means completing a prescribed sequence of courses. At another level, though, meeting this criterion has little meaning because the American system accommodates almost everyone who has any interest in pursuing education beyond high school, even if they are not ready to do so.

The challenge is not simply to get students into postsecondary programs, as daunting as that challenge might be in some high schools and communities. It is to prepare them to succeed in those programs. In essence, it means students ready to learn beyond high school, not simply to complete high school. A high school diploma awarded to a student who is not capable of performing successfully in any formal learning program beyond high school amounts to a false promise to its recipient. Focusing high school solely on awarding diplomas to students is to ignore the reality of the world into which those graduates enter.

That world demands specific knowledge and skills, not a certificate that has come to reflect attendance and perhaps perseverance for many students but not any identifiable level of performance in areas key to full participation in the economic and social systems.

Federal and state education officials spend an inordinate amount of time specifying the means to determine how many students have graduated from high school and how many have dropped out. High school administrators and teachers suffer angst and frustration over the reported graduation and dropout rates for their schools. Herculean efforts are made to improve graduation rates and increase student retention through to graduation. But seldom is equivalent effort devoted to ensuring that students who do receive diplomas are ready for what awaits them after high school and throughout the rest of their lives because we don't have the means or proclivity to measure these important outcomes.

To their credit, many high school educators have begun instituting programs that require students to demonstrate their skills, generally during the senior year and often through some sort of culminating process, and several states have made it a requirement that all high school students do so. More often, though, states have implemented a test that purports to ascertain whether students have reached a level of knowledge and skill that the state designates as adequate.

Several problems exist with using state-based tests as the sole or primary gauge of readiness for college or life. When compared to a consistent nationwide measure such as NAEP the proportion of students deemed to meet a standard of proficiency differs dramatically across states. On other measures, such as the SAT or ACT, moderate correlations can be found between the state measures and these admissions tests, but little evidence exists to demonstrate that performance on the state test is preparing students to perform better in college, that the state tests are particularly good measures of college readiness, or that schools are doing much specifically targeted to get students ready for college as a result of the state testing requirements. To the contrary, many schools essentially abandon a college preparatory focus in favor of intensive test preparation in order to get many students ready to meet state requirements, particularly when those requirements are tied to public accountability systems and the awarding of high school diplomas.

As we shall see later in this book, postsecondary readiness requires specific skills and capabilities that are not being developed in the head-long rush to increase graduation rates or to create accountability for high schools and their students. The goal of more college-ready students cannot be achieved without much closer coordination between high schools and colleges, a point that is taken up in the chapters in Part One of this book.

This, then, is the challenge facing American high schools. Can they be reengineered so that they offer programs designed to enable as many students as possible to be prepared to participate successfully in formal learning beyond high school in a variety of settings, but with the majority going on to some form of postsecondary education either immediately after graduation or within several years? Can high schools shed their current deep connections to reinforcing social stratification by graduating students equally prepared for a range of challenging, rewarding futures? Can the compulsion to judge and sort be overcome by the impulse and drive to empower all students to pursue additional education beyond high school? Can we believe we should expect this of all students? Can we believe this is right? Can we believe this is possible?

Redefining College and Career Readiness

CHAPTER 1

The Four Key Dimensions of College and Career Readiness

Historically college admission has been determined based on a rather narrow set of measures. However, actual success in college seems to be more dependent on a much wider array of skills, knowledge, attitudes, behaviors, and strategies than are currently considered for admission. What we need is a more comprehensive conception of college readiness.

This chapter presents a four-dimension model that serves as the basis for determining how prepared students are for college and careers. The model considers the capabilities, skills, knowledge, and behaviors students need to demonstrate to be ready to pursue learning beyond high school. The elements of this model can be applied to a broad range of learning settings in high school and beyond. Although the dimensions match up well with traditional core academic courses, they are just as applicable to a wide range of applied courses and learning experiences that help students prepare for postsecondary career studies.

The four dimensions derive from recent research on the key elements of college success. Most important is the finding that the development of a range of metacognitive capabilities, that is, key cognitive strategies, has been consistently and

Parts of this chapter are adapted from Conley, D. (2007). *Redefining College Readiness*. Eugene, Ore.: Educational Policy Improvement Center. http://www.epiconline.org.

emphatically identified by those who teach entry-level college courses as being as important as or more important than any specific content knowledge taught in high school. Key cognitive strategies are used in activities such as formulating problems, conducting research, interpreting conflicting evidence, communicating conclusions and findings, and completing all work with precision and accuracy.

Inextricably bound with key cognitive strategies is key content knowledge. Greater consensus is emerging regarding the content knowledge associated with college and career success. These big ideas of each content area are important building blocks that can serve as frameworks for the development of individual high school courses and an integrated, sequential program of study over four years of high school.

Similarly important are the attitudes and behavioral attributes that students must demonstrate to succeed in postsecondary education. Among these are the ability to study, manage time, be aware of one's performance, demonstrate persistence with difficult tasks, and set and achieve academic and personal goals. These academic behaviors require mastery of specific skills combined with a mind-set and attitude toward learning. The common element across all of these is a high degree of self-management, self-awareness, and intentionality on the part of the student. These attitudes and dispositions need to be developed systematically over time if they are to become habitual for students by the time they reach a postsecondary program where they will be expected to take much more responsibility for their own learning.

Finally, an increasing number of studies have highlighted the importance of students' possessing knowledge of how the postsecondary system operates and the differences between high school and college. These studies have identified the adjustment challenges students face when attending postsecondary programs because, for most students, going to college is like entering a new culture. This profound transition, disorienting for even the best-prepared students, is particularly difficult for students from communities that have little prior experience with postsecondary education. All students, particularly those without prior knowledge of the college-going culture, lack critical information in a number of areas and the ability to read important cues. Examples range from procedural tasks, such as how to choose among colleges and how to apply to college and for financial aid, to more sophisticated insights into how college is different from high school, how to interact with professors and peers in college, and a host of other types of knowledge critical to student success in applying to and matriculating at college.

GENERAL ELEMENTS OF A MORE COMPREHENSIVE DEFINITION OF COLLEGE AND CAREER READINESS

In a general sense, *college and career readiness* can be defined as the level of preparation a student needs in order to enroll and succeed—without remediation—in a credit-bearing course at a postsecondary institution that offers a baccalaureate degree or transfer to a baccalaureate program, or in a high-quality certificate program that enables students to enter a career pathway with potential future advancement. *Succeed* is defined as completing the entry-level courses or core certificate courses at a level of understanding and proficiency that makes it possible for the student to consider taking the next course in the sequence or the next level of course in the subject area or of completing the certificate.

The level of performance necessary to succeed in these courses in the manner just described is calibrated against what recent research has come to define as "best practices" entry-level college courses, which are quite different from the stereotypical freshman course. These courses require students to engage significantly with the course content and topics and to use key cognitive strategies. Students who succeed in these best practices courses will be ready to pursue further studies in a range of fields and to continue on in the major or certificate program of their choosing.

The college- and career-ready student envisioned by this definition is able to understand what is expected in a college course, can cope with the content knowledge that is presented, and can take away from the course the key intellectual lessons and skills the course was designed to convey and develop. The student demonstrates self-management skills that lead to success in the course. In addition, the student is prepared to get the most out of the rest of the college experience by understanding the culture and structure of postsecondary education and the ways of knowing and intellectual norms of the academic and social environment in which he or she is participating. This student has both the mindset and disposition necessary to enable this to happen.

This definition can facilitate several important actions. First and foremost, it can be used to judge the current system by which high schools calculate student readiness for college and careers. High schools should be prepared to measure student readiness in all four dimensions and ascertain how each high school course or learning experience contributes to each of the readiness dimensions. When high school staff engage in such systematic analysis, they are able to shape the high school's instructional programs so that it does a better and more intentional job of developing student capabilities in all of these areas.

In addition to judging how well the high school program is designed, the four dimensions can be used to provide better information to students at key points in high school while they still have time to address deficiencies in any of the four readiness dimensions. Nothing is potentially more powerful than enabling students to take control of their own learning and preparation by providing them with longitudinal information on how close to college and career ready they are along each of these four dimensions.

In short, a more robust, inclusive definition of college readiness can help shape high school practices and student behaviors in ways that lead to more students who are ready to succeed in college and careers.

CURRENT MEANS TO DETERMINE COLLEGE AND CAREER READINESS

It is beyond the scope of this book to present a full critique of current conceptions and constructions of college and career readiness. Nevertheless, it is worthwhile to consider briefly some of the limitations of the key measures used currently to determine readiness for postsecondary programs of study, most notably course titles, grade point averages, and tests, as well as a related measure, performance in entry-level general education courses subsequent to admission.

This brief overview is presented to accentuate the need for new tools, methods, and indicators that will help students understand how ready they are for postsecondary studies. It will serve as well to help high school educators in particular reflect on the limitations of current measures and the potential power of new sources of information on college and career readiness that reflect more fully the four dimensions outlined in this chapter.

Course Titles and Grade Point Averages

The most common approach is to define readiness in terms of high school course-taking patterns, including the titles, perceived challenge level, and the total units required for graduation, combined with the grades students receive in those courses. What this widely held definition presumes is that the number of courses that high school students take, and the units and names assigned to them, are accurate, comprehensive proxies for postsecondary-level success. Generally the course titles that meet requirements for entry into a baccalaureate program must be approved by college admissions officers, who engage in an uneasy but highly choreographed interplay with high school administrators to identify which course titles will be approved. The net effect is to produce course titles that appear standardized on transcripts but are almost certainly not comparable in terms of content coverage or challenge level.

Course requirements for certificate programs are much more variable. Some certificates have demanding prerequisite requirements, and few students enroll directly out of high school because they end up needing to take at least some college courses before they are ready for the certificate program. Others are less demanding of entering students. However, the administrators of certificate programs do not review and approve high school course titles the way that admissions officers review college preparatory course titles. Even this minimal quality control step is lacking for the career-oriented programs in most cases.

Federal studies using transcript analysis reach the conclusion that completing a challenging high school curriculum is the strongest precollegiate indicator of bachelor's degree completion. The impact of a strong high school preparation program is even greater for black and Hispanic/Latino students. This measure, important as it is, remains based on course titles as the primary measures of quality. When this approach is used, the only way to increase rigor is to increase the number of courses taken in a subject area. States, however, are learning that simply increasing the number of prescribed courses students take may not be sufficient, particularly for students who attend high schools that have low academic standards and low expectations for their students.

The nature and quality of the courses students take are ultimately what matters, and few true measures of course quality currently exist. A key necessary component that could address issues of course quality would be a set of criteria that specified the performances necessary to complete the course successfully. States have invested heavily in standards and tests, but have paid much less attention to the actual content of courses. Some states offer curriculum frameworks to guide local course development, but these generally fall short of identifying and prescribing how to measure key course outcomes or how these align with other courses and with college readiness.

Course requirements for the high school diploma have increased in a number of states, but scant evidence exists that these reforms have led to significant improvements in student performance in college. For instance, since 1987 many states have increased their mathematics and science requirements, but enrollment into engineering majors, which require healthy doses of math and science, remains flat, even while the number of students attending college has increased. Nor have scores on twelfth-grade National Assessment of Educational Progress (NAEP) tests shown improvements in core academic skills commensurate with increases in required courses in English and math. Remediation rates at most two-year colleges remain constant or are increasing. Time to degree completion is not shortening. This lack of improvement in a number of areas related to college success, even in the face of increasingly demanding high school graduation requirements, demonstrates how difficult it will be for states or districts to improve college and career readiness by simply having students take more prescribed courses without a greater understanding by governing agencies of what is actually going on in those courses.

If we use student high school grades as an indicator of improvement, here again we see increases in the average grades of high school graduates over the past thirty years. This has occurred even as measures of college success have fluctuated or worsened. Studies of high school transcripts undertaken by ACT researchers in the 1990s and again in the 2000s found compelling evidence of grade inflation in each decade. Data from high school transcript analyses performed as a component of NAEP confirmed this finding. The data revealed that high school graduates in 2005 had an overall grade point average (GPA) of 2.98 in contrast to 2.68 in 1990. In other words, a B average in high school now may reflect knowledge and skills equivalent to something more like a C+ average only fifteen years earlier. This is particularly problematic because many colleges have raised their GPA requirements over the same period of time. Grade inflation may help explain why college students who appear better prepared on paper are struggling much the same as did students who in the past took fewer English and math courses.

Rather than leading to an improvement in student readiness for college, these increases in GPAs appear to have resulted in the compression of grades at the upper end of the scale. This has led to any number of attempts to compensate for the compression, primarily through the weighting of particular courses, which has the practical effect of raising the top of the scale. The University of California (UC) system, for example, weights Advanced Placement (AP) and honors courses, so that many UC applicants now have GPAs that exceed 4.0 on a scale on which 4.0 is hypothetically the maximum. It's not just the UC system that gives higher weight to college prep courses; 49 percent of colleges and universities in the United States are doing it. Many less selective colleges and universities are choosing to employ weighting strategies rather than increasing GPA requirements. Private institutions in particular appear to be raising GPA requirements the most, leading to what amounts to an arms race among colleges to match one another in these increases. Individual high schools have adopted their own weighting criteria, leading to myriad ways to compute a student's GPA.

Many colleges take matters into their own hands and develop their own systems to adjust high school GPAs to combat this problem. In practice, this means lowering the GPAs of students from high schools whose students have historically not done as well in entry-level courses. Many of these schools have higher concentrations of students from low-income families and who are members of ethnic minority groups underrepresented in college. Students at these high schools may be at a competitive disadvantage and not even know it because they assume that their good grades are preparing them for college success, when in some cases, nothing could be further from the truth.

Tests

Beyond using high school course titles to define college readiness and grades to measure performance, a more direct approach is to test a set of the knowledge that students are presumed to need to know in order to succeed in college entry-level courses. Admissions tests are the vehicle of choice for this type of testing. These tests have recently attempted to transform themselves from aptitude-based measures that employ norm-referenced scoring models that make no reference to where on the scale a student is college ready to new models that establish college readiness benchmarks empirically and then identify cut scores associated with college readiness.

For example, ACT has defined college readiness by establishing College Readiness Benchmarks representing the minimum ACT test scores required for students to have a reasonable probability of success in corresponding credit-bearing first-year college courses. The benchmarks reflect the ACT scores students need to earn to have at least a 75 percent or greater chance of obtaining a course grade of C or better. This is not a direct measure of necessary content knowledge and thinking skills, but a gauge of probability. Moreover, the ACT test itself was never designed to make these types of distinctions. Instead, its purpose has always been to provide a student score on a continuous scale that admissions officers were then free to interpret as they saw fit. The inclusion of college-readiness benchmarks as a means to interpret student test scores is a new and still relatively unverified addition to college admissions tests. This development reflects the emerging importance of being able to specify college and career readiness more precisely in terms of a set of knowledge and skills that can be measured.

All states have adopted some form of high school examination in English, math, and science for a variety of reasons, including requirements contained in the federal NCLB Act. Research conducted by Standards for Success and published in 2003 found that most state standards-based high school tests were not well aligned with postsecondary learning and that the areas where alignment did exist were at the basic skills levels. These tests are perhaps good measures of a set of core academic capabilities, but not necessarily of the knowledge, strategies, and dispositions needed for college success.

In other words, knowing what successful performance on a state test really means is difficult. As a result, the scores that students receive on state tests are not necessarily good indicators of college readiness, even if states can show correlations between these test scores and grades in entry-level college courses. Nevertheless, this does not stop students and parents from believing that passing the state test is an indicator of college and career readiness.

This belief creates serious problems when high schools focus exclusively on getting students to pass state tests. When students do pass the state exam, perhaps in the tenth or eleventh grade, their program of study may be hopelessly out of sequence with what college eligibility requires. One possible means to help address this disconnect would be to revise state assessments so that they connect with outcomes beyond high school and, in the process, provide students with solid information on how ready they are and what they need to do to be college and career ready. NAGB is investigating ways in which the NAEP twelfth-grade exam might become a better measure of college and career preparation. If this could be achieved, states could have a reference point for determining how well their own tests measured these constructs. Similarly, the college and career readiness common core standards developed nationally and adopted voluntarily by states serve as a reference point for aligning state standards and assessments with a clear outcome level that corresponds with postsecondary success.

Performance in College Courses

An obvious but frequently overlooked fact is that the final arbiter of readiness for postsecondary education is student performance in college courses. Students who must enroll in remedial courses or fail entry-level courses find graduating from college much more difficult. One of the first orders of business in improving postsecondary readiness is to reduce the number of high school graduates who end up in remedial courses in college, particularly community colleges.

The high proportion of students who are identified as needing remedial or developmental education is frequently cited as evidence of the limitations of current preparation programs and admissions measures. Although the precise number of students requiring remediation is difficult to ascertain, federal statistics indicate that 40 percent of admitted and enrolled postsecondary students take at least one remedial course, which reduces dramatically their probability of graduating and costs an estimated $1 billion or more per year. The California State University (CSU) system, which draws its students from the top third of high school graduates in the state and tracks remediation rates more precisely, reported in 2007 that 37 percent of first-time freshmen required remediation in mathematics and 46 percent in English. Interestingly, the average high school GPA of students requiring remediation was approximately 3.15 on a four-point scale, just below the overall average GPA of all CSU-entering students of 3.27, illustrating the limitations of relying on high school grades to predict who will need remediation and who will not.

Remediation rates at community colleges are much higher. Some campuses see 80 percent of their students placing into remedial classes, particularly in mathematics. Some students come in at such a low skill level that they must complete several courses in a subject area before reaching a credit-bearing course. Students placing into the lowest levels of remediation have major skill deficiencies. Nationally, only 17 percent of students who must take a remedial reading class receive a bachelor's degree or higher; of those taking two remedial classes (other than reading), only 20 percent receive such a degree or higher.

Children from low-income families and some ethnic and racial minority groups are particularly likely to end up in remedial courses. In the CSU system in 2007, just under 64 percent of African American first-time freshmen required remediation, as did approximately 53 percent of Mexican American and other Hispanic/Latino freshmen. These students are the most dependent on the ability of their high schools to prepare them properly for college success because they are often the first in their families to attend college. The family members of these students rely on grades as a primary measure of ascertaining how well their children are doing in high school. The evidence suggests that these students may be receiving good high school grades, with GPAs over 3.0, and yet placing into remedial education. That students who do well in high school end up in remedial college courses can be frustrating for families who have encouraged their children to go on to postsecondary education and thought they were ready to do so.

Only 60 percent of students from minority groups and low-income families can expect to graduate from high school, only one in three will enroll in college, and only one in seven will earn a bachelor's degree. Students from these groups who do succeed in earning a college degree are taking longer to do so now than twenty years ago. These figures suggest that many, perhaps most, students from groups underrepresented in college are not fully prepared for what will be expected of them.

Just as important, this suggests that their high school program is not adequately geared toward preparing these students for college admission or success. These students are subjected to considerably lower expectations and demands in courses that have titles that satisfy the needs of college admissions offices but are not well aligned with the actual content knowledge and intellectual skill levels freshman college students need to survive in the general education courses that they normally take first. Often these students end up in courses that are neither college preparatory nor well aligned with certificate programs at two-year institutions. The courses may in fact be terminal in nature, that is, not clearly connected to any program beyond high school.

Current remediation statistics reveal only the tip of the iceberg. The tests used to determine who places into remedial courses vary from institution to institution. Placement criteria vary tremendously from institution to institution and are often set at a low level to begin with, identifying only students with the most serious deficiencies. Many colleges allow students to choose not to take remedial courses, even if the student is identified as needing such a course. Students also may choose not to take the remedial course until several years into their program, when they must do so in order to take a required course.

These factors in combination mean that many students, particularly those from low-income families and first-generation college attendees, struggle during the first year of college. For students who do remain beyond the freshman year, their time to degree completion often increases dramatically. According to federal statistics, just over half of students seeking a bachelor's degree beginning in 1995–1996 had attained that degree from that institution six years later. In short, relying on remedial education to solve the problems of inadequate preparation in high school does not seem to be a viable policy, particularly if the goal is to increase the proportion of first-generation college attendees and move students through the postsecondary system quickly and efficiently.

General Education Requirements for a Baccalaureate Degree

Baccalaureate education in the United States is distinguished from many other undergraduate systems around the world by its inclusion of and emphasis on general education requirements that all students must meet in order to graduate, regardless of their major. This model is not at all common in other countries. In fact, many other postsecondary systems around the world admit students directly to what we would call a major and do not expect students to take courses that do not relate directly to this area of study. Specialization and focus on a potential major often begin in high school.

The general education model employed in this country means that incoming college students who wish to pursue the baccalaureate will be expected to be capable of performing in a number of subject areas, not just their area of interest or strength. These courses are often prerequisite to courses in a major and are often taken during their first or second year in college. Being prepared to succeed in general education courses is key to success for U.S. college students. It is one of the key reasons why the high school curriculum needs to be well aligned with postsecondary expectations across its entire breadth.

Poor student performance in these general education courses has long been an issue among postsecondary faculty, who have historically used these courses as the real arbiter of admission. These courses have been designed to weed out students who faculty judge are not prepared to succeed in college. Regardless of which students the admissions officers deem worthy of entrance to the institution, the faculty have enforced their own ad hoc admissions process through these courses. Although the practice of weeder courses is falling out of favor at many colleges and universities, the rigorous entry-level general education course is one of the reasons that the first year of college sees the highest rate of failure of any year.

Some notorious courses have failure rates in the 50 percent range year after year. Some argue this is the fault of poor college teaching, but others assert that this phenomenon can be explained equally by deficiencies in content knowledge and thinking skills, poor study habits, and a lack of understanding of the expectations of college instructors, combined with poor attendance. Struggling in entry-level courses often results in the abandonment of whole areas of potential study. If students cannot get through an entry-level course in a subject area successfully, they are then closed off from any major for which the course is a prerequisite. This ends up limiting choice for students who cannot succeed in a particular general education course. When students struggle in multiple general education courses, they may find they have few viable choices for a major. And although colleges are beginning to provide much better advising to students in their first year of postsecondary study, the student remains responsible for choosing the major. Poor preparation for general education courses limits those choices.

A first step toward defining what students must know and be able to do to succeed in college is to define what it takes to succeed in entry-level courses in baccalaureate and demanding certificate programs. College and career readiness standards that represent the knowledge and skills students should have before entering their first postsecondary course can send clearer messages to high schools regarding course content and to states about their high school standards and assessments. College and career readiness standards are not geared to what should or does occur in high schools, but to what will be expected of students in postsecondary education. They have a clear reference point—clearer than the oft-cited goal espoused by many state policymakers to have "well-educated citizens." College and career readiness standards are clearly derived from the expectations that students will encounter in entry-level postsecondary courses.

No fewer than a half-dozen such sets of standards exist currently at the national and state levels. They largely concur on what students need to know and be able to do to be ready for college. All are focused expectations attendant with entry-level college courses. The Standards for Success project, sponsored by the Association of American Universities, developed a comprehensive set of readiness standards in six subject areas that outline the knowledge, skill, and habits of mind necessary for success in research universities. Washington, D.C.-based Achieve, Inc., an organization sponsored by state governors, organized the American Diploma Project. Its goal was to develop standards that reflect both college and work readiness in mathematics and English. The College Board and ACT have published their own versions of college readiness standards and criteria. In addition, several states, most notable among them Washington State and Texas, have published or are in the process of developing sets of college readiness standards that connect to state high school academic standards. Finally, as will be discussed in more detail later, the national effort to define a set of common core standards for college and career readiness is moving forward, and its effects are just beginning to be felt.

AN EXAMINATION OF THE FOUR DIMENSIONS OF COLLEGE AND CAREER READINESS

College and career readiness is a multifaceted concept comprising numerous variables internal and external to the school environment. In order to provide a functional representation of the key facets, all of the factors affecting college readiness that a high school can be expected to address are organized here in a four-part model. The four areas identified here emerge from a review of the literature and from original research my colleagues and I have conducted and are those that can be most directly affected by high schools. Other factors exist outside this model, such as student motivation and family support, but the four dimensions of this model encompass all of the areas for which high schools can reasonably be expected to take primary responsibility to provide all students the necessary learning experiences and programs of preparation.

The four basic dimensions are key cognitive strategies, key content knowledge, academic behaviors, and contextual and awareness skills. In practice, these facets are not mutually exclusive or perfectly nested. They interact with one another extensively. For example, a lack of college knowledge often affects the decisions students make regarding the specific content knowledge they choose to study and master. Additionally, a lack of attention to academic behaviors is one of the most frequent causes of problems for first-year students, whether or not they possess the necessary content knowledge and key cognitive strategies.

This model argues for a more comprehensive look at what it means to be college ready, a perspective that emphasizes the interconnectedness of all of the facets contained in the model. This is the key point of this definition: all facets of college readiness must be identified and measured if more students are to be made college and career ready. The following discussion explains each dimension in greater detail, but ultimately the four combine in practice and are not entirely separate constructs (see Figure 1.1).

Key Cognitive Strategies

The success of a well-prepared college student is built on a foundation of key cognitive strategies that enable students to learn, understand, retain, use, and apply content from a range of disciplines. Unfortunately, the development of key cognitive strategies in high school is often overshadowed by an instructional focus on decontextualized content and facts necessary to pass exit examinations or simply to keep students busy and classrooms quiet.

For the most part, state high-stakes standardized tests require students to recall or recognize fragmented and isolated bits of information. Tests that do

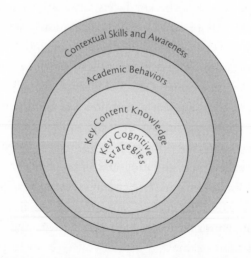

FIGURE 1.1 FOUR DIMENSIONS OF COLLEGE AND CAREER READINESS

contain performance tasks requiring more complex cognitive processing are severely restricted in number and time available to complete them, which limits their breadth or depth. The tests rarely expect students to apply their learning and almost never require students to exhibit proficiency in higher forms of cognition. Even before high-stakes exams were an issue, however, studies found an emphasis in high school classrooms on rote learning techniques that did not engage students deeply and did not lead to development of key thinking skills. Much learning for high school students is simply figuring out the "right" answer, or what the teacher wants to hear, and does not involve much active cognitive engagement.

Several studies have found college faculty members nationwide, regardless of the selectivity of the institution, to be in near-universal agreement that most students arrive unprepared for the intellectual demands and expectations of postsecondary faculty. For example, according to one study, faculty reported that the primary areas in which first-year students needed further development were critical thinking and problem solving. Other studies noted similar observations regarding the ability of students to handle ambiguous information or problems without one simple answer.

The term *key cognitive strategies* was selected deliberately to describe the intentional behaviors students must be able to employ situationally and to emphasize that these behaviors need to be repeated frequently over an extended number and variety of situations so that students learn when and where to employ them. In other words, key cognitive strategies are patterns of thinking that lead to the development of a variety of specific ways to approach and attack challenging learning situations. The term *key cognitive strategies* evokes a more disciplined approach to the development of cognition than terms such as *dispositions, habits of mind,* or *thinking skills.* It indicates intentional and practiced behaviors that, rather than being habitual, remain strategic in nature, with students making conscious decisions when to apply which for the optimal effect in a variety of learning situations.

Our research has found the following key cognitive strategies to be embedded in entry-level college courses across the disciplines. Although the case can be made that other forms of strategic thinking are equally important, the mental capabilities identified here are highly representative of those necessary to succeed in most postsecondary educational environments and to pursue a wide range of career pathways successfully.

- *Problem formulation.* The student develops and applies multiple strategies to formulate routine and nonroutine problems and uses method-based approaches for complex problems. The student develops a repertoire of strategies and learns how to select from among the repertoire based on the characteristics of the problem and the results from the administration of each strategy.

- *Research.* The student identifies appropriate resources to help answer a question or solve a problem by identifying all possible sources; collecting information from a variety of locations and sources; and distinguishing among the credibility, utility, and veracity of the information contained in the sources. The student learns the rules and ethics of collecting information and how to synthesize information so that it can be used to help identify possible solutions to a problem or illuminate all facets of an issue.

- *Interpretation.* The student analyzes competing and conflicting descriptions of an event or issue to determine the strengths and flaws in each description and any commonalities among or distinctions between them; synthesizes the results of an analysis of competing or conflicting descriptions of an event or issue or phenomenon into a coherent explanation; states the interpretation that is most likely correct or is most reasonable based on the available evidence; and presents orally or in writing an extended description, summary, and evaluation of varied perspectives and conflicting points of view on a topic or issue.

- *Communication.* The student constructs well-reasoned arguments or proofs to explain phenomena or issues, uses recognized forms of reasoning to construct an argument and defend a point of view or conclusion, accepts critiques of or challenges to assertions, and addresses critiques and challenges by providing a logical explanation or refutation or acknowledging the accuracy of the critique or challenge.

- *Precision and accuracy.* The student knows what type of precision is appropriate to the task and the subject area, is able to increase precision and accuracy through successive approximations generated from a task or process that is repeated, and uses precision appropriately to reach correct conclusions in the context of the task or subject area at hand. The student applies understanding of content knowledge appropriately and accurately, achieves accurate results, and reaches appropriate conclusions based on the data at hand and the problem or thesis presented.

These key cognitive strategies are broadly representative of the foundational elements that underlie various ways of knowing. Developing an understanding of these and facility with them is at the heart of the intellectual endeavor of the university. They are necessary to discern truth and meaning, as well as to pursue these goals. They are at the heart of how postsecondary faculty members think, and how they think about their subject areas. Without the capability to think in these ways, the entering college student either struggles mightily until these strategies begin to develop or misses out on the largest portion of what college has to offer, which is how to think about the world. Students pursuing careers similarly suffer from not being able to grasp fully the complexity of the material being presented and from not being as able to retain information because it is not well understood conceptually.

Key Content Knowledge

Successful academic preparation for college is grounded in two companion dimensions: key cognitive strategies and key content knowledge. Understanding and mastering key content knowledge is achieved by processing information so that its structure becomes more apparent and then probing, consolidating, and applying that information by means of the key cognitive strategies. With this relationship in mind, it is entirely proper and worthwhile to consider some of the general areas in which students need strong grounding in content that is foundational to the understanding of academic disciplines. The case for the importance of challenging content as the framework for applying key cognitive strategies has been made often and will be taken as a given here and not repeated.

In order to illustrate the academic knowledge and skills necessary for college success, a brief discussion of the key structures, concepts, and components of core academic subjects is presented. This presentation is not a substitute for a comprehensive listing of all essential academic knowledge and skills. Such a more complete exposition is contained in *Understanding University Success,* produced by Standards for Success through a three-year study in which more than four hundred faculty and staff members from twenty research universities participated in extensive meetings and reviews to identify what students must do to succeed in entry-level courses at their institutions in six subject areas. These findings have been confirmed in subsequent studies. The Standards for Success are presented as well in *College Knowledge* along with extensive discussions of the implications of the standards for high schools. Chapter Eight also contains an excerpt from the Texas College and Career Standards, which illustrates how one state is moving toward a common definition of college and career ready.

This overview begins with two academic skill areas that are repeatedly identified as being centrally important to college success: reading and writing. This is followed by brief descriptions of content from a number of core academic areas.

Overarching Academic Skills

Reading   Students in college read much more material in a much wider range of formats and types than high school students do. To be successful, entering students need to be able to understand the formats and important differences between and among different types of written materials. They must be able to distinguish between a descriptive paper and an opinion essay. They need to be able to read a textbook and possess the skills necessary to decode the text, but also to employ the strategies necessary to identify key concepts and terms and retain them. They will encounter source documents from other eras, cultures, and technical environments, and they will have to understand how to interpret meaning in the context in which the document was initially written and from the point of view of the audience for which it was written. They will encounter many unfamiliar words and will need to know how to find their meanings as well as being committed to doing so. They will also be expected to reread material in order to discern deeper meanings and nuances and to deconstruct texts. They will often be expected to read above and beyond the minimum assigned materials, investigating a topic on their own by independent reading.

Writing   Writing is the means by which students are evaluated to some degree in nearly every postsecondary course. It is the medium by which student thinking is expressed and assessed most frequently. In college, expository, descriptive, and persuasive writing, in particular, are important rhetorical modes. Students are expected to write extensively in college and to do so in relatively short periods of time. Students need to know how to prewrite, how to edit, and how to rewrite a piece before submitting it and, often, rewrite it again after it has been submitted once and the professor returns it with comments. College writing requires students to present arguments clearly, substantiate each point, and use the basics of a style manual when constructing a paper. College-level writing is largely free of grammatical, spelling, and usage errors.

Core Academic Subjects Knowledge and Skills

English   The knowledge and skills developed in entry-level English courses enable students to engage texts critically and produce well-written, well-organized, and well-supported work products in oral and written formats. The foundations of English are reading comprehension and literature; writing and editing; information gathering; and analysis, critique, and connection. To be ready to succeed in such courses, students need to build vocabulary and word analysis skills, including roots and derivations. These are the building blocks of advanced literacy. Similarly, they need to use techniques such as strategic reading that will help them read and understand a wide range of nonfiction and technical texts. Knowing how to slow down to understand key points, when to reread a passage, and how to underline key terms and concepts strategically so that only the most important points are highlighted are strategies that aid comprehension and retention of key content.

Math   Most important for success in college math is a thorough understanding of the basic concepts, principles, and techniques of algebra. This is different from simply having been exposed to these ideas. Much of the subsequent mathematics students will encounter draws on or uses these principles. In addition, having learned these elements of mathematical thinking at a deep level, they understand what it means to actually understand mathematical concepts and are more likely to do so in subsequent areas of mathematical study. College-ready students possess more than a formulaic understanding of mathematics. They have the ability to apply conceptual understandings in order to extract a problem from a context, use mathematics to solve the problem, and then interpret the solution back into the context. They know when and how to estimate to determine the reasonableness of answers and use a calculator appropriately as a tool, not a crutch.

Science   College science courses emphasize scientific thinking in all its facets. In addition to using all the steps in the scientific method, students learn what it means to think like a scientist. This includes the communication conventions scientists follow, the way that empirical evidence is used to draw conclusions, and how such conclusions are then subject to challenge and interpretation. Students come to appreciate that scientific knowledge is both constant and changing at any given moment and that the evolution of scientific knowledge does not mean that previous knowledge was necessarily wrong. Students grasp that scientists think in terms of models and systems as ways to comprehend complex phenomena. This helps them make sense out of the flow of ideas and concepts they encounter in entry-level college courses and the overall structure of the scientific discipline they are studying. In their science courses, students master core concepts, principles, laws, and the vocabulary of the scientific discipline they are studying. Laboratory settings are the environments where content knowledge and scientific key cognitive strategies converge to help students think scientifically and integrate learned content knowledge.

Social Sciences   The social sciences entail a range of subject areas, each with its own content base and analytical techniques and conventions. The courses an entry-level college student most typically takes are in geography, political science, economics, psychology, sociology, history, and the humanities. The scientific methods that are common across the social sciences emphasize the skills of interpreting sources, evaluating evidence and competing claims, and understanding themes and the overall flow of events within larger frameworks or organizing structures. Helping students to be aware that the social sciences consists of certain big ideas (theories and concepts) that are used to order and structure all of the detail that often overwhelms students and can help them learn to build mental scaffolds that lead toward thinking like a social scientist.

World Languages   The goal of second-language study is to communicate effectively with and receive communication from speakers of another language in authentic cultural contexts through the skills of listening, speaking, reading, and writing. Learning another language is much more than memorizing a system of grammatical rules. It requires the learner to understand the cultures from which the language arises and in which it resides, use the language to communicate accurately, and use the learner's first language and culture as a model for comparison with the language and culture being learned. Second-language proficiency can improve learning in other disciplines, such as English, history, and art, and expand professional, personal, and social opportunities. Language learners need to understand the structure and conventions of a language, but not through word-for-word translation or memorization of decontextualized grammatical rules. Instead, students of a language need to master meaning in more holistic, contextual ways.

The Arts   The arts refer to college subject areas including art history, dance, music, theater, visual arts, and humanities. Students ready for college-level work in the arts possess an understanding of and appreciation for the contributions made by the most innovative creators in the field. Students come to understand themselves as instruments of communication and expression who demonstrate mastery of basic oral and physical expression through sound, movement, and visual representations. They understand the role of the arts as an instrument of social and political expression. They formulate and present difficult questions through their personal artistic visions. They are able to justify their aesthetic decisions when creating or performing a piece of work and know how to make decisions regarding the proper venue for performing or exhibiting any creative product.

Academic Behaviors (Self-Management)

This dimension of college readiness encompasses a range of behaviors that reflects greater student self-awareness, self-monitoring, and self-control of a series of processes and behaviors necessary for academic success. These are distinguished from key cognitive strategies by the fact that they tend to be more completely independent of a particular content area, whereas the key cognitive strategies are always developed within the ways of knowing a particular content area.

Self-monitoring is a form of metacognition—the ability to think about how one is thinking. Examples of metacognitive skills relevant to self-management are awareness of one's current level of mastery and understanding of a subject, including key misunderstandings and blind spots; the ability to reflect on what worked and what needed improvement in any particular academic task; the tendency to persist when presented with a novel, difficult, or ambiguous task; the tendency to identify and systematically select among and employ a range of learning strategies; and the capability to transfer learning and strategies from familiar settings and situations to new ones. Research on the thinking of effective learners has shown that these individuals tend to monitor actively, regulate, evaluate, and direct their own thinking.

Another important area of college readiness is student mastery of the study skills necessary for college success. The underlying premise is simple: academic success requires the mastery of key skills necessary to comprehend material and complete academic tasks successfully, and the nature of college learning in particular requires that significant amounts of time be devoted to learning outside class in order to achieve success in class. Study skills encompass a range of active learning strategies that go far beyond reading the text and answering homework questions. Typical study skill behaviors are time management, preparing for and taking examinations, using information resources, taking class notes, and communicating with teachers and advisors. An additional critical set of study skills is the ability to participate successfully in a study group and to recognize the critical importance of study groups to success in specific subjects that assume students will be using them.

Examples of time management techniques and habits are accurately estimating how much time it takes to complete all outstanding and anticipated tasks and allocating sufficient time to complete the tasks, using calendars and creating to-do lists to organize studying into productive chunks of time, locating and using settings conducive to proper study, and prioritizing study time in relation to competing demands, such as work and socializing.

Contextual Skills and Awareness (College Knowledge)

The importance of this broad category has only recently been highlighted as an ever-wider range of students applies to college. Contextual factors encompass primarily the privileged information necessary to understand how college operates as a system and culture. This lack of understanding of the context of college causes many students to become alienated, frustrated, and even humiliated during the freshman year and decide that college is not the place for them. Examples of key contextual skills and awareness are a systemic understanding of the postsecondary educational system, combined with specific knowledge of the norms, values, and conventions of interactions in the college context and the human relations skills necessary to cope within this system even if it is very different from the community the student has just left. Examples of specific knowledge are how to select the proper postsecondary institution from among all available, how and when to apply, which tests and materials to provide with an application, how to complete a financial aid form and the FAFSA, what the institution to which the student is applying requires for placement purposes, and how to access the support resources available to students.

The fact that colleges have a culture, norms, and traditions does not necessarily mean that students have to disown their cultural backgrounds, heritage, and traditions, only that they need to understand the relationship between their cultural frame of reference and assumptions and those operating in college. Even though students do not need to disown who they are, success in college comes to students who possess interpersonal and social skills that enable them to interact with a diverse cross-section of academicians and peers. These skills include the ability to collaborate and work in a team, understand the norms of the academic culture and know how to interact with professors and others in that environment, be comfortable around people from different backgrounds and cultures, possess informal communication skills, and demonstrate leadership skills in a variety of settings.

Another important area of contextual awareness is the information that is formal and informal, stated and unstated, and is necessary for gaining admission to and navigating within the postsecondary system. College knowledge encompasses an understanding of processes such as college admission, including curricular, testing, and application requirements; college options and choices, including the tiered nature of postsecondary education; tuition costs and the financial aid system; placement requirements, testing, and standards; the culture of college; and the level of challenge present in college courses, including the increasing expectations of higher education.

Admissions requirements, and time lines in particular, are extremely complicated, and students often do not know or understand the importance of either until it is too late. Specific institutions have additional special requirements and exceptions that are not immediately evident. Financial aid options are largely unknown or substantially misunderstood by many of the students who are most in need of such support. The economically well off are more likely to have this knowledge than working-class families or families whose children are the first generation to attend college.

DIFFERENCES BETWEEN HIGH SCHOOL AND COLLEGE COURSES

It is worth noting that college courses, although different from high school courses, are not necessarily "better." Nor is college teaching superior to high school teaching. They are, however, different in a number of important ways, and understanding those differences is a crucial first step in improving alignment between high school and college.

Secondary and postsecondary instructors and administrators need to enter into a consideration of these differences with an open mind, devoid of preconceptions regarding the teaching and learning that takes place at each level and, perhaps more important, without judgment regarding whose teaching is "better" and the ways in which the other level is flawed in its approach to instruction and student learning. With an open mind, it is possible to see and appreciate what is valued at each level, what is expected of students, and how students are likely to respond to the demands at each level. This understanding is the necessary underpinning to the conversation about how high school and college courses differ.

Why is it important to understand and be fully cognizant of the differences between secondary and postsecondary education? We cannot fully comprehend and act on what it takes to make students ready for learning beyond high school until we have taken into account the ways in which the two environments differ along a number of dimensions.

Over the past eight years, our research has focused on analyzing entry-level college courses to determine what these courses expect and require of students. The primary source of data we have used has been the instructor's view of what is important to succeed in the courses cross-referenced against the content of the syllabi from the entry-level courses they teach. These are all credit-bearing courses that fulfill general education and certificate requirements at two- and four-year postsecondary institutions across the United States.

The instructor input, syllabi, and related course documents have proven to be a rich source of information about and insight into the expectations college instructors have for their students and what they are trying to accomplish in their courses. A close analysis also reveals many of the assumptions these instructors harbor about the nature of their students. These data are informative of the expectations that students will encounter in college courses.

We have concentrated our efforts on what we identify as "best practice" college courses. Our studies begin by specifying the key characteristics that should be present in entry-level college courses to make them consistent with the best thinking of national organizations and experts in the field regarding content they should include and the instructional methods they should employ. We use these criteria to identify such courses. We then verify these courses by collecting large amounts of information about them by having instructors complete extensive surveys in which they specify their practices and priorities. Finally, we subject all the collected data to the scrutiny of expert secondary and postsecondary educators who serve as independent judges to confirm whether a course truly represents best practices in a particular subject area. Based on these methods, our research findings have identified a number of characteristics that tend to distinguish college courses from high school courses.

Detailed analyses of both baccalaureate and certificate courses reveal that although a college course may have the same name as a high school course, college instructors pace their material more rapidly, emphasize different aspects of material taught, and have very different goals for their courses than do high school instructors. Students fresh out of high school may think a college course is very much like a similarly named high school class they have already taken, only to find out that expectations are fundamentally different.

College instructors are more likely to emphasize a series of key thinking skills that students typically do not develop extensively in high school. The instructors expect students to work independently to make inferences, interpret results, analyze conflicting explanation of phenomena, support arguments with evidence, solve complex problems that have no obvious right answer, reach conclusions, offer explanations, conduct research, engage in the give-and-take of ideas, and generally think deeply about what they are being taught.

College students are assessed in a variety of ways, including multiple-choice exams and much more sophisticated tests in which the answers must be inferred from readings and lectures rather than being verbatim restatements of those materials. It may not be enough simply to show up for class, take notes, and do the reading. Students may also be expected to apply what they have learned in routine and nonroutine situations.

We determined that college courses in general move at a more rapid pace than a typical high school course does. Literature courses, for example, frequently require students to read eight to ten books in a term. In these classes, students write multiple papers in short periods of time. These papers must be well reasoned, well organized, and well documented with evidence from credible sources. Students receive detailed critiques of these papers that can be frank and unvarnished.

Assessment in college courses generally consists of fewer elements than in a high school class, with each element being correspondingly more important. Typical college courses have a midterm exam, perhaps several papers, and a final exam. When homework is required, it is rarely graded and often not even collected. Students may be accountable for completing homework in order to participate in classroom activities, and instructors may then assign participation points that reflect student preparation and involvement, but not a grade on the homework assignment itself.

Writing assignments in entry-level courses tend to be moderate in length, generally in the range of three to five pages, with the expectation that the student drafts, revises, and edits each paper before submitting it. Most written work includes the expectation that the student has consulted source material and incorporated appropriate material into the paper as directed. Few assignments allow ungrounded expression of personal opinion absent significant justification and references. Postsecondary instructors have low tolerance for grammatical and spelling errors, poor sentence and paragraph construction, lack of an overall structure for the paper, inappropriate word choice, and lack of fluency in the paper. Their assumption is that these elements simply must be addressed by the student in order to complete the assignment successfully. The focus of the instructor's evaluation of the paper is the topic at hand as specified in the assignment, not grammar, syntax, and conventions, although deficiencies in these areas are duly noted.

Because entry-level courses may have relatively few grading elements, each grade is more important, and, consequently, students have fewer degrees of freedom to do poorly on one test or assignment and then be able to compensate by performing better on other elements. Some instructors do allow students to discard their lowest score from a series of exams, but few include opportunities for extra credit in the form of substitute assignments. While it may be possible for a student to rework an assignment under certain conditions, rarely can one requirement be met by completing an entirely different piece of work. Extra credit, where it is offered, most often takes the form of additional items on a test that students may choose to complete, or perhaps some augmentation to an assignment. Generally students must meet the standards set forth in the syllabus by means of the stated requirements without recourse to additional ad hoc work products that compensate for poor or nonexistent performance on required elements.

Science courses often have separate lecture and lab components, and students enroll in and receive credit for each separately. The labs take on a variety of forms, from very structured classes in their own right with extensive requirements, to more self-guided learning experiences in which students must take the initiative to complete the lab activities independently and ask for help if they need it. Lectures assume students have completed or will complete the lab, and if students make the mistake of viewing the lab as independent of the lecture and fail to attend one or the other regularly, they are likely to struggle mightily on exams given in the lecture section and on lab assignments. The idea that a lab may be required but that they might not receive any credit for attending is particularly difficult for students accustomed to trading time for credits to comprehend and accept.

Many science labs require descriptive and analytical writing skills. The lab section may require that students keep a log in addition to completing the exercises in the manual. The log consists of observations they make, descriptions of the procedures they choose and employ, and their results. These logs may run to dozens of pages and contain detailed illustrations along with descriptions that stretch on for pages. These logs are generally not reviewed weekly, but when they are reviewed, instructors place a premium on the accuracy of the observations and the precision of the descriptions. These are standards to which their work may not have been held previously, particularly in science courses.

Higher education faculty members typically are not particularly tolerant of work that is turned in late. There are various reasons for this stance, but at least part of the reason is that students are adults and should be expected to act as such. College syllabi typically contain a section addressing late work, and in that section the instructor anticipates the various situations and excuses students are most likely to present as explanation for late assignments or missed exams. The college syllabi lay out the consequences for late work and indicate the circumstances under which exceptions are granted. Given that many entry-level college courses have large enrollments, these policies tend to get enforced without significant exception. Instructors of entry-level courses can offer many examples of students who did not submit work on time and then expected special treatment or extension of deadlines. These students are often bitterly disappointed when no dispensation is forthcoming.

Plagiarism is a large issue in postsecondary education for a variety of reasons. First and foremost, most instructors are highly aware of the rules of scholarship and are therefore attuned to the significance of committing plagiarism. They consider it to be a serious infraction and are vigilant regarding plagiarism and inclined to punish transgressions rather than simply issue warnings. As noted, students must cite sources often in college writing, which leads to more temptations and opportunities for plagiarism. Almost every syllabus for an entry-level college course contains a definition of plagiarism and spells out the consequences of committing plagiarism. Most colleges and universities have an office devoted to student judicial affairs that may become involved if plagiarism is committed.

According to the NSSE, the vast majority of first-year college students are actively engaged in small groups and are expected to work with others inside and outside class on complex problems and projects. They are then expected to make presentations and explain what they have learned. In these courses, students are expected to be independent, self-reliant learners who recognize when they are having problems and know when and how to seek help from professors, students, or other sources. At the same time, college faculty consistently report that college freshmen need to be spending nearly twice the time they indicate they are spending currently to prepare for class. College freshmen who are most successful are those who come prepared to take responsibility for preparing for class in a variety of ways and for a significant amount of time.

Finally, the relationship between instructor and student in college is dictated by institutional dynamics to a significant degree. At colleges where students take at least some large classes, students need to take the initiative to connect with the instructor. That connection is best established based on mutual interest in the course content and the subject matter generally. Instructors appreciate students who have an interest in what is being taught because the instructors themselves are usually very interested in their subject areas and often passionate about particular aspects of what they teach. They connect well with students who share their interests and passions. They do not relate well to students who wait until the last week of classes to consult with them during office hours or tutorial sessions for the first time in order to demand special treatment and consideration.

College instructors expect students to be responsible for their own actions and for taking the initiative to resolve any outstanding issues. This means that instructors expect students to contact them, not the other way around, when a problem exists, and to do so while there is time to remedy the situation. While instructors understand that students lead complex lives with competing demands on their time, they also expect that the course they are teaching will be an important priority in the student's life when it needs to be. In general, they are willing to work with students who meet them halfway and make an effort to deal with situations before they spin out of control.

Most colleges have numerous resources available to students who need help: academic support centers, tutoring services, writing consultants, technology labs with instruction available, counselors, advisors, and student life and residence hall assistants. The student as young adult is expected to access the appropriate person or office when in need of assistance. While instructors may attempt to assist students by directing them to the proper resource, few instructors take on the assistance roles that are the responsibility of these various programs and individuals. Instructors will help students with problems related to the content area (and may develop close working relationships with students who show interest in the subject area), but the general expectation is that students will take care of themselves in significant ways through independent action and self-initiative when they have a skill deficiency or cannot complete assigned work due to an underlying lack of knowledge.

College instructors expect students to behave in class. They are not prepared to expend significant amounts of time on classroom management and do not tolerate repeated infractions. It is apparent from the contents of syllabi that instructors are adding more detailed behavioral expectations to their courses in response to what they perceive to be declining student civility. Areas of concern include tardiness and inattentiveness, smoking, reading newspapers, or inappropriately using personal electronic devices in class. Of greater concern are behaviors such as hostility toward others, lack of tolerance for differing points of view, unwillingness to accept feedback on ideas or on pieces of work, and what might best be categorized as generally rude behavior. The remedies most instructors employ are a consultation after class or exclusion from the class altogether, which continues to be very rare but is then dealt with by the office of student judicial affairs in most institutions.

Online discussions among postsecondary instructors regarding student behavior frequently mention a growing phenomenon: a sense of entitlement among students who believe that they should receive a good grade if they attend regularly and make a good-faith effort. They conflate effort with achievement. In other words, if an assignment takes them a long time to complete, they expect a good grade for it based not on the quality of the work but on the time it took to complete. Many students have never experienced failure before or received a grade on an assignment much lower than a B. For a growing number of students entering postsecondary education, the act of participating is considered equal to the act of achieving. Anything less they view as unfair or unjustified.

In short, the expectations students encounter in college can be quite different from those to which they are accustomed. They must be prepared to use a quite different array of learning strategies and coping skills to be successful in college. Current measures of college readiness do not necessarily capture these many dimensions of readiness well.

While many adults are aware of these differences, many young people are not. As high schools prepare students for postsecondary education, the students should at the very least be made aware of these differences. Beyond simply informing students, high schools may want to consider creating situations that start to parallel a college classroom or learning environment in important ways. Examples of ways in which this can be done are presented in Chapters Three, Four, and Five. For now, it is worth noting that the transition from high school to postsecondary education is particularly challenging for students who have little or no opportunity to understand the ways that the postsecondary world they are preparing to enter is different from the high school world they are about to leave.

The next section adds detail to the definition of college readiness derived from the conceptual model. It includes specific statements that illustrate all of the dimensions of college readiness. These are statements that could conceivably be measured or gauged. The net result would be a profile of college readiness that would help students know the degree to which they were college ready and could eventually help high school educators know how well their school's program of study is preparing students to be ready for college success and which students it is preparing.

OPERATIONAL EXAMPLES OF COLLEGE READINESS

It is possible to compile lengthy and detailed lists of the content knowledge students must know and the key cognitive strategies they must possess to be college ready. In fact, a variety of such compilations have been produced. In addition, others have identified the academic behaviors and context knowledge students need. Rather than repeat each of these previous lists in detail, it may be more useful to consider a highly representative set of examples of the knowledge, skills, and attributes a student should possess to be ready to succeed in entry-level college courses across a range of subjects and disciplines. This set attempts to capture keystone skills—ones that can be demonstrated only if a set of subordinate and prerequisite knowledge and skills is in place. The examples are not intended to be inclusive, but to suggest the types of indicators necessary to gauge the more comprehensive notion of college readiness presented in this book.

General Characteristics

Students who possess sufficient mastery of key cognitive strategies, key content knowledge, academic behaviors, and contextual knowledge are defined as being college ready to the degree to which they can demonstrate the following:

- Consistent intellectual growth and development over four years of high school resulting from the study of increasingly challenging, engaging, coherent academic content

- Deep understanding of and facility applying key foundational ideas and concepts from the core academic subjects

- A strong grounding in the knowledge base that underlies the key concepts of the core academic disciplines as evidenced by the ability to use the knowledge to solve novel problems within a subject area and demonstrate an understanding of how experts in the subject area think

- Facility with a range of key intellectual and cognitive skills and capabilities that can be broadly generalized as the ability to think

- Reading and writing skills and strategies sufficient to process the full range of textual materials commonly encountered in entry-level college courses and to respond successfully to the written assignments commonly required in such courses

- Mastery of key concepts and ways of thinking found in one or more scientific disciplines sufficient to succeed in at least one introductory-level college course that could conceivably lead toward a major that requires additional scientific knowledge and expertise

- Comfort with a range of numerical concepts and principles sufficient to take at least one introductory-level college course that could conceivably lead toward a major that requires additional proficiency in mathematics

- Ability to accept critical feedback, including critiques of written work submitted or an argument presented in class

- Ability to assess objectively one's level of competence in a subject and devise plans to complete course requirements in a timely fashion and with a high degree of quality

- Ability to study independently and with a study group on a complex assignment requiring extensive out-of-class preparation that extends over a reasonably long period of time

- Ability to interact successfully with a wide range of faculty, staff, and students, including many who come from different backgrounds and hold points of view different from the student's

- Understanding of the values and norms of colleges and, within them, disciplinary subjects as the organizing structures for intellectual communities that pursue common understandings and fundamental explanations of natural phenomena and key aspects of the human condition

Example Performances

The general characteristics listed are suggestive or descriptive of tasks that students will have to be able to complete in college courses. The following examples illustrate what a student who has sufficient competence in the general areas would be able to do in a college course. Any student who can do the following with proficiency will likely be ready for a range of postsecondary learning experiences:

- Write a three- to five-page research paper that is structured around a cogent, coherent line of reasoning; incorporates references from several credible and appropriate citations; is relatively free from spelling, grammatical, and usage errors; and is clear and easily understood by the reader

- Read with understanding a range of nonfiction publications and technical materials, using appropriate decoding and comprehension strategies to identify key points, note areas of question or confusion, remember key terminology, and understand the basic conclusions reached and points of view expressed

- Employ fundamentals of algebra to solve multistep problems, including problems without one obvious solution and those requiring math beyond algebra; do so with a high degree of accuracy, precision, and attention to detail; and be able to explain the rationale for the strategies pursued and the methods used

- Conduct basic scientific experiments or analyses that require the use of the scientific method; an inquisitive perspective on the process; interpretation of data or observations in relation to an initial hypothesis; possible or plausible explanation of unanticipated results; and presentation of findings to a critical audience using the language of science, including models, systems, and theories

- Conduct research on a topic and be able to identify a series of source materials that are important and appropriate to explaining the question being researched, organize and summarize the results from the search, and synthesize the findings in a coherent fashion relevant to the larger question being investigated

- Interpret two conflicting explanations of the same event or phenomenon, taking into account each author's perspective, the cultural context of each source, the quality of the argument, its underlying value positions, and any potential conflict of interest an author might have in presenting a particular point of view

- Communicate in a second language, using the language in a culturally appropriate fashion for common daily tasks and interactions, without resorting to literal translation except for certain specific words

- Punctually and regularly attend a study group outside class with students who represent a continuum of academic abilities and cultural backgrounds, incorporating the strengths of group members to complete the assignment or project at hand or prepare successfully for the exam or presentation in question

- Complete successfully a problem or assignment that requires about two weeks of independent work and extensive research, using periodic feedback from teachers and other pertinent resource people along the way to revise and improve the final product

- Create and maintain a personal schedule that includes a to-do list with prioritized tasks and appointments

- Use key technological tools including appropriate computer software to complete academic tasks such as conducting research, analyzing data sets, writing papers, preparing presentations, and recording data

- Locate Web sites that contain information on colleges, the admissions process, and financial aid, and navigate such sites successfully, in the process comparing the programs and requirements of several colleges and assessing the financial requirements and feasibility of attending each

- Present an accurate self-assessment of readiness for college by analyzing and citing evidence from classroom work and assignments, grades, courses taken, national and state exams taken, and a personal assessment of maturity and self-discipline

CHAPTER 2

Ways to Develop Key Cognitive Strategies and Key Content Knowledge

Few would deny the importance of strong thinking skills and foundational content knowledge to college and career success. An observer of high schools, however, finds little in the way of systematic integration of key cognitive strategies and key content knowledge into all courses. Granted, some schools have adopted packaged thinking skills programs, but these operate separately from the key concepts, principles, laws, ideas, and terminology that define the essence of foundational content knowledge. They teach thinking independent of content knowledge. Similarly, content knowledge is generally taught independent of the key cognitive strategies. The focus in teaching content is on retention of information, not extension or application of what is taught through cognitively challenging tasks. This disconnect leaves students struggling to make connections between what they know and what they should and could be doing with what they know. This lack of an integrated model has led to the need for tools and methods to address the challenge of getting high school students to develop their thinking skills while mastering the key content knowledge they will need to succeed in entry-level college courses for baccalaureate degrees or certificates.

This chapter addresses this challenge by presenting some specific approaches, methods, and techniques. The chapter begins with a brief overview of the importance of identifying the big ideas of each content area and organizing instruction around these big ideas. Once the big ideas are identified, it is possible to align the high school program in ways that lead to mastery of the big ideas. However, equally important is the development of key cognitive strategies that students learn to use to understand content more deeply. The chapter concludes with a consideration of how to support students through scaffolding so that high expectations can be established and sustained for all students.

FOCUSING ON THE "BIG IDEAS"

Postsecondary success most assuredly requires a strong content knowledge base. Although some professors assert that students are better off entering their class without any prior conceptions or knowledge about the subject, this is perhaps a bit of hyperbole. Students do need strong grounding in the academic disciplines, an understanding of the big ideas of each subject area, and an awareness of how knowledge is structured within the subject area. Most postsecondary faculty, if pressed, can identify a body of content knowledge that will help students be better prepared to succeed in entry-level college courses.

The content of a high school program of study is often determined paradoxically by what students have been taught in middle school. The high school course offering is restricted to some degree by what students bring to high school in terms of basic skills and content knowledge. This is an odd notion in some senses because it reflects a "design-up" rather than a "design-down" model of curriculum and content specification. In other words, rather than identifying clearly what students need to know to be college ready and then designing high school and middle school educational programs accordingly, the system has inadvertently moved to a model in which offerings are determined in large measure by what the previous level of education has accomplished, not by what is required to succeed in current and subsequent levels of education.

The key component to remedy this situation is a set of college readiness standards that define where students are expected to end up by the conclusion of high school. As noted previously, most states have signed onto national efforts to identify a set of common core standards for college and career readiness.

State standards can then be aligned to these standards, increasing the confidence that teaching to state standards will result in students who are college and career ready. Several sets of college readiness standards are readily available for review as well. Educators can benefit by noting the commonalities among all these efforts.

The way that content knowledge is organized for presentation to students is a key consideration. One of the main goals and purposes of introductory college courses is to help students understand the structure of knowledge within the discipline, along with the ways of knowing entailed by the subject area. High school courses should strive to help students understand the big ideas of the subject being studied, key controversies in the subject area, and how knowledge is generated in the subject area.

One important means to enable students to understand the big ideas and the structure of subject areas is to adopt a set of college readiness standards and then align the high school's instructional program with it. In this way, students develop the understandings and specific knowledge that prepare them to engage in these subject areas more deeply in postsecondary education.

The task of identifying the big ideas has become somewhat easier in the era of educational standards. Not only have states established academic content standards, but, as noted previously, a number of organizations have also identified the knowledge and skills necessary for college and career readiness. Educators will be able to draw on these documents as convenient reference points when considering how best to organize the high school program of instruction so that it is focused on big ideas.

ALIGNING COURSES AND EXPECTATIONS BETWEEN HIGH SCHOOL AND COLLEGE

One of the most challenging and yet powerful places to begin to improve the connections between high school and college is to align course content and student performance expectations. This approach has rarely been undertaken outside of a small group of private preparatory schools and some public high schools geared almost exclusively to college preparation. These schools find ways to ensure that the courses they offer students align well with college courses. They pay particular attention to the types of instructional experiences offered in the senior year to ensure that they will most closely approximate what students will encounter several months hence in a college classroom.

Most public schools, by contrast, rely on a combination of AP courses, dual credit, and perhaps a home-grown honors program to address the alignment issue. More often than not, these courses neither connect well with the high school courses that precede them, nor link all that well with college courses that follow. High schools that depend on AP courses to bridge the gap often overlook the fact that the AP course is supposed to represent the first year of college, not the last year of high school, so most students are still left with the need for a transition between a typical high school course and an AP course that represents college-level work. The lack of a clear progression toward college and career readiness makes it more difficult for students to know where they stand at any given moment relative to the expectations they will face in postsecondary education.

Similarly, postsecondary institutions do not necessarily build their entry-level courses in relation to what students are doing in high school courses. Colleges rely on placement tests in English and math for the purpose of a coarsely grained sorting of those who are minimally prepared for college-level work from those who do not reach minimum necessary skill levels. Rarely, if ever, do college instructional faculty and program designers sit down with or include their secondary peers in any consideration of the content and structure of entry-level college courses, the level of challenges they present, and any assumptions about prerequisite knowledge and skills. College instructors rely largely on their own experiences with freshmen as the reference point for the expectations that accompany their entry-level courses. None of this gets communicated to high school educators in any systematic fashion.

Tackling this fundamental disconnect requires rethinking relationships and assumptions about the content of courses and how the senior year of high school and the freshman year of college are connected. Several strategies are discussed here. They are presented in ascending order of challenge to implement. The first strategy is to use programs such as AP or International Baccalaureate as reference points. These programs are familiar to educators and parents and can be implemented with relative ease. Next in challenge level are processes to develop high school syllabi that are more consciously aligned with postsecondary readiness, seminars that mimic many aspects of college courses, and assignments that similarly reflect postsecondary expectations. The final strategy presented is to design paired courses in which an exit-level high school course is connected with a corresponding entry-level college course. The chapter concludes with a description of ways to develop and measure the key cognitive strategies that are so important to college success and to support students for whom mastery of the key cognitive strategies will be more challenging.

Aligning with Advanced Placement or International Baccalaureate

Once a high school has identified the big ideas of the subject areas and has agreed on the key cognitive strategies that will be developed throughout the curriculum from course to course and year to year, it is possible to think more deeply about aligning the curriculum. Alignment is the act of settling on an explicit program design in which knowledge and skills develop systematically, sequentially, cumulatively, and purposively toward an overall goal, in this case, readiness for college and career.

Advanced Placement (AP) and International Baccalaureate (IB) represent possible reference points for alignment. The difficulty is that neither program had explicit standards until recently. Each had exams and some specification for courses, but neither had standards at a level of specificity and comprehensiveness necessary to identify the prerequisite knowledge and skills that students needed to master to be ready for the course. Although each program is in the process of developing more detailed standards, even in their current state they can provide invaluable information about how the curriculum should be aligned toward college and career readiness for all students.

Advanced Placement is an appropriate target because the AP exam is supposed to represent college-level work. Preparing for AP means preparing for entry-level college courses. Although IB does not claim to be college level, its exams are designed in a way that the highest levels of performance on them reach college level. Furthermore, IB courses, which are more highly specified than AP courses, demonstrate many of the attributes of entry-level college courses, particularly around the key cognitive strategies, so that advanced-level IB courses represent a worthy target toward which the secondary curriculum should aim.

Schools or districts choosing to align toward AP or IB have several options. The sponsors of each provide materials and programs to help develop "pre-AP" and "middle years" knowledge and skills. Adopting these programs can be an important first step toward improved alignment. However, most schools can benefit from a deeper exploration of curricular relationships, which will be discussed later in this section.

The fact that most states have not aligned their high school content standards and assessments with college and career readiness frameworks makes it more difficult for high schools to undertake the alignment process on their own. However, tools are being developed to help educators align state standards with a designated set of college readiness standards selected by the educators as their desired reference point. When these tools are used, the alignment process becomes more manageable and within the grasp of districts and even some individual schools.

Aligning Syllabi

Aligning syllabi is a way for high school and postsecondary courses to be connected without extensive direct interaction between faculty. Other methods described subsequently utilize more direct contact, but for many high schools, it may be most feasible to begin alignment by working independently, then building on initial successes to contact postsecondary institutions and work more directly with them. To align syllabi, course developers at both high school and college levels work in relation to a common set of standards and expectations for college and career readiness. Each can thereby calibrate expectations, challenge level, and content coverage to maximize continuity and alignment, but they can do so without the time and expense of meetings or joint development activities.

The key to making the aligned syllabi process feasible is a clear, specific reference point for college readiness. That point needs to be sufficiently detailed to enable course developers to know what is to be taught at each level; the cognitive challenge level and its progression; expected skills and prerequisite knowledge for success in the course; teaching and learning strategies; tests, assessments, and assignments; overall workload expectations; and grading standards and methods. Accompanying this information are examples of student work at each level that demonstrate more definitively how requirements and expectations play out in terms of products. Once agreement has been reached on the knowledge and skill necessary for postsecondary success, the next step is to collect existing syllabi for a course and then analyze the syllabi to determine their alignment with the college and career readiness standards. Through this process, the commonalities among the existing courses can be identified and synthesized. This analysis can be used to create a syllabus that contains detailed information on course goals and objectives, necessary prerequisite knowledge, assignments, readings, tests, grading criteria, and teaching methods. With this syllabus in hand, developers can then identify student work and other artifacts that illustrate what college and career readiness looks like in practice.

Once this extensive process is completed, individual teachers and instructors align their courses with the master syllabus. Each instructor can make decisions about areas of alignment and areas of individuality, which can ease the development process somewhat. Afterward, a review of syllabi will indicate how successful the alignment process has been. Any areas of concern or weakness identified can then be addressed by adding materials in those areas or providing teachers and instructors with sample language to incorporate specific areas.

The aligned syllabi model is not without its challenges. The single greatest one is getting teachers to commit to developing and using quality syllabi consistently. The approach does, however, have the advantage of permitting considerable autonomy by individual teachers within a common framework. This sort of compromise may be desirable and necessary in situations where individuals on one or both sides of the high school–college divide view alignment between high school and college with some concern and trepidation.

College-Ready Seminars

A college-ready seminar is a specially designed course that seeks to challenge students in ways that begin to approximate what they will face soon in college. This seminar has a set of features that distinguishes it from a normal high school class.

The pacing is faster than in a typical high school course. Where students may be accustomed to reading two or at most three pieces of literature in a semester-long English course, the college-ready seminar may expect them to read eight to ten selections, at least several of them novel length. Students are expected to keep closer track of when they are to complete each reading assignment because they typically would have several selections they were in various stages of reading at the same time. This requires students to develop their self-management skills, including tracking and prioritizing due dates and the attendant scheduling required to do so.

The seminars tend to have fewer assignments, with each being more substantial in nature. Here again, students need to be cognizant of due dates and the time required to complete assigned tasks by deadlines. The courses rely much less on daily homework assignments that high school teachers typically collect and grade and for which students receive points that comprise a substantial portion of their grade in many classes. Students are expected to complete homework, but the homework largely relates to the larger assignments and is not checked because the effect of not doing the homework is clear when the assignment is turned in.

The assignments themselves require a great deal of writing, including editing and redrafting. Although no one essay is necessarily more than about five pages, students may be expected to complete five of these at three-week intervals. This requires almost continuous drafting and editing to produce quality products on such a regular time line. Falling behind can be disastrous, as students soon come to realize.

These writing assignments are not ones that can be completed through expressive or narrative writing alone, nor can students simply make claims that are not supported or documented. These require well-developed research skills, including the ability to locate a range of relevant sources, make determinations about the credibility and relevance of sources, and know how and when to cite, paraphrase, and quote. This type of writing also requires the ability to synthesize information from multiple sources in order to present a coherent argument, point of view, or interpretation rather than simply repeat information verbatim.

The grading criteria that teachers employ in these seminars are clear, consistent, and tied directly to college readiness skills. One of the first casualties of this policy is extra credit, at least as commonly practiced. When extra credit is offered, it is in the form of additional work directly related to the topic at hand or additional questions on a test.

Students are more accountable for their performance, and they receive more candid and useful feedback on assignments. This can be something of a shock to students who are accustomed to generic positive feedback on everything they turn in. Receiving back a paper that is scored as not being well organized, well researched, or particularly convincing is not a familiar experience for many high-performing students. For students at lower achievement levels, feedback is also honest and direct, but it is presented with more detailed instructions on the changes that need to be made. These students have too often received globally positive comments from teachers concerned about damaging their self-esteem. Although they will have further to travel to be fully college ready, the college-ready seminar can help them begin to close the gap and understand the need to focus and improve in specific areas.

The college-ready seminars emphasize deeper understandings of content knowledge previously taught and an emerging awareness of the structure of knowledge in core academic subject areas. To accomplish this, the seminars focus on developing the key cognitive strategies outlined in earlier chapters. Students learn to think about central questions of the disciplines, engage in discussion about enduring issues, consider emerging explanations and theories, and begin to develop an awareness of how experts in a discipline think about knowledge and understanding. By not introducing significant amounts of new content, the seminars can serve as a form of review and consolidation of conceptual understandings, not simply a reteaching of basic terminology or facts.

Instead the seminars are integrative in nature, helping students make connections among material they have learned and developing insight into why this is important to know and understand. In the process, they become better at formulating and solving problems; considering multiple, competing, and conflicting explanations of the same phenomenon; viewing knowledge as evolving and subject to verification and proof; and accepting that not everything they have been taught to date will be forever and always true. This type of intellectual maturity helps students prepare for college learning environments in which exactly these sorts of conceptions of knowledge are central to engaging in more of a give-and-take process that can include challenges, from student to instructor or instructor to student, and relies much more heavily than high school on the rules and conventions of disciplinary knowledge and scholarship to establish the ground rules for learning and interaction.

College-ready seminars may also contain one other unique element, although not all do: independent, third-party evaluation of student work. Ideally the person providing the evaluation is a college-level instructor or someone with previous experience teaching entry-level college courses. However, other subject matter experts from the community can also serve in this role. This outside perspective provides a scale against which student work can be judged in ways that match more closely how similar work would be evaluated in college.

The college-ready seminar can present an opportunity for high school faculty to work collaboratively to design challenging instructional opportunities for students, opportunities that foreshadow what they will encounter in college. The advantage of this type of collaboration is that it focuses on teaching and learning. Such interactions can contribute to substantial change in teaching and learning because they revolve around professional interchange. When educators interact as peers to solve a commonly held problem, the results can be surprising in both their scope and impact.

The college-ready seminars can model a level of expectation that can serve as a benchmark against which other high school classes can also be gauged. The college-ready seminar helps to contribute to the creation of a college-going culture—one that signals to students the efforts they should be making to be college ready and the importance of focusing on postsecondary education as a key goal.

The other advantage of the college-ready seminar, particularly if it is developed in partnership with local postsecondary faculty, is that the rigor and challenge level of the course can be demonstrated for parents and community members. This is particularly important in communities that hold high expectations for their schools, but it is equally relevant in schools that historically have not sent a large proportion of students to college. Establishing that a set of courses has a legitimate, explicit connection to college readiness is important in all schools.

Although AP courses are the coin of the realm for college readiness in many schools, it is worth remembering that those courses are supposed to contain content and performance expectations reflective of the first year of college. The college-ready seminar functions as a step before AP, the highest level of high school performance toward which students should strive, whether or not they intend to take an AP course or a dual-credit course. Knowing with some certainty that the college-ready seminar is properly calibrated between high school and college expectations is an important aspect of its role as the highest level of high school course.

College-Ready Assignments

Less daunting to develop and implement than aligned syllabi or college-ready seminars are college-ready assignments. Many high schools already have some form of assignment in the form of a senior project that functions as a capstone experience. The key distinguishing factor in terms of college readiness is that the senior projects in most high schools are not tied directly to college readiness standards or assessed against them. This results in a range of interesting projects that do not necessarily reveal much about whether the student is ready for postsecondary education. The senior project is not generally designed to develop and measure precisely the knowledge and skills needed for college and career readiness and success.

The college-ready assignment is different in this respect. This category of assignment is carefully crafted to represent something that students will have to do in college and is scored against postsecondary readiness criteria. The precise nature of the assignments varies from subject to subject, but all college-ready assignments will be similar to college assignments.

A research paper is perhaps the most common form of college-ready assignment, and because these papers may be relatively short, in the five-page range, students might be expected to produce more than one of them. This helps mimic what they will encounter in college. English courses may already have some requirements for students to complete papers, but this assignment would necessitate their going into greater depth and documenting their assertions with more supporting evidence. In science, students may be asked to conduct a research review or examine conflicting scientific evidence and reach a conclusion about the nature of the differing perspectives and the strength of the evidence, not the "correct" explanation of the phenomenon in question. In the social sciences, students could be required to investigate a social issue and provide evidence for several likely futures derived from differing sets of assumptions. Math college-ready assignments may consist of complex problems that derive from other subject areas and are not easily solved with simple solutions or routine methods.

In all cases, the college-ready assignments are scored with criteria that are made available to students throughout their work on the assignment and tied to the types of grading criteria the students will face in college. At the least, the paper is expected to be well written without major grammatical and usage errors, well organized, well argued, well documented, and devoid of unsubstantiated personal assertion. Ideally the paper represents an original take on a problem or issue and puts forth a cogent, compelling point of view. Finally, the paper is sufficiently robust to be subjected to public presentation and critique by teachers and fellow classmates. All of this helps prepare students better for the give-and-take of a postsecondary learning environment.

Paired Courses

The paired-course model is based on a partnership between a high school (or group of high schools) and one or more postsecondary institutions. The purpose of the partnership is to develop guidelines that apply to exit-level high school courses and entry-level college courses. The guidelines are used to develop syllabi that align in a number of specific areas, including the important content topics the course addresses, assumptions about prior student knowledge and skill, the assignments students are expected to complete, grading criteria and methods, overall workload, and the specific educational materials used, such as texts and supplemental readings.

Once the partnership has been established, teams comprising high school and college instructors who teach these courses convene to develop the details to accompany the guidelines. In the process, course outlines and syllabi emerge. Continued dialogue and review lead to a carefully sequenced pair of courses in which instructors develop student knowledge and skill in a complementary fashion that is appropriate for the entire range of potential postsecondary students when they are in high school and then is appropriate for those who reach college.

The course pairs emphasize continuity in expectations and coordination in content coverage. While a well-designed course pair may include significant content review at the college level, this review is undertaken intentionally and not as the teaching of previously learned content as if it were new material. Coordination of grading practices, another important element, is generally accomplished through the use of scoring guides that are consistent across levels. The pairs pay close attention to ensure that the high school course reaches a pace at which the college course can begin so that students won't be totally thrown by the more rapid content coverage associated with the college course. Attention is paid to the instructional methods used to ensure they are consistent with student developmental level and that high school students are exposed to the instructional methods they will likely encounter in the paired college course. Finally, the pairs encourage the development of student knowledge of how to interact with a college professor by having the high school teacher model some of these behaviors as well.

The argument can be made that not all students will attend an institution of higher education that is involved in developing the course pairs and that this will dilute the effect of pairing courses. In practice, many commonalities exist across colleges in the content of entry-level general education courses. This is so for a number of reasons, including the texts that are used, the fact that such courses often receive the most scrutiny from departments because they are taught by both regular and adjunct instructors and require more standardized syllabi, and that greater agreement has been reached about the general outlines of most survey-type courses. This means that if a student completes the high school version of the course pair, the student will likely be better prepared for almost any entry-level college course that corresponds with the high school course, even if the college has not specifically adopted the paired course model.

The logistics of creating these development partnerships can be complex and can be a limiting factor in the creation of paired courses. Ideally the framework for such courses would be developed at a system level for local adaptation, but few states currently have the kinds of cooperation between state secondary and postsecondary education agencies necessary for a collaborative project of this nature to be initiated without some sort of legislative mandate. The state's role is taken up in Chapter Eight. The key point here is that local action can be undertaken to improve alignment between high school and college.

FORMATIVE ASSESSMENT FOR COLLEGE READINESS

One of the key findings from essentially every study of the expectations of postsecondary instructors is the importance they give to students' ability to employ a range of cognitive strategies in their college courses. These skills are used to formulate and solve complex problems, conduct research, evaluate the credibility and usefulness of source information, interpret findings, weigh conflicting claims and arguments, construct a logical argument or present a hypothesis or thesis based on evidence, and do all of these things with precision and accuracy appropriate to the task at hand.

Developing these skills in high school students can be challenging for a number of reasons. Often students have had their success defined by the ability to retain and repeat factual information, and they resist anything that makes more cognitive demands on them. They want to get the right answer and then move on to a new task. When challenged more fully, many students find this sort of learning to be not as "efficient" as memorizing facts. They resist engaging deeply in problems or open-ended tasks and lack the will and the intellectual stamina to pursue an answer for more than a couple of minutes. On the positive side, some students immediately appreciate finally being allowed to engage in something that is intellectually compelling and fully challenging to them.

Many high school teachers are reluctant to devote the time necessary to develop these skills in students, in part because they feel pressured by state and federal testing requirements (and even by parents) to teach a set body of knowledge that is clearly identifiable and easily quantifiable. Another reason many teachers avoid delving into this type of learning is that the methods of teaching required to engage students fully in activities that are intellectually challenging require skills that many teachers who have not been explicitly prepared to teach in this fashion may lack.

This type of teaching and learning requires careful planning and sequencing of activities and assignments so that students explore a range of cognitive strategies in ways that successively approximate more closely what they will be expected to do in postsecondary programs. Research papers, experiments, literature reviews, problem-solving exercises, simulations, debates, carefully reasoned papers, and logically coherent presentations all require considerable preparation by students and teachers. These tasks entail multiple steps, including intermediate products and frequent revision and rewriting. Harried teachers find it difficult to manage the demands of these types of assignments, and students resist revising or revisiting work once they have completed it in even the most rudimentary form. In short, this type of teaching and learning must be built into the core expectations of the school and not just be the result of a heroic teacher striving for high standards in the face of overwhelming resistance and lack of support.

One way to build this type of culture of high expectations is to incorporate a system of low-stakes formative assessments designed specifically to gauge student performance in relation to the key cognitive strategies. Such an assessment system can provide a measure of student cognitive performance in five key cognitive strategy areas outlined in Chapter One: problem formulation, research, interpretation, communication, and precision and accuracy. Students complete an authentic performance task at regular intervals. The task is built into the teacher's program of instruction for the course and is not a stand-alone test. It is not separate from the course curriculum; it *is* the course curriculum. Each performance task is carefully designed to provide information on three to five key cognitive strategies. Teachers may adapt the tasks to their specific curriculum if they follow certain procedures.

Teachers score the task using guides on which they are trained and have demonstrated that they can score the tasks consistently. Ideally the teacher incorporates the results from the performance assessment into the student's grade for the course. This is done to ensure that students take the tasks seriously. However, teachers can award the grade separately from the score generated by the scoring guide used to determine college readiness. In other words, students can receive a college readiness score on a task and a separate score that contributes to the course grade.

Schools should be prepared to take steps to ensure that teachers are scoring the performance tasks consistently. This can be done by internal or external moderation, in which selected pieces of student work are rescored by trained scorers outside the classroom where the task was given. They then give the teacher feedback on how consistently the task was scored in relation to the scoring criteria. Teachers can also receive reports on how their average scores compare to all other teachers scoring the task. The goal is to help teachers determine if they are judging student work at the proper challenge level.

The net effect of a program of formative assessment that meets these requirements is to be able to gauge student performance in each of the key cognitive strategies. Information can be used to help gauge the overall challenge level within the school by examining the number of students who meet or exceed the readiness level in each of the five key cognitive strategy areas as compared to the proportion of students who approach or do not meet the readiness level. Teachers can review class-level information to determine the current level of performance for the class as a whole, which is useful in identifying appropriate activities to develop skills in the key cognitive strategies. Students can review their progress over time to see if they are likely to be ready for college-level courses in which they will be expected to use the same key cognitive strategies on which they are being assessed.

Because this is a formative system, no conclusions can be drawn about an individual student based on any single administration of the assessment. Similarly, it would be inappropriate to judge a teacher based on how an individual class performed on a single performance task. The scores are sufficiently reliable to identify trends at the school or grade level or within a subject area or for a student over several years. This level of aggregation is still useful for a series of instructional and program design decisions, as well as to inform professional development planning and individual student goal setting.

We have noted in our work with schools that have implemented this type of formative assessment of key cognitive strategies that teachers and students develop a common language of college and career readiness that includes the key cognitive skill areas as part of their vocabulary. Partly as a result of using common scoring guides regularly, they become familiar with the components of problem formulation or research or interpretation and can identify the presence or absence of these in student work. This leads them to make better decisions independently about instructional content and challenge level for all students and to take into account the developmental range represented by all students in the class.

Agreement within a school about the importance of developing these behaviors in students and on how these terms translate into practice creates the kind of commonality of purpose that connects faculty efforts across classes and grade levels, even in the absence of formal planning to do so. Students who are exposed to the model consistently across all classes and assignments become accustomed to producing work that conforms to these expectations. In the process, they become better and more prolific thinkers who can manage their own learning with greater facility.

What of students who lack many of the basic skills necessary to complete complex tasks? Is the only hope to "dumb down" the system and use tasks designed for elementary grade students? The answer is a resounding no. Many tasks can be cognitively challenging and not require high levels of literacy or numeracy. These tasks can be constructed so that the content knowledge required is still important to postsecondary success. For example, poetry can be linguistically simple and still be quite complex cognitively, or at least evoke complex responses. Similarly, in mathematics, some problems that require a great deal of mathematical reasoning can be approached at varying levels of content expertise, with different strategies being employed to solve the problem based on the mathematical knowledge possessed by the student working to solve the problem.

Performance tasks can be important pedagogical resources precisely because they can be made to offer challenges to students with emerging literacy and numeracy skills. High school students in the United States, when polled on the degree to which their high school education challenges them, consistently respond that they are nowhere near as challenged as they could be. Most students are holding back to some degree, in part because they do not want to have to work harder; paradoxically, they then are unhappy because they are not more engaged and do not have more meaningful work to do.

For more information on the methods and strategies presented in this chapter, go to http://CollegeCareerReady.org.

The Role of Scaffolding

The type of learning necessary for students to be prepared for college and career requires high school educators to adopt specific instructional strategies and techniques. Examples of these are contained in a wealth of other publications, and their content will not be repeated here. Instead, several key principles of teaching to college and career readiness will be presented and briefly discussed.

Perhaps the key foundational instructional principle necessary for all students to be more college ready is to keep the challenge level constant and vary the amount of support, or scaffolding, that is provided. In practice, this means that all students are given intellectually engaging assignments drawn from content that reflects the big ideas of the subject areas necessary to be ready for college and career. These assignments require all students to develop the key cognitive strategies identified as so important to postsecondary success.

What happens more often in practice is that different students are given fundamentally different materials at different challenge levels. The problem with this approach is that it is difficult to determine with any precision whether the student is capable of coping with more challenging material and is simply unwilling to do so. Paradoxically the more material of a less challenging nature that students receive, the lower their performance level is likely to be. Teachers observing this phenomenon then determine that the best solution is to lower the challenge level even further, perpetuating this downward spiral of expectations.

In fact, students can demonstrate their capabilities only if they are fully challenged and stretched beyond their comfort zones on a regular basis. If this happens only occasionally, students develop coping strategies to get them through the infrequent situations where more is asked of them, and they do not develop the kinds of cognitive strategies necessary for successful learning in academically demanding contexts. In other words, they will not be preparing for college and career pathways and will be overwhelmed by the demands and expectations of the postsecondary classroom if they do choose to continue their education beyond high school at any point.

Rather than devising fundamentally different assignments for different students or assigning students to courses that cover very different content, it makes more sense to provide supports to students based on their needs and then to remove the supports as they prove more capable. It may still be necessary to have some grouping of students by degree of scaffolding required, but this is not the same as grouping them based on the content itself that they are taught, the assignments they are given, the overall level of expectation held for them, or some determination about their innate ability.

Grouping practices are contentious in most high schools and are based on a combination of folk information and superficial data generally derived from course grades, which are themselves composites of many aspects of performance. Adopting the principle that all students are challenged at comparable levels within a subject area but provided varying degrees of support is not easy to accomplish in most high schools without significant planning and attention to the nature of the content to be taught, the expectations to which all students will be held, and the supports that will be provided.

Examples of supports include the use of exemplar papers for key assignments so that students know the target toward which they are aiming, tutors, study groups (discussed in greater depth in the next chapter), study guides, and greater specification of assignment elements. For example, all students might be assigned a five-page research paper in which they must include five citations to support their conclusion regarding the phenomenon being investigated. Students who do not require scaffolding are expected to locate all five sources themselves. Students requiring scaffolding may be given anywhere from one to five citations to help them develop their argument. Over time, the number of citations provided is reduced as all students become more familiar with what constitutes an acceptable citation. The reason for providing this support is to reduce the number of places where a student can become stalled on the project and to have the student who is receiving scaffolding focus on the key task of integrating the sources. Some students may then require support integrating the provided citations as well. This may represent the highest level of scaffolding.

Keep in mind this approach to learning does not work if students are not exposed to enough assignments or challenges that allow or cause them to develop some understanding of the underlying skills, in this case selecting and integrating sources into a research paper to support one's basic findings. If they write only one research paper a year, they will need the same level of scaffolding each time they undertake the task. However, if they are expected to write many research papers each year, they will become more proficient using sources and will not need to have as many provided to them on successive papers. The teacher's job is to determine when each student is ready to have the scaffolding removed, in the form of resources or detailed examples. As students develop a mental model of the nature of the task and the skills needed to master it, they become more self-reliant learners, a key capability for college success.

Scaffolding requires careful and deliberate planning by teachers. However, many of the basic techniques generalize well across subjects and assignments, and teachers are already intuitively familiar with the idea in most cases. Professional development activities devoted to developing extensive scaffolding resources that can be reused in a variety of settings help ease the burden for individual teachers having to engage in too much lesson planning and redesign. The professional development also helps ensure the quality of the resulting scaffolding options and the consistency with which scaffolding is offered and implemented in classes.

If a high school has aligned its instructional program with college readiness standards, the types of activities that all students should be expected to do become much clearer. This can lead to the implementation of plans to have students complete challenging assignments at each grade level in each course. When students realize they are going to have to complete challenging assignments in all classes, they are much more motivated to use scaffolding as a means to develop learning strategies that make it easier for them to complete the challenging assignments. In this fashion, a common schoolwide framework of expectations and supporting instructional practices can lead to more students engaging in challenging learning and completing assignments that build college readiness.

CHAPTER 3

Ways to Develop Self-Management Skills and "College Knowledge"

Many students enter college with strong academic knowledge and skills but struggle nevertheless. The reason, in many instances, is that they did not necessarily develop the self-management skills or the knowledge about how to succeed in college that becomes much more important in postsecondary education.

High school students can succeed by following directions and completing assigned tasks in a prescribed manner. They often have additional options, or safety valves, available to them should they falter in following procedures or attending class. Postsecondary education, however, expects students to function more independently and to take initiative when they need help or assistance.

Although many high achievers struggle, another group of students suffers even more: those who are the first in their families or communities to attend college. They lack awareness of the implicit, often unstated knowledge about how college really operates—everything from selecting courses to studying, accessing resources when in trouble academically, talking with professors, interacting with students with differing perspectives and beliefs, and knowing how to cut their losses in particular academic situations. All this and more is information that those who have experienced college pass on to their children or members of their community. This knowledge can make the difference between persisting and withdrawing when students face challenges during the first year of college.

This chapter presents and discusses a range of behaviors, skills, strategies, and knowledge associated with success in college. All of these are necessary in addition to the content knowledge and cognitive strategies students should be acquiring in high school classes. Unfortunately, few high school programs attend to these self-management skills and college knowledge in any systematic fashion. Part of the reason is that these crucial capabilities are not systematically measured or taken into account in the admissions process at the vast majority of colleges. The net result is that the students with the most advantage—those who have access to information on how to master these areas and understand the importance of doing so—have a distinct advantage over students who lack such awareness and access to successful coping mechanisms.

ELEMENTS OF SELF-MANAGEMENT

The term *self-management* describes a category of behaviors and attitudes by which students take greater responsibility for their actions and become significantly more proactive. In many ways, the presence of self-management behaviors can be considered to be evidence of maturity.

This type of maturity is important not only to academic success, but to success on career pathways and in real-world settings outside school. Self-management is part and parcel of a much larger set of behaviors and attitudes associated with making the transition from childhood to early adulthood. For this to happen, the secondary school environment must create the need for students to acquire these behaviors and attitudes and have consistent expectations that they be evidenced with increasing reliability as students progress through high school.

Time Management

The ability to manage one's time is a fundamental skill for success in postsecondary education and, for that matter, in much of life beyond high school. Many programs, tools, and techniques have been created and marketed to help students manage their time. Schools that we have studied use a variety of methods, but few have a systematic program extending continuously from ninth through twelfth grades in which students are expected to become progressively more responsible for managing their own time in anticipation of postsecondary education, where they will be entirely responsible (and faced with many temptations).

Some techniques are fairly simple, such as having students keep a planner in which they enter all the tasks they have for the upcoming academic term immediately when they begin a class. A more sophisticated approach is to use a common method for all classes, not just one or two where the teacher chooses to require it, and have teachers help students learn how to allocate an amount of time to each task each week. This allows students to get a better perspective on when in the semester they will face multiple demands on their time, a situation they will encounter frequently in postsecondary settings. The next layer of planning is for students to add their personal obligations to this time map. Such obligations include extracurricular activities, jobs, family obligations, volunteering, church-related commitments, and any other predictable encumbrance of their time. Understanding that they will be expected to balance academic and nonacademic activities and allocate between the two proportionally is an important first step in gaining control of time management.

With this full view of the match between obligations and available time, students can begin to prioritize activities and time and think more strategically about how much time they choose to devote to any given activity or task. This strategic thinking is just as important as, if not more important than, the act of recording all of one's obligations. In college, students are likely to encounter new opportunities and distractions and can easily become overloaded. Knowing how to prioritize by identifying the relative importance and urgency of any particular activity or task is a survival skill under these circumstances.

Academic planners are available free or at low cost from a number of sources that can be located relatively easily on the Internet or locally. However, there is nothing magical about the planners themselves. It is how they are used in a school. They will be more effective if all teachers agree to require them, check them, and help students learn to use them effectively. They are also effective when students take more ownership over the planning process each subsequent year of high school until, during their senior year, they are fully independent planners.

This is a behavior we see frequently with the highest-achieving students—those who must track multiple major assignments, prepare for AP or IB exams, and juggle a full load of outside activities. This level of skill needs to be transferred to the average student, particularly the student for whom such behaviors do not come naturally and will not necessarily be developed or supported at home. A comprehensive program of time management throughout high school will help these students be ready to live and work independently in college or while pursuing a career.

Study Skills

Many commercial programs exist to improve student study skills. Few high schools have adopted a schoolwide program for study skill improvement, and many have no clear expectations of the study skills that their students will develop. When schools do have such programs, they tend to focus them on either the very low or very high achievers, for quite different reasons. The net effect is that the vast majority of students do not develop systematic study skills and are left to fend for themselves when it comes to studying.

It may not be necessary to have a formal program of study skills if all teachers in the school agree to emphasize a series of key strategies and mind-sets related to study. These metastrategies help all learners to think much more consciously about how they are approaching studying. Here are some examples of the kinds of strategies students need to master to be successful in college.

Distinguish Between Material You Understand and Can Pursue Independently and Material You Don't Understand and Need Help to Complete

This rather straightforward metacognitive ability is a key skill. Without it, students don't realize they have a problem until it's too late, generally the night before an assignment is due or a test is to be given. Knowing whether you can realistically study something on your own is perhaps a key skill for college success. If students can identify areas where no amount of individual studying is going to help them, they have the opportunity to take advantage of help offered in most classes or to try to form or join a study group.

This may seem like an obvious principle, but in high school, students, particularly average performers, are much more focused on completing tasks than on being aware of how well they understand what they are doing. This leads to a whole series of coping strategies focused on submitting a completed assignment and turning it in on time rather than understanding the subject matter in question. Students receive points for completing assignments, not mastering material, and the incentive system is simply to complete the assignments. Getting students to step back enough to be aware when they are just going through the motions and do not truly understand what they are doing is the first step in selecting a more constructive study strategy.

Know How to Work with Others in Study Groups

This skill consists of a series of subskills, beginning with the ability to select appropriate members of the study team. High-performing students are often proficient at assembling ad hoc study teams, particularly to prepare for AP exams or similar high-stakes tests and assignments. These students make strategic decisions about the composition of study groups, basing their choices of participants on finely honed judgments about the contributions each participant will likely make to the group.

This is not necessarily a bad thing: the students are not systematically exclusionary; they are very concerned about someone's willingness to contribute. "Contribute" in this sense means showing up for the group meetings, being prepared, and being able to answer at least some questions or contribute to some degree to group understanding of difficult concepts or complex tasks or problems. Sophisticated study group organizers take mental notes about who is serious enough about learning to make the effort necessary for the group to be effective.

Students in effective study groups monitor the use of time carefully. They insist that participants show up on time, that the group have an overall agenda or structure for each meeting, that the conversation remain on topic, and, often, that each member has a particular role to play within the group. In this way, they emphasize the importance and seriousness of the group and the time spent on it.

The challenges for students who have not participated in study groups before they reach college are manifold. They do not comprehend the importance of such groups, do not know how to get invited to participate in such groups, often do not take them seriously enough even after being invited, and may violate one of the key group norms by taking much more than they contribute. Any of these actions limits for these students the degree to which study groups help them succeed in college. This is particularly so during their first year, when many study networks are forming and competing social opportunities are most tempting.

First-generation college attendees and students from groups historically underrepresented in college face a particularly daunting challenge getting involved with study groups. These students may be outside the social networks that take the initiative to create study groups. If they are invited to a group, they may feel ill at ease with the other members, the group's location, or the social norms shared, often unconsciously, by the group members. The groups may only strengthen for these students a sense of being an outsider and of not really belonging on the college campus.

The challenge with relying on students who do not have prior knowledge about study groups to form their own groups consisting only of students of similar backgrounds is that, based on what is known from research, students from these groups are more likely be struggling academically; moreover, fewer of them will have deep insight into the college knowledge about how to succeed on assignments or tests. If a study group consists of students who have no previous experience with such groups, they will have to go through a learning process simply to establish how a study group should operate and what it can accomplish. In the meantime, they may be losing ground academically to their peers who are more adept at using groups and have access to a wider range of strategies to succeed academically. Failure to keep up academically can lead first-generation college attendees to conclude that they do not belong in college. These first-generation attendees from groups that are underrepresented in college need to be particularly skilled at techniques such as study groups when they enter college and not expected to learn about them once they are enrolled.

One of the key contributions a high school can make is to ensure that students use study groups periodically. Teachers can help to organize the groups initially, but the groups rarely teach necessary study skills when they only meet during class. Study groups by their very nature must occur outside class time, which limits the school's ability to control or monitor them. Many high school teachers shy away from any expectation of out-of-class cooperation by students for fear of criticism by parents, potential legal liability, or simply a lack of belief that such techniques will work with their students.

Clearly teachers must give students guidelines on how such groups function and then create structured assignments in which students must meet to accomplish a particular task together. It may be discussing a passage or researching a topic, but it should be something that requires all students to participate, and it should not be a group project. Most important, the entire process should be debriefed and discussed in class after it is over. How did the groups work? What would make them work better next time? What rules and regulations need to be in place? What characteristics must individuals demonstrate to be fully contributing members of the group? What happens if someone is not contributing or is actually disrupting the group? Simply reflecting on these types of issues can be quite useful as a precursor to the types of independent study groups in which students need to engage if they are to be successful in college and in career preparation.

Know How to Prepare for Tests

Tests in college tend to be fewer in number, so each test tends to have greater significance in determining the final course grade. This means students cannot learn about what an instructor expects on a test primarily by failing the first one. College students must prepare for all tests, including the first one, with equal diligence and strategic thought.

High school students may not be as accustomed to this level of consequence being associated with every test or assignment, even the first one. They may be accustomed to do-overs of various types, including the results of the first test being thrown out if most students do not do well on it. Although many college courses do have a provision to allow an individual test or assignment score to be excluded from the computation of the final grade, it is a dangerous strategy to always be in the position of having to discard the first grade. Savvy college students keep that option in their back pocket until they need to use it. Less strategic students burn through their options quickly and find themselves in a corner by the time midterms arrive.

Studying for a test or major assignment successfully has many components all of which do not need to be explicated here to make the general point about the importance of doing so and the means by which high schools can begin to develop these skills in all students. Preparation begins at the most basic level of all, attending class and, in cases when it is impossible to do so, making sure to obtain all material covered in class that day and learn it.

Effective studying requires good organizational skills so that students have easy access to all required materials. Time spent looking for lost handouts or downloading material again from the course Web site detracts from developing an overall understanding of the materials by keeping them in an order that makes sense in relation to key course concepts and topics. Similarly, being far behind on readings creates an almost insurmountable problem in terms of digesting and understanding material at the last minute. Test prep consists largely of taking a number of steps during the course to be ready for the test so that the final studying push as the test approaches is largely to consolidate and review understandings, not to learn material from scratch.

Goal Setting

Goal setting involves the ability to set short-term and longer-term goals simultaneously. Goals are important to have because they help motivate actions that may be less enjoyable at the time but lead to more desirable results over time. This behavior, sometimes called deferred gratification, is an important part of preparing for success in a variety of environments in which hard work can lead to rewards over time.

Not all goal setting is about deferring gratification. High school students need to take pleasure and pride in small as well as large accomplishments. However, they generally need help formalizing their goal setting. Some remarkable young people need no help at all, and we are often amazed at their self-discipline and single-mindedness. However, most students do not fall into this category and require considerable support to set goals in the first place, gauge their progress toward achieving goals, and celebrate the achievement of goals when benchmarks are met.

Goal setting can be accomplished on multiple levels within a school. Students can be encouraged to set goals as they enter as high school freshmen, and college and career readiness most certainly should be one of those goals. This exercise requires times and places during the school year when goals can be set and assessed and students can receive guidance and support in stating their goals and in being acknowledged for the progress they have made or the challenges they have faced.

Goal setting also entails an understanding of what needs to be done to achieve the goal. This is necessary so that goals that are set have a reasonable probability of being met. Students need guidance and help shaping their goals so that they are potentially attainable but still result in a stretch from where they currently stand. One way to help them do this is to present examples of the performance level they need to be striving to reach so that they recognize the gap between where they are currently and where they need to be. Exemplar papers and documents can be useful in this regard.

Students also benefit from hearing from others who have set and achieved similar goals previously. Visits with students who have successfully prepared for college and can discuss how they did so can help inspire a wider range of students to set higher goals. Working closely with peer support and mentors can also help students craft ambitious yet achievable goals. In general, goal setting requires or is improved by interaction between the person setting the goal and someone encouraging the person and helping him or her to formulate a plan that demonstrates how the person can accomplish the goal. In other words, goal setting as a private activity is fine for some, but by no means all, students, and goal setting as an impersonal class activity is not as powerful as when human interaction can be introduced into the process.

High school and middle school faculty and administrators can encourage the creation of a college-going culture by infusing goal setting into the school's program at multiple points. For example, when students do schedule planning, they might also be required to complete goal-setting activities. Each course might include in the syllabus a section in which each student sets goals for the course and has this reviewed and signed by a parent or guardian and the teacher.

Goal setting is much more common in the athletic arena, and educators can learn from these models, emphasizing concepts such as "personal best" and getting students to "benchmark" their performance against external performance standards. Breaking improvement goals up into discrete, manageable steps can also help students achieve small successes on the way to larger accomplishments.

Goal setting, like all the other academic behaviors, must be practiced repeatedly under a variety of circumstances and in a range of settings if students are to internalize and generalize them to new settings, such as postsecondary education. Here again a college-going culture becomes the larger frame within which goal setting resides and serves as the focal point for most goal setting. In order to reinforce student participation, numerous opportunities to recognize successful achievement of goals need to be incorporated into the classroom life and culture of the school. In addition to the standard year-end award and recognition assemblies, each class can find ways to acknowledge successful achievement of goals. Letters to parents can be a simple yet significant way to demonstrate that someone noticed that the student had achieved an important academic goal. Parent conferences can focus as much on student goals as on performance, emphasizing where students have yet to go and what they need to do to get there. But recognition needs to be for real, significant accomplishments. Students will know when they are being patronized. A well-designed and coordinated program of goal setting schoolwide can yield changes in student behavior, particularly if students see many ways to set and achieve goals successfully and are recognized for doing so.

Persistence with Difficult Tasks

High school educators walk a precarious tightrope in their expectations for students. Ask too much, and students and parents may rebel. Ask too little, and students become bored and disaffected. How is the balance to be achieved? Some educators believe the best way to make a course challenging is to give lots of homework and grade in a rigorous fashion. This approach has its merits and drawbacks, but may be missing the point at some level, particularly if the content itself and the assessment methods do not stretch students in certain ways.

High school students become accustomed to being able to complete most tasks with little effort and not much time. They learn how to give back to teachers what they think the teachers want to hear or see. They calculate how little they can do to receive a minimally sufficient grade. They continue to test the system to see what is really required of them.

As a result, they are not accustomed to persisting with a task that takes a great deal of effort over an extended period of time or one where the answer is not readily apparent. This is perhaps even truer of higher-achieving students, although average students are experts at this as well. Students in the lower quartile so rarely encounter any material or assignment that is truly challenging that they don't even have the opportunity to develop a set of strategies attuned to filtering out such tasks.

In short, students and teachers often arrive at an uneasy truce under which neither bothers the other too much. In the average course, this results in a series of assignments that are completed and submitted without a great deal of thought or effort. In more academically challenging courses, more work may be assigned, but teachers have learned that high-achieving students do not tolerate ambiguity well and that these students require or even demand clarity in their assignments.

These coping strategies do not prepare students well for college or career preparation. Because college courses and many career preparation programs tend to emphasize more complex problems and require students to cope with the unknown to a greater degree than in the past, students who are unwilling or unable to cope with ambiguity or the need to be highly self-directed will struggle with many of the assignments and tasks they encounter in college courses.

Students do not have to be brilliant to cope with these expectations, only willing to persist in the face of a new or challenging task that they cannot resolve immediately or with little effort. Many postsecondary assignments are designed specifically to stretch students' thinking and cannot be completed with available knowledge or strategies. Students must have the tenacity to attack a problem from multiple perspectives and consider a range of strategic thinking skills until they seize on the right combination for the problem at hand.

One of the simplest ways high school educators can begin to acclimate their students to this type of learning is to begin in the ninth grade giving assignments that require multiple days to complete. These may be relatively straightforward initially, but they should have enough parts to them so that students cannot do them in one sitting. This is perhaps the first step in getting students accustomed to working on tasks that require some planning and decisions about how best to complete them.

A second technique is to introduce problems that have no one right solution, or at least no obvious solution. For example, in social sciences, students might read two documents that contain conflicting explanations of the causes of a particular historical event or social phenomenon. Rather than determining which one is "right," which will be the students' first instinct, the assignment would require them to research how each author reached her or his conclusion, the social context within which the conclusion was reached, and the relative merits of each argument. Such an assignment could require several iterations, each including a defense of the conclusions reached.

In the sciences and mathematics, it is relatively easy to think of problems or questions for which the answers are less clear or multiple correct answers exist. Sometimes the value of an assignment is not the answer at all, but the process of determining that no simple right answer exists. Instead of filling out lab manuals that always lead to a "correct" answer or solving problems that offer little insight into the mathematical concept they represent, students need to be engaged in more complex tasks that require presenting findings and defending them publicly, explaining how they reached their conclusions, and even going back and reanalyzing data to understand why an incorrect result was achieved or to reach a new conclusion when the problem is restated.

Another example of persistence is being able to improve on a draft of a piece of writing. High school students rarely have to rewrite a paper and almost never have to do so repeatedly until it reaches an acceptable standard before it can be submitted for a grade. Part of the reason this is so is that most written assignments are not long or complex enough to justify significant editing, and the feedback provided by teachers, who have little time to undertake in-depth analysis, tends not to be terribly informative of the redrafting process.

Many teachers shy away from complex writing assignments under the belief that they do not have the time to grade them in the first place, so why assign them at all? However, complex writing assignments do not necessarily require teachers to read every draft from every student. By reading a few carefully selected drafts covering a range of student performance, the teacher can discern the problems students are having and then offer a lesson directed at exactly those points. No individual student receives detailed feedback, but all are privy to instructions and guidance on how to improve their next draft. This can be supplemented by example papers with annotations noting the problems contained in the example and how best to address that problem. When final drafts are read and graded, a scoring guide can speed the process, allowing for more skimming of papers and fewer comments on the papers themselves.

Having students understand that writing well requires persistence can pay off in other subject areas where they can be introduced to projects and studies that require more of them in terms of engagement and willingness to learn. Advanced classes in particular should be showcases of appropriate, challenging work and not simply content mills designed to grind through as much material as possible in the time allotted. While students may not applaud a shift toward work that requires them to engage more deeply and to confront the fact that they may not know how to proceed with an assignment without significant thought and planning, they will nevertheless benefit from a high school education that consistently expects them to persist in situations where they are not entirely proficient or even fully confident.

Self-Awareness of Academic Strengths and Weaknesses

First-year college students are often shocked by many of the ways that the expectations they face in their entry-level courses differ from what they had become accustomed to in high school, but no change is more jarring to them than the grades they receive on their first college assignments. Having done much of what they did in high school and for which they received high marks and positive feedback from their teachers, they now earn grades that are considerably lower, accompanied by comments that are far more critical of their thinking, organization, and general attention to detail. How can students be prepared to cope with this reframing of expectations?

The most important single step a high school faculty can take is to grade student work, at least some of it, against standards that provide students with a clearer picture of where they stand relative to college and career readiness. Perhaps it will remain necessary for high school teachers to inflate grades so that students remain competitive for admission to colleges and universities, which continue to raise their minimum GPA requirements, thereby fueling this very inflation. But it will be in the best interests of students to ensure that they receive unvarnished feedback at least occasionally.

One strategy is to grade papers against a set of high school–referenced standards and provide a separate scoring against college readiness standards. The college readiness–referenced comments might tell students how the paper would have fared had it been submitted in a college course. Feedback of this nature might point out the places where the students have not devoted sufficient time and effort to preparing a position, documenting a point of view, constructing a logical argument, using sources appropriately, and rewriting or editing for precision and accuracy. Many teachers provide this type of general feedback, but for it to have an effect, students need to know the mark that their paper would receive in a college course as a part of the feedback. Many may be surprised to learn that a paper that receives an A from the high school teacher would likely be graded as C work in college. This realization helps students understand that they have considerable room to improve—and a need to do so.

Another strategy for anchoring grading practices so that all students receive comparable feedback is to have a common assignment that all students complete at a particular grade level. The assignment can even be labeled the "college-ready assignment," as described in Chapter Two. Typically this would be a research paper or a lab exercise in which they must draw conclusions from observations, not merely record data. The resulting papers are then graded by all teachers against a common set of standards that are tied closely to those that might be found in a college course. These standards can be derived from "reference courses" that are amalgams of entry-level college courses that were described earlier in this chapter. The EPIC has developed twenty such reference courses that are representative of the subjects that entering college students commonly take.

While care should be taken not to discourage students who are some distance away from college and career readiness, students who have set their sights on postsecondary programs (which may be over 80 percent of students at a typical high school) should have the opportunity to gauge how well their work measures against the expectations of an entry-level college course at a two-year or four-year institution. For students who have further to go to be college ready, feedback can be more selective and supportive without diluting the message that the student needs a realistic view of the distance yet to travel to be college and career ready.

Students, for their part, should be encouraged to reflect on the quality of the work they produce, independent of the grade they receive on it. This can be accomplished in a variety of ways. The common assignments provide one possible means to begin such a reflective process. Upon receiving feedback, students might discuss in groups their perceptions of the differences in high school and college expectations, without ever revealing anything about how well or poorly their own work stacked up against such standards.

For students who have a high opinion of their own academic work, it may be worthwhile to have opportunities for guided reflection on the quality of the work and areas in which it could be improved. This could lead to more formal goal setting, in this case focused much more clearly on the skills, techniques, and habits they need to develop to result in work that will meet college standards. This sort of activity is particularly important for "4.0" students, who may be the most shocked when they receive the first C of their lives in college.

High achievers from schools with large concentrations of low-income students, members of ethnic and racial minority groups, and students who would be first-generation college attendees are particularly vulnerable to the shattered self-image phenomenon. Many of these students are the academic stars of their schools, but are likely to find that they are more in the middle of the distribution once they arrive at college. The differential expectations present in U.S. high schools between those serving privileged communities and those serving the poor show up when students encounter the college instructor who cares little what high school a student attended and looks only at the quality of the work produced. Students in these high schools need clearer understandings of postsecondary expectations before they get to college to prepare them if they receive lower grades initially. Even better, these students need curriculum and assignments that challenge them to reach their full potential and that are well aligned with college and career readiness standards.

One of the ways to do this is to introduce the gap between the high school's expectations and the college's expectations. In addition, these students can be provided with transitional experiences that expose them to college-level grading while still in high school through dual-credit and AP courses. Finally, these students can benefit from mentor relationships designed to help them reflect on how to use their strengths in combination with new strategies to cope with potentially deficient areas.

Almost no student enters college with an objective sense of his or her own academic strengths and weaknesses. High schools that provide all students with opportunities to reflect on their academic performance in relation to postsecondary expectations they are likely to encounter will help ease the pain that many will experience on getting back their first college paper. This psychological toughness will help many students remain in college and seek help, rather than assume they are not capable of doing the work and give up.

"COLLEGE KNOWLEDGE"—CONTEXTUAL SKILLS AND AWARENESS

Nowhere more so than in the United States is information about college access and success privileged knowledge. Every aspect of getting into college, it seems, requires students (or their adult advocates) to take affirmative steps to learn what is required, how to apply, the programs available, the standards for admission and requisite tests, placement requirements, financial aid policies and practices, and a plethora of other information.

It is worth noting that it is not necessarily the case in other countries that students must pass through such a gauntlet to apply to a postsecondary program. Many countries have a much closer connection between their secondary and postsecondary systems, in part because their educational systems are not as decentralized as in the United States. I do not mean to imply that a centralized system is necessarily better. I do suggest that if U.S. secondary and postsecondary educators wish to retain a more decentralized governance and policymaking structure, they have a greater responsibility to ensure that all students have access to the basic knowledge necessary to be admitted to a postsecondary institution and that all students have the opportunity to do so without the need for extraordinary effort on their part.

In short, the reality of the U.S. educational governance system suggests that high school and college administrators and faculty have a greater duty to ensure that all relevant information related to college admission is available to all students, not just to students who pursue it or possess it already. If young people are left primarily to their own devices to gather the information necessary to be eligible for college and acquire necessary financial aid, those who fail to do so will be disproportionately from groups underrepresented in postsecondary education already.

In short, without increased simplification and transparency on the part of colleges' admissions procedures and a redesign by high schools of the systems they employ to get necessary information to all students in a timely fashion, it is unlikely that college-going rates for underrepresented groups will increase very dramatically. If they do increase, it will largely be in enrollments to two-year institutions, where students can apply as late as the first day of class and need to meet far fewer requirements.

While enrolling more students in two-year institutions is certainly a positive thing to do, this should not become the default option because students are simply unaware of what they need to do to be eligible for a larger set of postsecondary options. Even students who arrive at the doors of a community college the first day of class with little preparation are at a severe disadvantage compared to their peers who have been preparing for some time to make the transition. Evidence from recent studies suggests that many of these students are eligible for admission at more selective institutions but may not be aware of this fact or know how to access these institutions. All students need full access to the college knowledge that is necessary to be able to make an intelligent decision about where to pursue postsecondary education and then to be prepared to meet all relevant requirements to do so.

The second form of college knowledge is how to function within the postsecondary environment once admitted. This includes awareness of the resources available to students once they arrive at college, such as tutoring services, advising, special courses to help build core academic skills, developmental education programs, and student support groups and organizations.

Part of this college knowledge is having a general sense of the opportunities beyond classes available in the postsecondary community of learners. For first-generation college attendees in particular, college represents a case of severe culture shock. How does one behave with instructors and professors? With other students from different backgrounds? How does one develop a relationship with these people? Knowing, for example, that professors and instructors really enjoy talking about what they study and not just about the problems students are having in a class can provide an edge to the savvy student seeking to develop more personal relationships with faculty. Those relationships pay off in a number of ways through access to support and opportunities that are not available to students who are simply going through the motions. Understanding how the academic community functions is extremely important to students who are attempting to navigate an unfamiliar and potentially disorienting new system.

Most high schools offer a set of services that students must access themselves, such as scholarship night or college visits, or they have a set of cursory mandatory activities, such as a required meeting with a counselor to review their transcript. Addressing the college knowledge problem requires significant redesign and investment of time and energy by high schools and their postsecondary partners.

This implies that the high schools have one or more postsecondary partners in the first place. Here again, some high schools aggressively pursue such relationships, while others do not. And here again, the high schools that do develop these relationships tend to be those that already send a large proportion of students on to college, while those that don't also have far fewer students attending postsecondary institutions and far higher enrollments of students from low-income families and first-generation college attendees. One of the first steps a high school can take to build student college knowledge is to develop stronger partnerships with local postsecondary institutions. The effect of partnerships is to improve alignment between secondary and postsecondary levels and to help educators at each level discover the ways in which they can change programs so that more students acquire the college knowledge necessary to be ready to make the transition from one system to the other.

Building Cultural Capital

Cultural capital can be defined as the knowledge, experience, and values that enable individuals to succeed within a particular social and cultural context. Individuals with cultural capital are more likely to attend and complete college and career-preparation programs because they understand the institutional values and norms associated with those programs. The amount of cultural capital necessary to succeed depends in part on how individuals are socialized. Thus, students whose parents did not attend college are less likely to possess cultural capital than students who parents completed college and understand college culture and values. Nevertheless, cultural capital can be built over time.

One way is by closely mentoring a group of individual students. These students learn etiquette, social skills and norms, and financial planning in these mentoring sessions. Participating students are those who may not typically learn these skills from family or friends. Students may also gain access to social capital as they have opportunities through mentorships to interact with community leaders. Participating students then are expected to help their peers learn these same skills. The goal is to prepare students to be comfortable in a variety of settings, including college campuses.

Postsecondary institutions can offer an introductory course where advisors teach students the importance of attending all college courses, managing time and studying, and communicating with professors. Such a course can also be a place where advisors explain how the organizational structure and social system of college is different than that of high school. Students can learn an array of strategies, such as meeting regularly with academic advisors; learning how to select instructors by reviewing online evaluations and student comments on a course; joining a study group early in the first year; and accessing special programs that create cohorts of students who take courses together, engage in social activities, and receive specialized support.

Navigating Admissions

Students need help in a number of specific areas as they approach the process of selecting a postsecondary program, applying to it, and making all the necessary arrangements to be admitted and initiate studies successfully. Students need help and support in a variety of areas if they are to be prepared to choose a college and enroll successfully.

College Search and Selection Practices

Families in which one or both parents have attended college usually have a basic understanding of postsecondary options. In contrast, potential first-generation college attendees are less likely to be aware of college options, which include public, private, in-state, out-of-state, four-year, two-year, technical colleges, and proprietary programs, and how to select a college that will be a good fit with their academic and social needs. Research indicates that students are more satisfied with their choice if they have received high-quality information about college during high school. Students who have more information are likely to make better decisions about where to enroll and more likely to remain at the institution they chose initially.

High schools can provide a variety of resources and programs to help students select a college appropriate for their needs and goals. College fairs are a common way to expose students to a variety of colleges. High schools invite a range of postsecondary institutions to participate in a local fair. If it is not possible to host a college fair on-site, it may be possible to collaborate with another high school in the area to organize a multicampus fair. Free transportation for students to off-site venues makes college fairs accessible to all students. Some schools require students to attend a college fair in tenth or eleventh grade. In addition to college fairs, schools can invite college representatives throughout the school year and encourage interested students to attend their presentations. Publicizing these visits through public announcements and flyers is useful.

Assignments that require students to research several colleges and report their findings help students learn how to conduct college searches independently. Online programs contain detailed databases of colleges and can be searched with multiple criteria. Some schools require students to conduct research at the college fair. Others help students register for online accounts with service providers such as the College Board. These accounts function as the jumping-off point to exploration of college options using a range of resources available on the Web site in conjunction with the user account. Schools can also post a list of the colleges that their teachers attended. This may give students access to an adult to whom they may pose questions about particular colleges.

Field trips to college campuses encourage students to consider college as a realistic option. These visits help students become more comfortable in a campus environment and help them identify specific programs and characteristics of colleges that may be important to them. Ideally students can visit more than one college so that they are able to compare possibilities.

These visits include the opportunities for students to sit in on a class, take a tour, and talk to students enrolled at the institution. Some schools use state assessment days to take students who have already passed the state exam to college campuses. High schools with large concentrations of second-language learners may need to consider bringing along a translator for students who are not yet fully fluent in English so that those students can participate fully in the visit. To help students learn more about the college experience, schools can also require them to interview a college graduate or college student about what to expect in college.

The main challenge to all of these suggested activities is that the groups most likely to avail themselves of these activities tend to be those that need them least. High school administrators and educators need to make special efforts to ensure that all students participate in these exposure-to-postsecondary-education activities. This may require making some activities mandatory combined with carefully identifying and encouraging those not likely to participate on their own.

College Admissions Exams

Most colleges require students to submit the results of a college admissions exam as part of the application process. In an effort to reduce the barriers to enrollment in college, a number of states and many high schools now require all students to take tests such as the PSAT, SAT, PLAN, or ACT. Some states, districts, or schools subsidize the exams so that costs are not a prohibitive factor. Others help students who cannot afford the exams apply for fee waivers.

One advantage to this approach is that the school then has information on all students, not just those who choose to take the exam. School staff members can discuss the results of the exams with one another and with students. The results can be used to automatically enroll students who obtain particular scores in more challenging courses or to call attention to the student's college potential by making parents more aware of their student's test scores and the course opportunities available to students who show promise on the tests.

In communities where few students go on to college, it is often necessary for high schools to offer or arrange for optional preparation for these exams outside regular school hours at little or no cost to students. Exam preparation can also be integrated into course work. Instruction on test-taking strategies is likely to improve scores on college admission exams, as well as on college midterms and finals. Writing prompts from past exams give students the opportunities to practice for the exams in class. Some teachers routinely begin class with an SAT or ACT question of the day, which is readily available from each organization's Web site, while other teachers include regular assessment items that mimic the format of SAT and ACT questions to help students to be more confident when they encounter these item types on the actual exams. Even if these activities do not increase student scores dramatically, they do tend to signal the importance of college and career readiness and also make students more aware of things like testing requirements and test registration deadlines and administration dates.

Assistance with College and Financial Aid Applications

Offering assistance with college and financial aid applications to all students and parents conveys a message that submitting college applications is encouraged and valued. This is so important that some schools offer workshops during the summer for students to receive help with the college search, application process, and college essays. Counselors often visit required courses during the year to discuss critical steps for applying to college. In ninth grade, this addresses the importance of GPA and challenging courses. By twelfth grade, counselors are providing detailed guidance regarding specific college application time lines, how to secure recommendations, and how to write an effective college essay.

The application forms, particularly for financial aid, can be daunting, and even intimidating, to families not accustomed to government forms. Workshops for students and parents make completion of these forms less cumbersome. Instruction on how to complete the Free Application for Federal Student Aid (FAFSA) may be necessary to get parents to submit the form in a timely fashion or to submit it at all. Even with government efforts underway to simplify the FAFSA, many parents will still be intimidated by or wary of even a simplified version. Similarly, help completing the Common Application is equally important. This is a form that, once completed, can be used to apply to nearly 350 public and private postsecondary schools, many of which then ask for specific supplemental information. Computers that are available for and set up for the application process enable parents and students to work on their own time to complete these forms and explore admissions options.

Another practice that may improve college admission success is help on composing a college essay, preparing a personal statement, and compiling a list of accomplishments. Assignments of this nature can be included as a regular part of first-semester twelfth-grade English classes. This provides an opportunity for students to receive feedback and make revisions to these materials. Alternatively, counselors or advisors can provide feedback. An increasing number of high schools require students to complete a college application, and others expect all students to take the final step and submit an application to at least one postsecondary institution. This practice may require coordination from staff members to secure waivers for application fees, but it ensures that students are learning the necessary knowledge for applying to college.

Recognition of College Admission and Success

Enhancing college knowledge in ways that facilitate college enrollment and success requires schoolwide effort. One small practice that schools can implement is public recognition of success. All schools can publish newsletters with the names of students and the college they plan to attend. These newsletters can be distributed to all students and parents. Announcements over the school PA system, the school radio station, or TV station also provide public recognition of college acceptances.

Other schools use central bulletin boards where students can post their college acceptance letters. Some school bulletin boards connect students' names or photos to a map with the location of colleges that they are accepted to or where they decide to enroll. At schools with very large graduating classes, it may be possible to present similar displays within classrooms. Smaller schools may be able to post even more detail about students' achievements, including scholarship awards or updates from recent high school graduates. These types of public displays help to create a school culture where admission to and success in college are valued goals for all students.

While important in helping to shape a college-going culture in a school, these symbolic gestures do not substitute for challenging academic expectations and a program that is well aligned with postsecondary readiness. A school that undertakes only the activities described to this point in this section on college knowledge without addressing the other three dimensions of college readiness thoroughly will not see much of an improvement in student performance in college, even if more students do somehow advance to a postsecondary program. The college knowledge dimension is one of four, and all four must be addressed systematically for students to have an improved chance of postsecondary success.

Developing Postsecondary Partnerships

Collaborative relationships or partnerships between a high school and postsecondary institution are an important conduit for developing and transmitting college knowledge. Partnerships can lead to a variety of interactions and programs. One of the most common is some form of enrollment of high school students in college courses, often in a dual-credit program, which will be discussed in more detail in a following section. Less challenging than dual credit is to have students audit a section of a course. Participating students have to complete all reading and assignments and initiate contact with the professor during office hours, but they do not have the stress of a grade to contend with. Such experiences provide high school students with a better understanding of college expectations and course structure, and teach them how to seek help in college. The more time students spend on a college campus, the more comfortable they feel and the less intimidating it becomes.

High schools, especially those with large proportions of first-generation students, can develop strong relationships with one or more colleges that receive large numbers of students from the school. Colleges that participate in these types of partnerships may offer students from the partner high school special consideration during the admissions process along with favorable financial aid packages. In fact, some colleges cover full tuition and room and board for students from designated partner high schools who meet specified criteria.

Other school partnerships focus on tutoring and mentoring. Many college students are looking for volunteer opportunities and are willing to tutor or mentor local high school students. High school students are able to learn about the college experience from current students. In addition to tutoring and mentorship programs, some schools invite college students to tutor high school students.

Partnerships between high school and college may ease this transition process by offering early placement testing, priority course registration, assistance with college applications, scholarships, and counseling in both high school and college. All of these practices help students navigate the college admissions process and adjust to college.

Regional Alignment Workshops

The regional alignment workshop model connects high schools and postsecondary institutions within a region of a state or within a service area with the goal of solving problems, exchanging information, and creating programs that are uniquely adopted to local needs and challenges. These workshops are designed under the premise that although students can choose to attend college at any of over forty-two hundred institutions in the country, most choose a local institution, and most postsecondary institutions enroll a majority of their students from a relatively small group of secondary schools.

It is neither necessary nor possible to align a high school program closely with all colleges and universities, nor is it possible for a single college or university to take into account the programs of all high schools that send students to the institution. Therefore, the regional alignment workshop focuses on a set of high schools and their relationship with a single institution or group of institutions that capture many of the students from those high schools who go on to postsecondary studies. It makes the most sense to begin by pairing high schools with local colleges that receive a large proportion of their students. Community colleges fill this bill, but regional four-year institutions are often major recipients of students from a geographically identifiable group of high schools.

These regional workshops are often best organized by a state agency, ideally a partnership between the state postsecondary governing board or boards and the state K–12 education agency. In the alternative, a group of schools can collaborate locally and organize their own regional alignment workshop. The most challenging step in the process is getting one group or another to start the ball rolling by contacting the other. Once the invitation is made, the response is generally quite positive, regardless of which side of the divide issues that invitation, and the general structure of the workshops is the same.

Planning for the workshops begins with the collection of a significant amount of information well before the meeting. Ideally, information on student preparation in high school and subsequent performance in college is assembled and disaggregated by relevant groups. The first step is to ascertain the boundaries of the problem and not operate in the world of broad generalizations or assertions regarding how well students are prepared for college and which students are well prepared for college. The intent is not to embarrass high school educators or criticize postsecondary instructors. Instead, the goal is to set a baseline from which progress can be gauged. The analysis serves as the framework wherein specific planning and problem solving take place.

Participants should be faculty who can make natural connections with one another, for example, those who teach entry-level college courses and those who teach exit-level high school courses. Voluntary participation is important, at least initially, because the emphasis is on creating connections that will strengthen over time. The first session of the regional workshop is devoted to participants' getting to know one another because it is most often the case that local high school and postsecondary faculty and administrators are not well acquainted.

Once they have become more familiar with one another (or if they are so already), the workshop focuses on a topic of mutual interest, such as the skill level that students demonstrate in writing or the expectations they will encounter in college courses with respect to workload. This can be accomplished through shared documents consisting of actual student work or syllabi, in the case of these examples. Using actual work products helps to make the conversation concrete and avoid the broad generalizations about high school or college that can derail the workshop. These conversations need to be carefully structured to build trust and avoid blame. The goal is to come up with solutions, not rehash old gripes.

The resulting solutions can take a number of forms. For example, it may become clear that no one at the high school—neither counselor, teacher, nor student—knows much about the placement exam policies or instrument of the regional university or local community college. This may be contributing in some measure to high placement into remedial courses, say, in math. One result of the workshop might be a plan to share more information about placement testing with students, but also for high school teachers to examine the content of the placement tests and determine ways to prepare students better for those tests. Colleges, for their part, could consider more sophisticated ways to place students into entry-level courses, perhaps working more closely with feeder high schools to gather information on student performance.

Dual Credit

Dual credit, also known as *dual enrollment,* refers to the participation of high school students in courses for which they receive credit at both their high school and at the college level. The most successful dual-credit programs encourage all interested students to apply, but require students to meet specific academic eligibility requirements before participating in these courses. Most schools that have wide student participation in dual-credit courses are either located near a college or provide transportation to the colleges.

Another common practice of schools with successful dual-credit programs is an adequate orientation process. All participating students receive instruction on the expectations and structure of college courses, effective note-taking techniques, and other study strategies. Tours of the college campus are useful for students to become familiar with the college surroundings and learn where the library and student support services are located. Many high schools encourage or require students to seek out support services or contact their college professors outside class. It is beneficial if students can obtain a college ID card that provides them with access to the library, college events, and the recreation center.

In addition to orientation, high schools with successful dual-credit programs often help students register for appropriate courses and carefully monitor student progress in these courses. This helps to ensure that high school students do not inadvertently enroll in overly difficulty courses. Close communication with college faculty serves this purpose. Careful monitoring of student progress helps the high school identify large knowledge or skill deficiencies that necessitate adjustments to the high school curriculum and additional support for students who are struggling in dual-credit courses. It is important that high schools offer tutoring and advising for dual-credit students and helpful for high school faculty to observe dual-credit courses on occasion in order to improve preparation and target student support.

Dual credit is an integral part of the curriculum at early and middle college high schools—high schools located on or near college campuses that provide coordinated programs between high school and college. Students take courses at both the high school and college and can graduate with both a high school diploma and an associate degree within four or five years. One middle college high school requires students to complete internships on the college campus for credit. In exchange for this student labor, students gain additional experience on a college campus and possibly recommendations from supervisors.

Some of these high schools provide a gradual transition to college through other means. For example, schools may offer courses at the high school that are taught by college faculty or taught jointly by college and high school faculty.

The following year, students may attend courses on the college campus that are taught by college faculty but in classes with other high school students. Finally, students may take college courses with other college students. This progression steadily reduces the support for students as they become accustomed to college-level instruction.

Dual-credit courses allow students to earn valuable course credit and possibly reduce the number of credits required to earn a bachelor's degree. Perhaps more important, these courses provide students with firsthand experience on college expectations and the structure of college course work. Courses that take place on college campuses help students become familiar with the college environment and its resources. Another advantage of dual-credit courses is they encourage students' beliefs in their ability to succeed in college. Finally, these courses allow small schools to supplement their curriculum with a wide range of challenging courses that the high school is unable to offer.

Supporting Postsecondary Participation

Schools can do a great deal, large and small, to support students around postsecondary participation. Some of the ways necessitate changes in school structures and the way time is organized; others require little other than agreement among faculty to engage in certain practices. When schools can combine the larger structural changes with the myriad small symbolic behaviors, students receive a consistent message about the importance of setting their sights on college readiness and participation.

College Preparatory Organizational Structures

High school counseling departments that have high student-to-counselor ratios are often overwhelmed with a range of responsibilities, such as scheduling, discipline, and testing, along with advising students adequately on postsecondary options and expectations. One strategy many high schools employ is to assign students to a counselor or advisor who follows the same group of students across multiple years. This helps counselors become more familiar with individual students, monitor their progress, and be aware of their interests and skills. A counseling center that provides access to computers is a central organizing component of college readiness at many schools with an explicit emphasis on college preparation. Students can receive support using computers for college and scholarship searches, for compiling an online portfolio of information necessary to apply, and for learning more about myriad program options and opportunities available to them. Counselors can reach out to teachers in a variety of ways, such as sending brief e-mail messages with bits of information on college preparation that teachers read in class to students. In some schools, counselors and teachers work together to coordinate classroom presentations by counselors, followed by student assignments related to college and career readiness.

In addition to counseling departments, some schools use structures that mimic college characteristics. For example, schools can require students to register for courses in much the same style as a college registration process. Students are guaranteed enrollment in a section of their core academic courses, but may not get the teacher, section, or elective courses they prefer. Students learn how to design a course schedule and select classes according to requirements, interests, and preferences, a skill useful in college. Other effective schools offer block courses that mimic college scheduling by not meeting every day. Some schools require or strongly encourage teachers to offer office hours outside class and encourage students to contact them for extra assistance.

Some schools have a strong emphasis on creating a language around college readiness and academic achievement. For example, some schools label a set of courses pre-Advanced Placement (pre-AP). Although the College Board does not offer any formal set of courses that can be called pre-AP, the inclusion of pre-AP courses creates a pathway to AP courses and instills higher expectations for students who participate in these classes.

Career Exploration and Planning

The process of setting long-term college and career goals and developing plans to achieve those goals encourages students to consider life beyond high school. Goals help to motivate students. Developing detailed plans breaks large goals into more attainable steps. Many schools require students to participate in career assessment, exploration, and planning beginning in middle school and continuing through each year of high school.

Aptitude tests, interest inventories, and skills assessments are a starting point for students to consider career options. Many schools require all students to complete such assessments and then participate in small group or individual discussion of results. Most students need assistance interpreting the results. Some online career assessments integrate students' results with research on related careers. Students are then required to integrate the results into portfolios where they can track their progress over time and see how their thinking about college and careers evolves. Another option is to assign students to research several of the recommended careers and then identify the education and skills necessary for entry into these careers. They then compare the results to their planned program to determine if they are going to be eligible for postsecondary programs necessary to achieve their goal.

Career exploration activities expose students to the variety of occupational and professional fields. Career fairs give students the opportunity to explore careers further and interact with professionals in the field. Teachers can invite speakers from career fields that are relevant to course content. Professional development and teacher collaboration may improve teachers' awareness of associated career fields and enable them to integrate this information into their instruction. Courses that integrate career information help students to understand the relevance of subject matter to future goals. Class field trips may allow students to observe professionals in action. For example, science classes may schedule a trip to a hospital so that students see how content from chemistry and biology is critical to understanding problems in the medical field.

More active career exploration activities include internships, job shadowing, and interviewing professionals. Job shadowing, like class field trips, provides opportunities for students to observe career professionals, with the additional component of individual interaction between students and professionals. Internships for credit let students attain direct experience in a career field of interest. Finally, some teachers assign students to interview career professionals in the field of their choice. Teachers can help students develop appropriate interview questions, learn interview techniques, and learn how to set up interviews.

Counselors, advisors, or other trained staff members can use the results of career assessments, career exploration activities, and knowledge of students' goals to help them plan beyond high school and select courses that will prepare them to achieve their goals. The most successful schools help students review and modify their plans multiple times a year as student aspirations change. It is often helpful to involve parents and teachers in long-term planning meetings as this helps them to understand and support their students.

Student Advisories

Student advisory periods can be used to improve academic behaviors and convey information about college. The most effective advisory systems are those that reinforce a personal relationship between each student and an adult. Advisories are especially important in schools where counselors do not have the opportunity to meet regularly with each student. Ideally, teachers and administrators who serve as advisors should be trained by and work in collaboration with school counselors. With appropriate training, advisors can help students develop and monitor long-term plans, select appropriate courses and activities to achieve those goals, and overcome obstacles to success.

Effective advisory programs can take several forms. All of them involve a relatively low student-to-advisor ratio. Many schools set aside time for advisory classes during the school day. In such a model, advisory classes usually meet at least once a week in order to help build meaningful staff-student relationships. Other successful models require students to meet regularly outside class time with their advisor.

Advisories that meet regularly need a structured set of activities and direct instructional activities. Otherwise they can deteriorate into study halls or open-ended conversation sessions. The content to be covered is wide ranging and can include information on college choices, financial aid, study skills, and time management, among many other topics. Increasingly, the content for this type of structured advisory can be gleaned from the Internet, where many free services are available to provide the type of information students need to make program choices and begin preparing for the application process.

Advisory systems provide opportunities for teachers to help students identify appropriate colleges and apply for admission and financial aid. In advisory classes, students often conduct research on colleges, report findings, and discuss the findings as a class. Teachers can help students register for college admission tests and prepare them for these tests. Other useful activities are completing application and financial aid forms and drafting and refining application essays.

Parent Communication

Parents who attended college themselves are likely to understand how to prepare their children for admission to and success in college. Although outreach to all parents is useful, it is particularly important to communicate well with the parents of potential first-generation college attendees. These parents may not be aware that college is an option for their son or daughter. They may also be fearful of sending their children off to a postsecondary program in the first place. Working with these parents so that they perceive learning beyond high school as possible and beneficial is a necessary step.

The high schools that are most successful with parent communication use a combination of methods. Traditional outreach methods include mailed letters, communications sent home with students, e-mails, automated phone calls, and home visits. In addition, many high schools provide a Web site where parents can monitor their child's performance and progress online and obtain information on college and careers. Other schools require parents to attend their students' presentations or conferences. This helps parents understand the school's expectations for their children. Some schools employ liaisons who facilitate communication between the administration and parents. Often the liaisons are parents of former students at the school who have gone on to succeed in college and careers.

At schools with large populations of parents who do not speak English, schools have to use a host of creative solutions to improve communication. Web site and written documents can be translated into the relevant languages. Professional development to help teachers communicate critical information to non-English-speaking parents over the phone is also helpful. Hiring bilingual office staff or parent liaisons further improves communication. Schools may need to offer separate parent nights in different languages or provide translators and headsets at larger parent events. In some cases, offering free evening classes for parents of current students who wish to learn English is an important way to connect with and involve parents directly with the school. Parent support groups can be organized to create comfortable environments for parents to learn and discuss education. In schools that draw from a large geographical area, it may be necessary to hold meetings closer to parents' homes and in conjunction with other trusted community organizations.

Tracking Alumni Progress

Data collected from high school alumni can serve several useful purposes. This information can be used to identify how well graduates perform at specific postsecondary institutions, inform curriculum and instructional practices by highlighting areas of strong and weak alignment, and inform current high school students about college expectations by showing them where previous cohorts have succeeded and struggled. An increasing number of states are tracking the enrollment and success rates of high school students when they move on to college. The type of information provided is generally enrollment by institution, performance in freshman courses, and retention beyond the freshman year. Scores on placement tests, enrollment in remedial courses, and performance in remedial courses also help high school faculty develop a better picture of how their courses align with college expectations. Using this information, many high schools adapt their practices. Others make their own efforts to keep in touch with their graduates.

Some schools require students to sign up for e-mail accounts that the high school can use to contact them after graduation. Online networking sites such as MySpace and Facebook provide a new way to connect with alumni. Schools that make a more serious commitment to keeping in touch with graduates employ an alumni liaison to maintain contact with graduates and even to visit students on their college campuses.

One reason for tracking alumni is to include them in college forums, a means to provide high school students with an opportunity to learn what to expect at specific colleges and how college in general differs from high school. Forums can address how high school students can better prepare themselves for college and serve as an opportunity for high school students to ask a range of questions about college. Parents can be invited to these forums as well. High school students should be encouraged or required to attend the college forums beginning in ninth grade.

In addition, some high schools send surveys to alumni. Electronic surveys can be developed, administered, and analyzed easily using utilities such as Survey Monkey. Results from the surveys can be distributed and discussed with current high school students as a means to convey information about the college experience. Like the college forums, survey results reinforce college attendance as an achievable objective. Schools can also use survey results to inform curriculum design and school practices in areas where many alumni are underprepared.

 For more information on the methods and strategies presented in this chapter, go to http://CollegeCareerReady.org.

CHAPTER 4

Key Principles of College and Career Readiness

The previous chapters have presented an expanded definition of college and career readiness and introduced a series of strategies that can be integrated into high school programs of study to make more students college and career ready. The findings presented in those chapters derive from research conducted at the Educational Policy Improvement Center (EPIC), along with findings from other studies in the area of college readiness.

Many of EPIC's findings derived from our study of thirty-eight high schools that outperform comparable schools that are preparing students for college and careers. Our study of these schools, sponsored by the Bill & Melinda Gates Foundation, yielded many practices and programs of particular interest because they appeared in so many of the schools we visited and were central to the mission and success of these schools.

From the lists of key practice and programs our field observations generated, we synthesized a number of key principles that describe what educators and administrators do in schools that have success in preparing a greater-than-expected proportion of their students for college and career readiness and are particularly successful with students who will be the first generation in their family to attend college. This chapter sets out seven key principles, introducing and explaining each and providing examples from the schools that we studied.

For more information on the schools presented in this chapter, go to http://CollegeCareerReady.org.

PRINCIPLE 1: CREATE AND MAINTAIN A COLLEGE-GOING CULTURE IN THE SCHOOL

Adults and children in high schools with cultures that emphasize readiness for college and careers habitually engage in behaviors and practices that demonstrate the pervasive schoolwide belief that all students can enroll in postsecondary education after high school graduation and be successful. These high schools institute a range of practices that encourage and in many cases require students to consider postsecondary options. They send the message that all students should be focusing on college as their goal. They have high common expectations for all students and organize their instructional programs accordingly. A high school that sustains a college-going culture focuses on how to prepare for college and how to make the transition successful, not on whether to attend college.

These schools tend to define college broadly to include all postsecondary programs. In fact, the majority of graduates from many of these schools will attend a community college and pursue a career-oriented certificate program. Although all the schools encourage students to aim as high as possible, students do not receive the message that pursuing a career-oriented option is less valuable or desirable. The key is that these schools have high expectations for all students, and those expectations are defined as participation in some form of postsecondary education.

We observed schools engaged in a range of practices designed to create a college-going culture. At the heart of creating this culture is the belief by all faculty that the school's mission is to enable all students to be able to go on to education beyond high school if they so choose. To support this goal, many schools we visited use default schedules in which students are automatically enrolled in a program of study designed to prepare them for college unless their parents specifically opt them out of that schedule. College acceptance letters are prominently posted so that all students are aware of their peers' success. Award ceremonies always focus on the academic accomplishments of students and provide public recognition of students who are accepted to college. A few schools even require all students to apply to at least one postsecondary institution.

Almost all of the schools we visited have special programs for their entering freshmen. These include bridge programs for the summer between eighth and ninth grades designed to inculcate students in the college-going mission of the school academically and culturally, separate freshman campuses, freshman seminars, and others. The programs help instill the school's culture as well as discern student skill levels, motivation, and interest. They are also a place where students connect with caring adults and form relationships that will last throughout high school.

Through the first three years of high school, faculty serve as advisors who meet with a designated group of students monthly to review grades, discuss course selection, and develop strategies to overcome any learning obstacles. College counselors in these schools take over at twelfth grade and work intensively with students, providing technical support related to college application, choice, and financial aid. Students, particularly potential first-generation college attendees, spend time on college campuses through multiple visits designed to demystify college. Senior seminars or advisements required of all twelfth graders provide even more information on college and financial aid applications and encouragement and support.

These schools find ways to lower student-to-counselor ratios. All counselors are college counselors in some fashion. The people who fill the counselor role are extremely dedicated to the mission of preparing all students for postsecondary education, to the point of pursuing students in the hallways to make sure they have filled out the Free Application for Federal Student Aid (FAFSA) form or completed necessary application materials on time. Some schools employ an alumni counselor to track graduates' progress and success in college.

First-generation students often do not have access to the financial resources required to visit multiple colleges. However, many faculty, counselors, and administrators agree that the act of visiting a college campus in person can have a profound impact on students who will be the first in their families to attend college. Often it is on these campus visits that students begin to see themselves as future college students. Several schools invest resources into college visits and tailor those visits to meet their students' needs, for example, by sending a Spanish-speaking staff person to accompany Spanish-speaking students and making sure the tour includes stops at campus resources such as the financial aid office and academic support offices.

Examples of How Schools Seek to Create College-Going Cultures

The Cristo Rey Network is a national organization of Catholic high schools focused on the needs of students in urban settings. The initial focus of the network was on connecting students with work experiences in order to help students pay for their schooling. However, the internships were so successful in engaging and retaining students that they were incorporated as a central element of each Cristo Rey school's design.

One of the results of the internships was that students were much more motivated to consider continuing formal education beyond high school. This led to an increased emphasis on preparing for a range of college programs. Over time, college and career readiness has become one of the central goals of all Cristo Rey schools. College counseling at Cristo Rey Jesuit High School in Chicago, Illinois, begins during freshman orientation when counselors meet individually with students to establish the expectation that all students will apply to and attend college. The school hosts two college fairs each year, and students across all grades are invited to learn about specific colleges and the application process. The college-counseling program intensifies in the junior year when all students participate in college visits, retreats, and individual sessions with counselors. Juniors are required to take the ACT and PSAT and engage in career exploration activities through IllinoisMentor.com. All juniors take the AP Spanish Language exam, and all seniors take the AP Spanish Literature exam.

Rising seniors are invited to attend a three-week summer institute to work individually with counselors on writing personal statements and completing applications. Some students are able to submit all of their applications during this time. Roughly half of the seniors complete the institute, while the others attend an after-school workshop held three days a week once the school year begins.

Cristo Rey's comprehensive and personalized college counseling program reinforces the school's expectations and offers students important contextual skills for college success. The caseload for a full-time counselor is eighty-five students, which allows time to work with every student individually during all four years of high school. Among many other examples, college counselors send students e-mail information about scholarship opportunities and summer writing programs offered at the local colleges to students and parents.

Building a strong culture around the standardized college preparatory curriculum is a shared responsibility at Sammamish High School in Bellevue, Washington. Since adopting a policy that all students will take at least one AP course, approximately 95 percent of students who enroll in an AP course take the AP exam in that course. The remaining 5 percent of students do not complete the AP course or opt to take an alternative test developed by the district and modeled after the AP exam. To remove financial barriers, the school offers a scholarship program for students who can't afford the AP exam registration fee, and all students eligible for free or reduced-price lunches automatically receive a scholarship.

School administrators estimate that the policy has a 75 percent overall approval rating with students, parents, and teachers and believe it takes up to three years to completely integrate into a school's culture. Administrators, department heads, guidance counselors, and AP teachers work collaboratively to raise awareness about the ultimate value of a rigorous curriculum—that advanced course work in English, math, science, and history leads to more options after high school. The expectation and consistent message to students is, "Taking AP courses is what we do here."

This message is reinforced in numerous ways. Administrators regularly meet with struggling students and their parents to discuss what employers and colleges demand and how advanced course work cultivates such knowledge and skills. During many of these meetings, they review the student's academic plan so that both student and parents can better understand how AP courses relate to the student's four-year schedule and college admission. This activity has proven to be particularly helpful with parents who did not attend college themselves and with the parents of students who are designated as English Language Learners (ELL).

The school pursues tailored solutions to remove barriers for individual students. The principal described one case in which she and an ELL student moved through five options to keep the student enrolled in an AP history course: individual tutoring with the assistant principal, additional group work to increase interaction with English-speaking students, a new schedule to accommodate work and school demands, and a school laptop to complete assignments at home.

Ultimately the student transferred to the regular history class but continued to audit the AP course in order to have a more college-like experience.

PRINCIPLE 2: CREATE A CORE ACADEMIC PROGRAM ALIGNED WITH AND LEADING TO COLLEGE READINESS BY THE END OF TWELFTH GRADE

We found schools going beyond alignment with state standards to consider how their curriculum—ninth through twelfth grade—could be designed to prepare students for college readiness generally and AP courses specifically. This process of vertical alignment is achieved by comparing course expectations, assignments, goals, and activities across several grade levels and using a set of college readiness standards as the common reference point. Although no one school employs all the elements of a fully integrated vertical alignment process, several succeed in achieving good continuity and consistency of expectations across levels within one or more subject areas. Smaller schools, newly constituted schools, and charter schools have more success than large, comprehensive high schools, but even some large schools demonstrate portions of the instructional program where alignment had been achieved.

An additional strategy we observed is requiring all students at a given grade level in a given subject to complete a common test or assessment. This helps enforce a form of horizontal alignment across all students at a particular grade level. This type of alignment helps determine if certain baseline expectations are consistent for all students across all courses, important as a means to establish that all students are on a pathway toward some form of postsecondary readiness.

All students taking a sophomore English course, for example, would be required to complete the same writing task, which their teachers then score using common criteria. This activity allows the school to calibrate expectations better across courses. Teachers meet to read student work and compare their expectations for their students. Similarly, all students enrolled in Algebra I take the same exam at a certain point, allowing teachers to get a better sense of how their students are doing in relation to a common standard. Teachers could then adjust the challenge level in the class accordingly. This strategy is particularly important in schools with diverse student populations and campuses with multiple small schools, where differing expectations can become established for different groups of students or for different programs.

Vertical alignment takes place across grade levels, within high schools or between high schools and the schools from which their students come and to which they go. Partnerships with middle schools, although complex to organize and implement, can foster a better understanding of what the incoming students are being taught and what will be necessary to prepare them for a college preparatory curriculum in the ninth grade. Summer bridge programs prior to the start of the ninth grade can address some of these gaps. Some schools work with feeder middle schools to develop coordinated, aligned pre-AP programs. However, the basic starting point for alignment between middle and high school programs is to establish what is being taught in each course at each level, identify redundancies and gaps, and commit to greater transparency and consistency in content and expectations across levels.

Alignment within high schools can be accomplished through a wide range of methods developed by organizations with interest and expertise in the progression of the high school curriculum. The following examples are of several of these organizations—those that focus on the progression of high school in relation to college readiness. The types of alignment processes these groups offer are designed to help ensure that the high school program of study leads more directly to and connects with postsecondary expectations and programs.

Over the past decade, EPIC has worked with a number of high schools to conduct alignment and challenge audits. This process analyzes the content of all core content courses against a set of college readiness standards. While any set of several possible sets of college readiness standards can serve as the reference point, including the Common Core Standards, we have utilized Standards for Success, developed by the Association of American Universities, a group of the nation's sixty leading research universities.

Teachers at the high school where the audit is taking place rate their courses against college readiness standards and submit copies of their syllabi for external review, which helps validate self-reported data. The resulting report details where the school's program of study is well aligned with college readiness standards and where gaps or redundancies exist. High school educators can then modify course content and sequencing to improve the continuity and flow across four years of high school to ensure that students are challenged at a level consistent with college and career readiness.

The College Board offers curriculum alignment analysis services to help high schools develop comprehensive plans for reshaping their overall program of instruction. As a result of participating in the College Readiness Systems process, school staff receive detailed information about all aspects of the school's instructional program. This comprehensive analysis then serves as a baseline to create a customized program for the school designed to improve college readiness. That program may include tools and services offered by the College Board or by other organizations. College Board resources include the SpringBoard program of courses and AP, along with the PSAT and SAT tests. Staff then complete a comprehensive school diagnostic instrument annually to gauge progress longitudinally and refine priority actions regularly, a process explained in greater detail in the next chapter.

The ACT program of high school alignment is called QualityCore. Its purpose is to provide educators with the resources necessary to align courses in ways that enhance rigor and improve outcomes for students. The program consists of twelve courses in English, math, science, and U.S. history. Teachers are provided course guides, descriptions and syllabi, instructional plans, and model instructional units. In addition, each course has formative assessment questions, and an end-of-course exam is also available. These resources are linked with the ACT battery of exams, EXPLORE, PLAN, ACT, known collectively as EPAS, which are administered in eighth or ninth, tenth, and eleventh or twelfth grades. The exams provide longitudinal information to help students begin career planning and prepare for college admission. Increasingly schools are using the test data to help shape the content of courses and improve alignment between middle and high school.

Numerous other organizations, companies, and consulting groups offer services to help high schools improve course alignment, although not all of these explicitly align with college and career readiness standards. At the heart of all of these systems and approaches is course-level analysis of offerings in relation to external criteria or standards. The ultimate goal in all cases is to improve consistency across courses. Some systems are turnkey, offering full programs of courses and assessments, while at the other end, many consultants offer processes that are entirely independent of any particular set of material, curriculum, or assessment and allow schools to make incremental modifications in their existing programs rather than adopting something new in a wholesale fashion.

Regardless of the strategy a school chooses, any effort to align curriculum and instruction across levels vertically and within departments horizontally will potentially lead to a more coherent program of instruction. When implemented properly, aligned systems enable students to become proficient with a specified set of knowledge and skills more systematically than a disjointed set of courses that may overlap or omit content and are not intentionally designed to develop key cognitive skills within the context of key content knowledge.

Examples of How Schools Seek to Develop Aligned Core Academic Programs

Mt. Abram Regional High School in Salem Township, Maine, has as its mission and curriculum a focus on personalized student learning. The school is organized around clearly stated learning standards, learner-centered classroom instruction, adaptive decisions regarding individual learners, and student engagement in constructing personal learning plans. Each student at Mt. Abram starts a personal learning plan (PLP) at the beginning of ninth grade and develops its content over four years. The purpose of the plan is to help students set and modify goals based on future aspirations and collect evidence that demonstrates how they are achieving their goals. PLPs are reviewed each fall during student-led conferences when students reflect on and assess what they've learned, as well as discuss academic goals and needs with teachers, advisors, and parents.

Students also present a standards-based career/life portfolio that integrates technology, showcases academic and personal achievements, and, by the senior year, outlines a specific postsecondary plan. The principal personally reviews and responds to every portfolio to support individual students as well as to ensure that academic expectations are being met.

George Washington High School in Denver, Colorado, has an overarching focus on improving instruction and student performance through teacher and administrator professional development and collaboration focused on improving instruction. The foundation for these practices is a well-established professional learning community that provides opportunities for all George Washington teachers and administrators to meet weekly to discuss issues related to instruction and student achievement. During professional learning community meetings, teachers and staff focus on three professional development and teacher collaboration practices: data teams, learning walks, and peer visitations.

Data teams, composed of three to four people who teach similar subjects, meet for two hours each month. The teams look at student performance data and work samples in order to focus on strategies to improve student performance and teacher instructional practices and find ways to align expectations.

All teachers and administrators participate in learning walks. Two to five teachers and one administrator visit George Washington classrooms on a rotating monthly basis to observe instructional practices and then develop strategies to improve practices based on feedback received and dialogue exchanged during the professional learning community meetings. Furthermore, all teachers are expected to complete a peer visitation once a month: they observe another teacher's classrooms and provide each other feedback on instructional practice. These activities help set the stage for enhanced alignment and coordination of curricular expectations across classes, subjects, and grade levels and create a strong norm for greater curricular coherence and consistency.

The E-Cubed School in Providence, Rhode Island is one of ten schools in New England to offer the Diploma Plus curriculum. Designed for small schools (generally around 250 students) by the Commonwealth Corporation, the model provides a rigorous alternative for at-risk students in urban centers who are poor or for whom English is not their first language. The Diploma Plus model challenges all students to demonstrate proficiency through a digital portfolio of work, which is required to advance from grade to grade. Schools agree to implement all three phases of the program model—the foundation, presentation, and plus phases—and all students at the school must participate in Diploma Plus.

The three phases proceed as follows. By the end of sophomore year, students create a portfolio that is used to judge whether they are ready to proceed to the eleventh-grade presentation phase. By the end of junior year, students defend their portfolio to determine if they are ready to proceed into the plus phase. The defense committee consists of plus phase teachers, administrators, parents, community members, two students, and occasionally central administration staff. By the end of senior year, students must present their senior defense in order to graduate.

Marshall Fundamental High School in Pasadena, California, takes a different approach to creating a strong core aligned to college readiness. The school is organized into six levels of courses through sixth through twelfth grades: intervention, strategic, benchmark, AP prep, honors, and AP. In sixth through eighth grades, all levels except AP are available to students. Beginning in ninth grade, all levels are available. Intervention, which emphasizes problem-solving skills, is the lowest-level course that the school offers and is available in English and algebra in the sixth, seventh, and eighth grades and for some in the ninth grade. It phases out at tenth grade as students become ready for more rigorous courses. In tenth grade, all levels except intervention and strategic are available. Because Marshall Fundamental enrolls the majority of its students before ninth grade, the school is able to get most students to benchmark course levels by ninth grade.

Having students attend Marshall Fundamental from sixth grade on decreases the disconnect between middle school and high school and enhances curricular integration. If students arrive at Marshall Fundamental in sixth grade and are in the lowest-level (intervention) courses, they still have the potential to be part of the AP program because the administration and teachers have more time to help students build their skills toward college-ready levels. Middle school students who are ready to progress are allowed to take high school courses; a number of eighth graders take biology and French, for example. The AP prep program in the middle school grades allows teachers and administrators to start moving students toward college readiness early on as they demonstrate readiness.

PRINCIPLE 3: TEACH KEY SELF-MANAGEMENT SKILLS AND ACADEMIC BEHAVIORS AND EXPECT STUDENTS TO USE THEM

Student self-management is an important dimension of college readiness and something that gets developed most often on a hit-or-miss basis in high school. Although educators may stress to students the importance of being organized and taking responsibility for their actions, these exhortations are not necessarily accompanied by carefully structured programs and requirements designed to have students develop and internalize these habits over the four years of high school. The result is that some students become highly proficient at self-management by the end of high school, while others have changed little, if at all, from the day they entered high school in their ability to manage key tasks and behaviors necessary for success in and beyond high school.

Schools are implementing a wide range of strategies and programs to develop self-management skills. These were discussed in some detail in Chapter Three. Areas of focus include techniques to help students learn how to manage their time and prioritize tasks, improve their study skills, learn how to set and achieve goals, and develop necessary academic skills systematically through a dedicated elective course. Other equally important areas include helping students learn how to persist at difficult tasks, organize and participate in study groups, and develop resilience in the face of academic frustrations and even failures.

In the area of self-management, many programs are available to help students develop these skills. Most notable and very widely adopted is the AVID program (Advancement Via Individual Determination), an in-school academic support program that spans fourth through twelfth grades. The program targets students in the academic middle but is potentially beneficial to all students. The program particularly emphasizes building the skills of students from ethnic minority groups traditionally underrepresented in postsecondary education, students from low-income families, rural students, and other students for whom college may not be a family tradition.

The program consists of two core elements: the AVID elective and the AVID curriculum. The elective is a course in which self-management, including personal organization and study skills, is intentionally and systematically developed. The elective also encourages development of cognitive strategies necessary for college and career success, such as problem solving and critical thinking. The course is taught by an AVID-trained teacher and is often augmented by peer tutors and mentors, many of them college students and former AVID students.

The AVID curriculum consists of a number of paths that emphasize at different grade levels reading, writing, study skills, test-taking skills, organization, critical thinking, goal setting, choosing a college, and preparing for college entrance exams. The AVID curriculum is designed to be used in combination with the elective to create a consistent educational experience that supports student development of a full range of knowledge and skills necessary for college success; it emphasizes self-management and self-awareness in particular.

Examples of How Schools Develop Academic Behaviors

At Corbin High School in Corbin, Kentucky, students receive rubrics detailing how they will be evaluated on specific activities and assignments in each class. Substandard work is returned to them with feedback for resubmission. Students are strongly encouraged to spend the end of each class period organizing and rewriting their notes and receive examples of high-quality notes from previous students to demonstrate the desired standard. Students with strong note-taking skills are also paired with those who need to develop this skill further. These classroom practices help students take ownership of their learning while developing specific skills, such as note taking.

The net result of all of these activities is that students begin to develop the strategies and mind-sets necessary to manage themselves effectively. This skill is necessary regardless of the path students choose after high school, and it is particularly important for students who go on to a postsecondary program. Those programs demand that students learn how to manage their time, prioritize their tasks, gauge their strengths and weaknesses, and persevere when they encounter adversity in order to achieve their goals. High schools can help students be better prepared for these challenges by offering a progressive set of experiences leading to greater self-management by all students.

Teachers at University Park Campus School in Worcester, Massachusetts, expect students to use a range of low-tech information management strategies that will be important to success in college. Examples include outlining, note taking, and summarizing texts. Some techniques are explicitly taught, while others are simply modeled, and students pick up on their use from their fellow students. Students are encouraged to keep their work well organized in a form that it makes it possible for them to easily access their papers and assignments.

The approach at Forest Park Street School in Forest Park, Georgia, is to infuse a "moral code and tools for self sufficiency" into every aspect of its program so that its students can grow into effective, autonomous adults prepared to pursue college and careers. Student advocates advance this goal by meeting with each youth at intake to initiate an ongoing dialogue about how to prepare not only for successful program completion, but also for life after high school. Staff members function somewhere between advocates and parents. Without a personal connection at school, many of the school's students would not remain motivated to follow through on their academic responsibilities.

While internal motivation is the goal, Forest Park Street School teachers and advocates acknowledge that the backgrounds from which many students come did not foster the type of academic behaviors that lead to success in the classroom; the brand of external motivation provided by advocates helps fill this gap. Forest Park Street School keeps in touch with its students for up to a year or more after they graduate, extending the opportunity for personal accountability into the next phase of a student's life, whether at college or in the workforce.

Students at the Gateway to College at Montgomery College in Montgomery County, Maryland, begin their program as part of a small cohort of twenty to twenty-five students who take a series of foundation courses designed to replicate the college experience. Foundation courses bring students up to speed in reading, writing, and math and offer career development and college survival skills, such as how to access support services and work with academic advisors. Many of the students in the program report belonging to peer groups or families that do not value education, so Gateway to College puts extra emphasis on why certain behaviors are necessary for school success.

During the foundation semester, instructors use a variety of strategies to break students of the unsuccessful patterns they developed in previous high schools. The program serves at-risk youth between the ages of sixteen and twenty who are not on a track to complete high school or have stopped attending another high school. To create circumstances students will likely encounter in college, two Gateway to College instructors might deliberately schedule exams for the same day, forcing students to manage their time wisely in order to prepare while under pressure. One class may provide a study guide while another may not, discouraging student reliance on predictable instructor behavior and putting the responsibility on students to be prepared. Using resources such as writing and math labs is required in some classes because instructors want to emphasize study and self-determination skills, as well as provide every opportunity for students who are behind to take the initiative to make up work.

PRINCIPLE 4: MAKE COLLEGE AND CAREERS REAL BY HELPING STUDENTS MANAGE THE COMPLEXITY OF PREPARING FOR AND APPLYING TO POSTSECONDARY EDUCATION

The simplest and most straightforward way to address this principle is to have all students apply to college. As simple as this sounds, it is much more complex in practice to determine that all students have accomplished this task. And in some communities, parents may object to this being a mandatory part of the senior year. We saw this requirement work best in schools where students enrolled voluntarily. These included charter schools and open-enrollment programs in large school districts.

Because many of the schools we visited had large concentrations of students who would be first-generation college attendees, administrators and faculty understood the need to provide a great deal of information to these students and to do so repeatedly and systematically over all four years of high school. One example was the practice of requiring all students to take one or more college admission–related tests, such as the ACT battery of EXPLORE/PLAN/ACT or the College Board sequence of the PSAT and SAT. Student advisors helped students interpret the results and make decisions about what they needed to do academically to be college ready.

Many of these schools have extensive programs of student and parent information to explain financial aid in particular. Some offer help completing FAFSA, the government-required form for financial aid. Most of the schools emphasize making college real to their students through visitation programs, dual-credit courses, and opportunities to take actual college courses. In all cases, the high schools provide support to students who are engaged in these activities and help the students learn from their experiences, in which students are generally successful overall and over time.

We also found schools where a proportion of parents were likely to object to this being mandatory. These schools require students to engage in all the steps leading up to applying without actually requiring submission of an application. They achieve this by requiring students to participate in certain prerequisite activities each year. For example, in the freshman year, all students engage in a general exploration of online college resources and options that helps them identify their general interests. Sophomore year includes activities that help students learn more about the relationship between particular career pathways and the type of education required to pursue that pathway. Juniors complete a more extensive research project on types of colleges, their varying missions and requirements, and how they select students and award financial aid. Seniors go through all the steps of applying to college and establishing eligibility for financial aid even if they do not actually submit an application.

The effect of these tiered activities is to make college much more real to all students in the school. The idea that they may actually go to college is an alien concept to most high school freshmen and even to the majority of juniors. They don't grasp that they will be expected to exert some control over the ways in which their lives evolve. These readiness activities, built into classes or otherwise required of students to complete independently, help them come to grips with a topic many would just as soon avoid: their transition to young adulthood and, with it, the need to make big decisions about their futures.

Examples of How Schools Help Students Manage the Complexity of Preparing for College

Annandale High School in Annandale, Virginia, is a large high school that integrates many of these strategies to ensure high rates of college application and acceptance. The school employs twelve counselors for its 2,350 students in addition to a career center specialist. These counselors work collaboratively with each other, the administration, and teachers. For example, a counselor attends each parent-teacher conference. This collaboration allows the school to determine the best way to address student challenges and support each student. One result of the close interaction between counselors and students is that counselors know students extremely well, which means few students can retain the anonymity that results in no one noticing if they are not preparing for their future. Counselor support extends to information on the college application process. Eleventh- and twelfth-grade students are pulled out of required classes once a year to attend assemblies where they learn about different aspects of the college and financial aid application processes in small groups.

A well-equipped career center doubles as a college center. Career exploration and other college search programs are available online. For example, the school uses a version of the popular online program Naviance to help students assess their qualifications for particular colleges and whether these colleges align with their desired program of study. The center is staffed after regular school hours one day a week.

The career center director, in collaboration with the guidance counselor, focuses on getting students to consider their career goals early in high school and then to work toward them. The career center director is very accessible and works closely with the guidance counselors to get to know the unique skills of each student. This collaboration enables the center to match scholarship and college information with individual students.

The school has a Pathways to the Baccalaureate partnership with the local community college that provides assistance with applications, financial aid, placement tests, class registration, and guidance. The participating students are primarily first-generation students. The funds to pay for the counselor who runs this program come jointly from the district and the community college.

A financial aid officer is funded by the county education office to work with Annandale fifteen hours a week. The officer is responsible for administering a student need survey, keeping evening hours for drop-ins once a week, and visiting every senior English class to advise students on financial aid and to answer questions, along with monitoring the financial aid application process.

The school schedule includes a flex period where students have the opportunity to spend one class period off campus in a college course or in a career academy, sponsored and operated by the county, that offers subjects such as animal science. This period is also used to bring college speakers to campus at a time when every interested student can potentially attend.

Hobbs High School in Hobbs, New Mexico, makes sure that all students receive extensive counseling services. Counselors establish relationships with students because they stay with the same class for four years. Each year has its own counseling focus. The tenth-grade year focuses on adjustment, eleventh grade on assessment and yearly progress reports, and twelfth grade on college preparation.

Counselors at Hobbs provide students with a great deal of information and assistance to help them with the college application process. Counselors put together the "Counselor's Corner" newsletter that also appears in the local newspaper to help parents stay informed on a range of issues related to the college admission. The newsletter gives information regarding upcoming testing, scholarship opportunities, and local college programs. A great deal of emphasis is placed on helping students obtain scholarships. Counselors provide a list of scholarships and their associated deadlines and give students a scholarship request form to expedite the process.

Counselors also provide a monthly task list to seniors with items such as what to look for when researching colleges, detailed FAFSA information, assessment information, and tasks to complete to be college ready. This is especially helpful to first-generation college attendees and others who have not been exposed to the college culture to understand how to prepare to apply to college. In addition to monthly task lists, the counseling department provides a senior-year calendar that contains a monthly guide to events, pertinent Web sites, and task information contained in a practical one-page document. The calendar helps students organize their year by providing them with as much information ahead of time as possible.

Through a partnership with Houston Community College, George I. Sanchez School in Houston, Texas, offers all students a college readiness course that focuses on the contextual knowledge and skills young people need for a successful transition to a postsecondary environment. Seniors are provided a detailed, month-by-month checklist to help them organize the process of applying to college. The school then monitors student progress closely to ensure each student can apply to college. If a student's family is unsupportive of their child's postgraduate plans or participation in the early college program, staff often can provide the background the student needs to see college opportunities as a positive and important next step.

PRINCIPLE 5: CREATE ASSIGNMENTS AND GRADING POLICIES THAT MORE CLOSELY APPROXIMATE COLLEGE EXPECTATIONS EACH SUCCESSIVE YEAR OF HIGH SCHOOL

One of the most traumatic experiences first-year college students encounter is the difference in instructor expectations on exams and papers between high school and college courses. If high school students are not given experiences that begin to approximate what they will encounter in college courses, they will have few coping mechanisms or strategies available to help them succeed. A progressively more challenging high school program of study in which students must take more responsibility for their own learning helps lay the groundwork for a smoother transition to postsecondary education.

We found some high schools that were calibrating their expectations year to year so that the quality and quantity of work that they expected from students increased from freshman through senior year. These schools employ a range of techniques and strategies, some well coordinated and others more episodic. Many of those techniques involve emulating one or another aspect of a college course, such as having fewer assignments with greater emphasis on each one, not accepting late work, having stringent rules regarding plagiarism, focusing more on concepts and less on facts, expecting students to cite sources to support their assertions, or spending time analyzing text in greater detail than is usual for a high school course.

Some schools employ methods that are not found in college courses but help determine how well their students are doing relative to college readiness standards. For example, some have benchmark assignments at each grade level that all students complete. These assignments are in the form of projects, papers, or problems that require significant thinking, analysis, and writing. Although they are not used to retain or promote students, the assignments help teachers calibrate their expectations for students and help students gauge the progress they are making toward postsecondary readiness. Most commonly, but not exclusively, these are in the form of senior assignments.

Research papers are by far the most prevalent assignment given to approximate the college experience. Schools vary in the frequency with which these are assigned, the required length, citation style requirements, and other elements. Many emphasize one large assignment later in high school. However, it may be more appropriate to have students complete a number of such papers each year, with the grading criteria becoming more stringent rather than the paper length increasing between freshman and senior years.

Putting any sort of progressive system of expectations in place in a large high school is challenging. The most prevalent strategy high schools use currently is simply to identify a progression of courses, each assumed to be more difficult than the previous one. In practice, the students often do not perceive an increased challenge, only new content to be learned. They attribute any success or failure in the more advanced classes to being "smart" or "dumb," not to developing cognitive and behavioral strategies to cope with increasing workload and more complex material.

The alternative is a deliberately sequenced learning progression where expectations are carefully set and monitored across grade levels and courses. We were more likely to encounter these coordinated approaches in smaller schools that accommodate and feature more personalized programs for each student. These schools often emphasize some sort of project-based learning or have internship requirements that make tangible the increasing expectations for independent work.

Of all commercially available programs, the International Baccalaureate (IB) comes the closest to offering a progressively more challenging set of learning experiences and expectations aligned with postsecondary readiness. The limitation of the IB, however, is that its Diploma Programme covers only eleventh and twelfth grades, leaving high schools to their own devices to determine what ninth and tenth grades should look like to align with the Diploma Programme's courses and the IB exams given during twelfth grade. Many high schools that have adopted IB have also then struggled to redesign ninth- and tenth-grade courses to align fully with the program. Using IB as a reference point can help set the expectations and workload for the lower-division high school courses, but creating progressive increase in challenge in practice from grade to grade is much more challenging.

Examples of How Schools Seek to Create Assignments and Expectations That More Closely Approximate College

The Metropolitan Regional Career and Technical Center in Providence, Rhode Island, known as the Met, requires all students to write an autobiography that must be a minimum of seventy-five pages. The paper is all about the student's life, broken down into chapters. Students usually initiate the project in tenth grade. Once students reach seventy-five pages, they must go back and revise what they have already written. Students are required to present the final product in an exhibition context, where they can read excerpts, use visual aids such as PowerPoint, and add posters, movies, and so on to inform the audience about their life to date.

The autobiography assignment may not have many of the elements of a traditional research paper, but it does cause students to write extensively, conduct informal research and fact check, and become more familiar with large, complex document structure, and engage in serious editing of their own writing. Manhattan Hunter Science High School in New York City takes a different approach. It invites a Ph.D. candidate from Hunter College to teach a formal course on research. Students spend three years learning how to identify research topics, find information on a topic, write a research paper, and present it orally. The research class meets weekly, and students are expected to communicate with the instructor and one another as necessary by e-mail. This helps approximate a college course that meets relatively less frequently than a high school course does.

Early college high schools are another means to help students make more direct connections between high school and postsecondary expectations. At Middle College High School at Contra Costa Community College in San Pablo,

California, students attend some high school classes and also enroll in community college classes from ninth to twelfth grades for which they receive college credit. The school is located on the college campus, and its students do not pay college tuition. The students learn about college by completing college course work instead of hearing teachers talk about what college-level classes are like.

The ninth-grade classes are designed to bring all students up to the same level of basic skills and prepare them for success taking college courses. After ninth grade, students may take more classes on the college campus. Classes where students struggle may be team-taught by high school and college faculty, or the high school faculty may observe the college course in order to provide better support to their students in tutorials.

All of the school's courses mimic college instruction in terms of the amount of independent learning, the number of assignments, an emphasis on class discussions, inclusion of more conceptual questions and issues, and use of college-level texts and vocabulary. The high school teachers provide extensive support and scaffolding to their students to help them cope successfully with postsecondary expectations.

The school also emphasizes reading and writing across the curriculum. Students write papers in most of their classes. In high school English and history classes, for example, they write ten-page research papers as take-home tests. High school English/language arts teachers assign at least one essay a week in tenth grade. All teachers also teach reading explicitly. They take passages from college textbooks and put them on the overhead. The class might spend twenty minutes learning to read one paragraph, a skill that will help prepare them for the technical reading required in college. Assignments are not always due during class time but have deadlines similar to those of college courses. No late work is accepted.

Teachers at Maryland's Baltimore Freedom Academy help create a more college-like atmosphere in classes by not simply giving students the answers to questions asked in class. Rather, teachers respond by asking the students a different question or enlisting other students to help fill out the response. Instead of focusing on right or wrong answers, teachers prompt the class to discuss the subject matter from a variety of perspectives, dissecting information, looking for patterns, and generalizing through description. After conducting this exploration process and orienting the class to the concept in broader terms, teachers can provide any necessary details that have not been discovered or contributed in the class exploration. The training students receive to learn how to approach new information with curiosity and a skill set of interpretive and analytical tools helps them develop key cognitive strategies such as inquiry, interpretation, analysis, and problem formulation.

PRINCIPLE 6: MAKE THE SENIOR YEAR MEANINGFUL AND APPROPRIATELY CHALLENGING

Twelfth grade at many high schools is an opportunity for some rest and relaxation for at least a significant proportion of the senior class. Unfortunately for educators trying to motivate students to stay engaged through graduation, even many parents believe their children have somehow earned the right to a year off after having ostensibly worked hard throughout their years of schooling. All the evidence suggests, however, that students who do not challenge themselves academically during the senior year are much more likely to place into remedial courses in college and to have lower college grade point averages in entry-level postsecondary courses. There's a price to be paid for coasting through the final year of high school.

These effects are particularly pronounced for students who will be first-generation college attendees, come from low-income families, or are members of racial or ethnic minority groups that have been underrepresented in college historically. Because many of the schools in our study had large proportions of such students, these schools paid much closer attention to the senior year in many ways. One of the most common practices was to require all students to enroll in an English, math, science, and social studies course along with any other academic or elective courses, regardless of the number of credits the student needed to graduate. Many also expected students to take a second-language or art class as well. The principal at one large high school went so far as to review the schedules of each incoming senior for challenge and rigor. Another school made participation in the senior trip contingent on taking an advanced science course from among several choices.

Senior seminars are by far the most common way that schools distinguish the senior year from the prior three. The most demanding of these require that the project have a strong content knowledge component and not simply be an expression of student interest, although in some schools, senior seminars focus on the college knowledge dimension of readiness, helping students select colleges, complete applications and financial aid forms, search for scholarships, and write the essays required by some colleges and universities. All place an emphasis on what students will be facing six months or so hence and what they can be doing to prepare in the time they have remaining in high school.

A few schools emphasize internships and field-based experiences for seniors. Many of these young adults are intent on experiencing the "real world" and are impatient at being in high school. Others need more exposure to reality to help them come to grips with their impending transition. One distinguishing feature of all of these internships is that they are designed in ways that help prepare students for continuing education, not for the world of work exclusively. This means that school personnel must work closely with employers to build into the internship duties, responsibilities, and tasks that will hold students accountable for developing and applying knowledge, skills, behaviors, and attitudes necessary for college success.

Examples of How Schools Seek to Make the Senior Year Meaningful

All students at High Tech High School in San Diego, California, complete an academic internship as a condition of graduation. These internships extend over one semester during which students work two afternoons per week. Students receive a grade for successfully completing their internship and simultaneously take course work related to the internship. They must write journals documenting their experiences and communicate with their employers, mentors, and the school internship coordinator in specified ways.

Throughout the internship, each student pairs with a mentor who understands and supports High Tech High and its philosophies. The school expects the mentor to include the intern in meetings and events in order to develop a fuller picture of how the business operates. The mentor works with the student to plan a project that meets the company's needs and is possible for the student to complete successfully. Some projects last an entire semester, while others are short enough to give the student an opportunity to work on several things throughout the semester. High Tech High students work on a range of projects: event and marketing support; Web design; recruitment and retention activities with human resource departments; networking, software, and hardware support; and public relations support positions. After students participate in these projects, they develop and present a report on their experience, which they deliver in a public setting to teachers, students, and community members.

Fenway High School in Boston, Massachusetts, has a series of requirements for its internships that include the following: (1) work at least thirty hours per week at the internship site; (2) return to school on Mondays for an early afternoon seminar; (3) work on a large project that is assigned by the student's internship supervisor and takes place at the internship site; (4) maintain a weekly hours log, which has to be signed by the internship supervisor; and (5) complete a senior portfolio that documents and presents work done during the internship.

Along with the required internship, the school requires seniors to take a class that allows them to practice professional skills. This class helps students learn multimedia skills, engage in a process to project what their life will look like in twenty years, and assess each other's time management skills. The class causes students to examine how their career interests align with colleges and majors and participate in skills assessments that provide additional information on career options. Students prepare cover letters and résumés, and they participate in role-play interviews. They also learn financial planning and other life skills.

During their final year, seniors at Polytech High School in Woodside, Delaware, complete a rigorous senior project called a Technical Exhibition, which includes writing a research paper that must conform to American Psychological Association style and demonstrates mastery of some sort of technical skills. They deliver the paper to judges in a thirty-minute oral presentation. Students also have the option to complete an even more rigorous project with a longer paper and a presentation. External community members evaluate these more rigorous projects. Students can ask teachers questions, but they complete the project largely independently. These senior projects prepare students for college-level independent writing, research, expectations, communication, and presentations.

As students at YES Prep in Houston, Texas, near graduation, they engage in a series of structured and cumulative self-actualization activities embedded within the curriculum. For example, seniors participate in an ethics seminar that focuses on key cognitive strategies. Students analyze and find evidence within work samples they have accumulated throughout middle and high school to show skills such as the ability to write clearly, support arguments with evidence, and interpret and analyze information. As they engage in this self-reflection, they are taught to focus not only on positive examples but also to include material where they fell short of achieving a desired level of performance in an area. This exercise helps ready them to take greater control of their learning once they go on to postsecondary programs, get a better picture of their own growth over time, and be prepared to accept more direct criticism and feedback on work in the future.

PRINCIPLE 7: BUILD PARTNERSHIPS WITH AND CONNECTIONS TO POSTSECONDARY PROGRAMS AND INSTITUTIONS

For all intents and purposes, U.S. high schools and colleges as they exist today could be on separate planets and still have students matriculate, assuming appropriate interplanetary transportation were provided. No direct communication is required between high school and college instructors or between high school administrators and college admissions staffs. This is very efficient but not very effective as the percentage of each successive high school graduating class that goes on to postsecondary education increases. Better communication and more programs that span the gap are necessary, and examples of local initiatives can be found around the country.

One key step that high schools take to prepare more students for college is to reach out to their postsecondary partners to find ways to work together much more directly and closely to understand each other's expectations for students. In many cases we have observed, though, it is the postsecondary institution that has taken the initiative to suggest ways in which high school students and staff could work more closely to enhance success of incoming students. This is the result of the experiences of entering students at campuses where large proportions of students cannot place into credit-bearing courses or drop out quickly.

The key to successful partnerships and connections is that they must end up leading to deeper understandings of what each institution expects from its students and how each is gauging academic performance and college readiness. This means that the relationships are more substantive and deeper than just having high school students visit a college campus or having a college admissions officer make a presentation at a high school. These deeper relationships lead to bridging programs, teams of instructors that work across institutional boundaries, richer data sharing, attempts to come to agreement on what constitutes adequate performance for college-ready students, and much more.

For example, simple partnerships begin with the exchange of more detailed data between institutions. What is the nature of the high school's population? What types of courses are the students taking? How well do they perform on admissions tests? This information is readily available to the colleges and the high schools, but in a partnership relationship, the two sides come together to discuss the data and develop plans to increase college attendance. High schools may agree to offer more college preparatory courses, ensure more students enroll in them, and encourage students to take admissions tests. Colleges, for their part, may offer support preparing students for admissions tests and may do much to help students become aware of the full amount of financial aid for which they are eligible. College personnel can even help high school students understand how best to complete college applications and be aware of the requirements of different majors and the wide array of options open to them in college.

As partnerships strengthen, faculty from the two institutions may begin to communicate more directly in ways that supplement, but do not replace, the role of high school counselors and college admissions officers. This more direct communication almost always focuses on student readiness in specific academic content and skill areas. The conversations must be carefully delineated, structured, and facilitated initially, because the historical separation between high school and college has led to a tendency for participants to be prepared to engage in a certain amount of recrimination and finger pointing initially without careful facilitation. College instructors often bemoan the poor state of preparation of incoming students, while high school teachers bristle at being told what to do by college instructors. However, when faculty get beyond these initial misgivings and miscommunications, they rapidly see that they share much more in common than they may have thought they did.

Each cares about the education and intellectual development of the student, and each is frustrated with the state of preparation of students arriving in their class. Each cares passionately about the subject matter and student intellectual development. Each works under institutional constraints that make it difficult for them to attain their goals, and each carries a personal definition of what constitutes adequate and desirable student performance in a particular class.

This internal definition of adequate and desirable performance needs to be surfaced and made explicit. When faculty begin comparing what they expect of students and what they are trying to teach them, it becomes clearer to them how best to align and sequence what is taught at each level and how best to reinforce and build on prior learnings so that students are ready to continue their education beyond high school and beyond entry-level college courses.

Colleges are increasingly offering programs to retain students and address the needs of groups that have been historically underrepresented in college. Such programs include special pathways or cohorts in which designated students take a predetermined sequence of college courses together and receive support collectively. Other initiatives include a variety of bridge programs offered in the summer between the end of high school and the beginning of college. In these intensive sessions, students learn about college, have their academic skills diagnosed more precisely, are introduced to the college's resource and support systems, and are given a head start toward success by gaining greater familiarity with the campus and faculty. Finally, many colleges are targeting financial aid at particular students in particular high schools to build stronger relationships with those high schools. High-priority students are guaranteed an identified level of support if they make adequate progress in core academic courses and participate in other preparatory activities.

Examples of How Schools Build Postsecondary Partnerships

One of the schools we studied, Brackenridge High School, near San Antonio, Texas, has undertaken a collaboration with the University of Texas at Austin as part of the Students Partnering for Undergraduate Rhetoric Success program. Eleventh-grade English language and composition students learn about rhetorical theory and analysis and then write extended rhetorical analysis and conduct research to buttress the arguments in their essays. This work is done in partnership with a lower-division college writing class. The high school students' work is peer-reviewed by college students, and their final drafts are submitted to the university instructor for assessment and additional feedback. Students communicate with their counterparts using e-mail, blogs, and discussion forums, and they travel to University of Texas at Austin for a campus visit.

Brackenridge also participates in Chem-Bridge, another collaborative program in which students can earn three hours of college chemistry credit from the University of Texas at Austin while simultaneously earning high school credit for an advanced science course. Brackenridge students use a college-level text to complete assignments, in addition to downloading online lectures and course work. They then combine online course work with the opportunity to visit the campus and the university's College of Natural Science.

A much more specialized form of partnership is the middle college high school, where a high school program is located on a college campus. One such program is the Middle College High School located at Contra Costa College. This partnership between the college and the West Contra Costa Unified School District began in 1989. The middle college gives underperforming and underserved youth access to college experiences while they are able to remain within the more supportive high school structure. Careful attention is paid to student schedules so that they can still meet the University of California's subject area requirements on the high school side while also taking a range of college courses.

Students at Middle College High School are largely treated like college students and consider themselves members of the campus community. The physical layout of the college campus and constant exposure to college students and faculty reinforce this culture. The administrative offices for both institutions are located at the center of campus. Middle College High School has two permanent high school classrooms; all other facilities—library, financial aid services, career counseling, college tutoring, clubs and activities, and study areas—are shared with college students. Middle College High School teachers sit in on college classes with their students and talk with college faculty about their expectations of college-level classes. Each teacher is assigned a college faculty member to work with. Particularly difficult college classes may be cotaught by a high school and college instructor.

Marshall Fundamental High School in Pasadena, California, has a number of partnerships with local colleges and community organizations that provide additional resources and opportunities to its students. The school partners with Puente (sponsored by the University of California) and Upward Bound (sponsored by California State University, Los Angeles) to help prepare minority students for college. Puente (meaning "bridge" in Spanish) is an academic preparation program serving Hispanic/Latino students that offers academic counseling, a writing component, and a mentoring program. Within the math component of Upward Bound, students from ninth grade up can stay for four weeks at California State University–Los Angeles during the summer and take math courses from college professors. This program runs throughout the year as well (with bus transportation provided to the students), and the program has study hall three days each week. Upward Bound has a senior seminar as well, and within the senior seminar, a college professor comes to the high school and goes through the application process with students. Upward Bound students can receive fee waivers on their college applications.

Pasadena City College (PCC) offers dual credit courses at Marshall Fundamental. Through these courses, students can earn both high school and college credits. PCC also sponsors the Computer Careers Academy, a school-within-a-school targeting at-risk students for college and careers in computers. This program is taught by five teachers, serves 120 students in grades 10 through 12, and is located on the Marshall Fundamental campus. The academy is a partnership of PCC, the California Department of Education, several private companies, and several governmental workforce and occupational programs. PCC also offers a college preparation class for all students at the high school, taught by college counselors, that focuses on skills and strategies for college success.

All of these activities are examples of ways in which high schools and colleges can work more closely to facilitate successful transitions for more students. Although states are focusing on college readiness as a policy priority and are establishing programs and requirements for high schools and colleges, our research indicates that locally developed and focused partnerships focused on mutually identified needs and priorities can play an important role within a state policy context. In short, secondary and postsecondary faculty and administrators need to make an active, sustained effort to reach out and connect with one another.

CHAPTER 5

Case Studies of Schools That Succeed

In the previous chapters I have laid out a four-part conceptual model for college readiness and illustrated how that model can be translated into seven organizing principles that lead toward specific actions. In this chapter, I adopt a slightly different perspective by presenting profiles of high schools that are demanding more of their students and achieving results that improve college readiness. I have drawn these examples from the thirty-eight high schools we studied in depth as described in earlier chapters. Each case study contains descriptions of key practices and programs that the school employs to help more students achieve college readiness. These summaries are taken from *Creating College Readiness*, which contains comprehensive descriptions of all of the schools.

 For more information on the schools described in this chapter, go to http://CollegeCareerReady.org.

It is worth keeping in mind that these are point-in-time descriptions of practices observed by Educational Policy Improvement Center (EPIC)

researchers during the 2007–2008 school year. Many of these schools will have changed in significant ways since then, in part because they continue to learn from their experiences and make changes accordingly. Some may even be dramatically different by now. It is not our intent to set these schools up as national models but rather to learn from their experiences. We did not find any of these schools to be doing everything necessary to maximize college readiness for all students, but all were doing some things particularly well when we visited. The case descriptions in this chapter seek to capture some of what each school was doing that was noteworthy and to present some of their effective programs and practices in the larger organizational context of the school.

A final caveat: educators have a tendency to reject programs that don't occur in schools with precisely the same student demographic profile as that of their own, and this would be a mistake in many instances when considering what other schools do successfully to enhance college and career readiness. Although the schools for which we present profiles may be different in one or more important ways from an average American high school, they nevertheless offer valuable lessons and insights that can be generalized to a wide range of school settings willing to adapt the practice to local conditions.

I present the school descriptions here in a narrative structure to allow their story to be told holistically and to provide a sense of each school's nature. For this reason, I have not organized the findings about each school into the four dimensions of college readiness that appear throughout this book. However, readers should be able to discern readily in each profile examples of programs and practices that align with each of the four dimensions. In fact, readers may want to look specifically for examples from each of these dimensions of college readiness while reviewing these case studies.

We visited six distinctly different types of schools: alternative, charter, comprehensive, early college, magnet, and private. I present here examples of each (and two examples of different types of comprehensive high schools) in order to paint a fuller picture of the range of strategies and approaches we observed. The careful observer may discern a practice or idea that is applicable to his or her school even if it comes from a different type of school.

ALTERNATIVE SCHOOL: UNIVERSITY PARK CAMPUS SCHOOL, WORCESTER, MASSACHUSETTS

Year established:	1997	**Enrollment:**	244
Locale:	Large central city	**Asian:**	18.0%
Free/reduced meals:	72.1%	**African American:**	9.0%
		Hispanic/Latino:	39.8%
Attendance rate:	95.4%	**Native American:**	0.0%
ELL students:	59%	**White:**	32.0%
AP participation:	0.0%	**Multiracial:**	1.2%

We'd seen a host of reasons why students with these challenges don't succeed. The expectations inform the curriculum. I'm sick of hearing outside of UCPS that students can't succeed.

UNIVERSITY PARK CAMPUS SCHOOL ADMINISTRATOR

Since University Park Campus School (UPCS) opened in 1997, it has shown that urban students can thrive in a small school with a rigorous college preparatory curriculum, regardless of their previous educational preparation. The school is in the poorest section of Worcester, Massachusetts, with a student body that reflects the surrounding community. Seventy-two percent of the 232 students receive free or reduced-price lunch, and 59 percent speak English as a second language. The majority of the students are students of color (68 percent), and among the white students, many are recent arrivals from eastern Europe who are learning English. University Park admits students through a lottery that accepts entries from students within a one-mile radius of the campus. When students enter University Park as seventh graders, they are typically significantly behind grade level, but six years later graduate essentially all of its students well prepared to succeed in college.

Operating with the same per-pupil budget as other high schools in the district, University Park has earned national recognition for ranking first among urban schools serving low-income students on state-mandated English and math graduation exams, and in the top quartile of all schools in the state. Student dropout and mobility rates are nearly zero, as are suspension and expulsion rates. Over 95 percent of graduates have attended college (80 percent going to four-year institutions). University Park's success with a student population with which many other schools have failed can be attributed to its mutually beneficial partnership with neighboring Clark University, a rigorous, data-driven college preparatory curriculum, and a culture of commitment to each student's success at every level.

State and Local Context

Worcester, located forty-five miles west of Boston, is an important manufacturing, insurance, and transportation center and the second-largest city in New England. The total population is estimated at 173,966, is predominantly white (78.5 percent), with 9 percent African American and 17.7 percent Hispanic/Latino. The demographics of students in Worcester Public Schools (WPS) closely parallel those of the University Park; WPS students are 39 percent white, 16.6 percent African American, 7.9 percent Asian, and 36.4 percent Hispanic/Latino. In 2008, Worcester Public Schools received a moderate Adequate Yearly Progress (AYP) performance rating in English/language arts and a low AYP performance rating in mathematics. African American, special education, low income, and Hispanic/Latino student subgroups in the district did not make AYP.

The largest employer in the area is University of Massachusetts Medical School, one of thirteen colleges and universities in the greater Worcester area. Massachusetts has endeavored to strengthen the connections between higher education and K–12 institutions in the state, as evidenced by the Massachusetts *School-to-College Reports*. Drawing from a database linking K–12 and higher education data, these reports provide data on graduates of Massachusetts public high schools who go on to attend a public college or university in the state. The first *School-to-College Reports* were released in 2008, providing data on 2005 high school graduates.

The University Park *School-to-College Report* indicated that 60 percent of 2005 graduates enrolled in a Massachusetts public college or university, which was nearly double the state average. The percentage of University Park students requiring remedial course work in college was lower than that of the district, most notably in writing, for which only 6 percent of University Park students required a remedial course, compared with the state and district averages of 15 and 19 percent respectively.

How It Began: Clark University's "Enlightened Self-Interest"

Clark University, a small, private university, has contributed in various ways to reverse the social and economic decline of the areas around its campus. Previous revitalization initiatives focused on the rehabilitation of abandoned and burned-out buildings, spurring business development, and increasing public safety. A 1995 grant from the U.S. Department of Housing and Urban Development for $2.4 million aimed to reverse the social and economic decline of the neighborhood and provided the funds for creating a neighborhood school with close ties to the university. Donna Rodrigues, a resident of the neighborhood and a veteran teacher in the local district who had recently completed a master of education degree at Harvard, was brought on as the school's planner and principal. Equipped with knowledge of the most recent research on effective schools and almost thirty years of experience teaching locally, Rodrigues hired three veteran teachers and set about developing an untracked academic program that would prepare all students for college.

The Academic Program: Closing the Gaps and Getting Students College Ready

University Park Campus School's initial focus is on literacy and getting all students up to grade level so that they can succeed in the rigorous honors class curriculum in ninth through twelfth grades. Teachers are expected to differentiate their instruction for students at all levels and encourage students to develop the ability to engage in self-directed problem solving. Scaffolded instruction builds on and celebrates student successes, gradually requiring students to become more independent. The instructional strategies used to scaffold learning are made explicit in the eleventh and twelfth grades so that students will be able to employ these strategies at the college level. English Language Learners (ELL) and special education students are in all the same classes as their peers; the school uses a full immersion model with no pull-out classes.

Group work is particularly emphasized at University Park, which functions to maximize student engagement and promote a culture of commitment to everyone's success. Writing and critical reading are also integrated throughout the curriculum, and teachers provide students with multiple opportunities to practice a variety of writing styles and techniques. Daily homework sessions before and after school provide additional opportunities for tutoring.

Students are usually at least two grade levels behind when they enter University Park in the seventh grade. An intense focus on literacy and developing critical thinking skills in the seventh and eighth grades addresses these gaps. Regardless of their literacy level, students are asked to show and explain critical thinking and problem solving; students conduct literary analyses using picture books as their texts when necessary. Instruction in higher-order thinking skills ensures that students develop an intrinsic motivation to learn and study. Teachers also often loop with students in seventh and eighth grades, remaining with the same cohort of students for two years in order to maximize efficiency and personalization in instruction.

University Park students are in a rigorous program consisting of all honors classes beginning in ninth grade. The college preparatory curriculum is vertically aligned with college standards for all grades and subjects. Classes are semester long and small, usually twenty-two students at most, and are taught in ninety-minute instructional periods. The rigid core curriculum consists of classes in English, math, history, science, and a foreign language for all students, including ELL and special education students. Few electives are offered on campus, but many students take additional classes at Clark University, for which the tuition is waived. AP classes are open to all students; it is assumed that the AP instructional level and format is good for all students.

As students approach graduation, the school structure provides assistance in navigating the college application process. Junior and senior seminars focus on the college selection and application process, ensuring that students understand the necessary steps to apply to college and receive assistance with writing college essays and college and financial aid applications. Teachers closely monitor the process.

The University Park senior year is carefully structured to parallel college. In addition to the semester-long ninety-minute courses and seminars, senior classes meet two or three times each week and are larger so as to more closely approximate the college experience. During the senior year, greater weight is assigned to midterms, exams, and papers, and the homework load is heavier. Class syllabi mimic college syllabi, and the pedagogy emphasizes note taking and self-management.

The first cohort of University Park graduates struggled with study skills in college, and the school has since increased its emphasis on teaching study skills, including time management.

Capitalizing on Substantive Ties with Higher Education Institutions

The partnership between the University Park Campus and Clark University partnership benefits both institutions in distinct ways. As a result of the relationship with Clark, University Park students feel they are a part of the college community early on, which is particularly meaningful to students who will be the first in their families to attend college and have little firsthand knowledge of the college experience to draw from. Clark has not only achieved the initial goal of improving the neighborhood surrounding its campus, but has also benefited from the contributions of University Park teachers and students to the university.

University Park students enjoy several tangible and immediate benefits as a result of the school's association with Clark. The school's physical proximity to the Clark campus affords students opportunities to use the Clark library, lab, and gymnasium and to interact with Clark students and faculty. In seventh through tenth grades, University Park students participate in miniseminars with Clark faculty to introduce them to college courses. In the tenth grade, each student is assigned an undergraduate mentor to introduce him or her to college life and expectations.

University Park juniors and seniors have the opportunity to take classes at Clark and earn college credit, and about half of them do so each year. Those who do not take classes at Clark audit an entry-level class at Clark for four weeks and are required to visit their professor during office hours to learn how to work with faculty.

Each year, four to five University Park graduates continue their education at Clark, where they benefit from the free tuition provided to University Park students who qualify for admission. Clark provides incoming students from University Park with a required precollege summer transition program, ACES, which provides targeted support to cohorts of students from University Park and other schools who could be at risk. Clark also has a designated full-time advisor for University Park students in their transition to Clark.

A particularly important feature of the University Park–Clark partnership is the pipeline created from Clark's Jacob Hiatt Center for Urban Education. Master's students from the program teach at University Park and are targeted for hiring;

the majority of the teachers at University Park studied at Clark. The expectations for University Park teachers are very clear: they are expected to be committed to the college-going mission of the school, passionate about teaching and their students, and invested in improving the lives of their students. The expectations for teachers are high, just as they are for students. The relationship with Clark facilitates ongoing mentoring of younger colleagues by veteran teachers and recruitment of teachers who will continue to serve the mission of the school.

Several veteran University Park teachers teach classes in Clark's program. University Park teachers can take up to five classes toward their master's degree in the program tuition free (this represents half the required course work for the degree). Clark faculty collaborate with University Park faculty on the school's curriculum team as well.

The benefits to Clark have been substantial as well. Not only has the initial goal of improving the campus neighborhood been achieved—people say that today there is a real sense of community in the neighborhood—but the school has gained recognition nationally as a leader in university-community partnerships and has been able to increase the diversity of its student population.

The School Culture: No One Is Allowed to Fail and Everyone Is a Learner

The University Park culture is articulated through four core values: pursuit of excellence, passion for learning, persistence until success, and support for others. The culture, described as one of excitement, engagement, and support, was deliberately crafted and nurtured from the school's inception to ensure alignment between the school's mission and daily procedures. Clear expectations and specific organizational practices foster and maintain the culture that explains much of what makes University Park uniquely successful.

The school culture is made clear to students and their parents from the beginning. Prospective students are required to attend information sessions before entering the lottery, where they learn that University Park students can expect to have two hours of homework each night and that there is zero tolerance for street talk, swearing, fighting, or disrespect. Incoming seventh graders are inculcated to the school's norms during the month-long August Academy, which introduces students to the school.

Great effort is invested to make University Park a nurturing environment for all students, many of whom initially struggle with a lack of self-confidence. Students feel valued and are included in decision making, including hiring decisions and developing school policies. For example, the first cohort at University Park developed many of the school's basic norms, such as no bullying or making fun of other students. Student involvement in decision making is reflective of the nonhierarchical nature of the school's structure and culture, which is evidenced through the role of teachers in school leadership. Important decisions are made collectively; a recent example is the restructuring of the senior year that involved all teachers.

University Park teachers expect their students to go to college, are emotionally committed to their pupils, and take the time to closely monitor their progress. This translates to going beyond teaching to act as mentors and advisors on academic and personal issues. It is not unusual for teachers to help students and their parents with housing, health care, childcare, taxes, and the like. Connecting with students and their families in such ways promotes stronger ties between the school and parents and demonstrates to parents that their children are valued, which fosters increased parental involvement.

Just as students are carefully prepared to be successful college students, teachers are carefully molded to be instructional leaders. Faculty mentoring of student teachers is strong, and as teachers master their practice, they become professional developers. Collaboration among teachers integrates instruction across grades and subjects and serves as a model to students as well. All teachers support one another and strive to improve their instruction. An open-door teacher observation policy is used for both formal and informal observation of classes. Teachers are encouraged to spend their nonteaching time in the back of a colleague's classroom and to solicit and provide feedback to one another. Classes are also observed more formally in rounds that follow the medical model: teachers convene prior to the class to discuss the day's objectives, observe as a group, and later debrief together. A teacher training binder is maintained with descriptions of strategies teachers can use to meet student goals and serves as an example of how professional development is embedded in the school.

University Park is vigilant in its use of student data to inform instruction. There is an ongoing formative assessment to keep a running record of each student, and teachers come together each week to collectively analyze student data (state test scores, results from computer-based added interim assessment system, student work, and alumni data) in the context of recent education research; they then make adjustments to instruction accordingly. The school maintains close ties to its alumni; a recent alumni survey netted an 87 percent response rate and provided valuable data on these students' postsecondary experiences.

MAGNET SCHOOL: FENWAY HIGH SCHOOL, BOSTON, MASSACHUSETTS

Year established:	1983	Enrollment:	290
Locale:	Large central city	Asian:	2.1%
		African American:	42.4%
Free/ reduced meals:	63%	Hispanic/Latino:	41.0%
Attendance rate:	95.5%	Other:	0.7%
		White:	13.8%

From the beginning, Fenway explains that college is an expectation.

FENWAY PARENT

Fenway High School, established in 1983 as a separate academic program for ninety disengaged students within an existing urban high school in Boston, became a Boston Public Schools (BPS) pilot school in 1994. One of the defining principles of the pilot school educational model is personalization of the academic learning environment. Therefore, Fenway has a small student enrollment of approximately 280 students in ninth through twelfth grades. Eighty-two percent of the students who attend Fenway are from minority backgrounds, more than 50 percent of Fenway students are eligible for free or reduced-price lunch, and 29 percent of all enrolled students have a documented disability. In addition, Fenway High School has an attendance rate of 95.5 percent, an overall graduation rate of 96 percent, and approximately 89 percent of all Fenway graduates apply to, and subsequently enroll in, two- or four-year colleges and universities. In 2003, Fenway High School was recognized as one of the nine highest-performing Massachusetts urban schools by MassINC, and in 2004, the American Library Association selected it as the recipient of the National School Library Media Award. The school's success at preparing students for college, and life after high school generally, can be attributed to programs and practices that facilitate the development of learning communities and personal relationships between students and teachers, a meaningful and challenging college preparatory curriculum and advanced assessment process for all students, and close and active collaboration with a local four-year college and other community partners.

State and Local Context

In 1993, the Massachusetts legislature passed the Commonwealth of Massachusetts Education Reform Act, which authorized the establishment of charter schools. The act indicated that groups desiring to receive a charter from the Massachusetts State Board of Education would have to complete a rigorous application process and demonstrate positive student academic achievement results within five years or potentially lose their charter. Following the 1994 passage of the Education Reform Act, Fenway High School applied for one of the first state charters, and the state board granted the charter. However, instead of accepting the charter from the state, Fenway decided to assume a leadership role in urban educational reform efforts in the city of Boston, and to that end, it collaborated with the Boston Public Schools (BPS) District and the Boston Teacher's Union (BTU) to create the pilot school model.

Both BPS and BTU agreed that in order for public pilot schools to be more innovative, they should be free of certain constraints. Therefore, pilot schools exercise much more flexibility over district policies and mandates, and pilot school governing boards have more authority than school councils. Specifically, pilot schools have autonomy over their budgets, staffing, governance, curriculum, assessments, and school calendar—the characteristics important in meeting the unique needs of students in urban environments. There are currently twenty-one pilot schools within BPS, and they serve students representative of the larger public school student population. Although pilot schools have the same per-pupil resources as other public high schools in Boston, compared to district averages, they have smaller class sizes, smaller teacher-student ratios, longer instructional periods, a nurturing school culture, and a practice of requiring students to demonstrate competency or mastery, rather than course completion, in order to graduate. Furthermore, these schools generally have extensive waiting lists, low suspension rates, and high college entrance rates.

Small Learning Communities Facilitate the Development of College and Career Readiness Behaviors and Skills

Fenway High School was founded on the principle that all students can learn when they feel safe and have opportunities to develop close personal relationships with their teachers. As a pilot school, Fenway still adheres to this founding principle, and therefore the school has implemented three programs that create small learning communities where students can develop college- and life-readiness behaviors and skills: freshman orientation and the Thompson Island trip, the house system, and advisory groups.

In order to help freshmen begin to develop a safe learning community and their capacity for working in groups, a skill that is necessary for college success and life in general, Fenway staff provides them with the opportunity to take a four-night trip to Thompson Island in the Boston Harbor Islands National Park. Freshmen spend time the first week of school each fall on this trip, learning about each other's strengths and weaknesses. The students participate in group activities that help them begin to trust one another and work as a team. According to school documentation, many seniors reflect back on this initial freshmen trip as important to their success at Fenway.

Another program Fenway implements in order to create small learning communities is the house system. All incoming freshmen are grouped into three learning families of approximately seventy-five students (encompassing students from ninth through eleventh grades), and they remain in these groups throughout their first three years of high school. Each house has its own faculty that teaches the core curriculum areas (math, science, and humanities) to the same group of students. In addition to the faculty, each house also has a student support counselor, a special education teacher or coordinator, and one or two teachers from minor content areas. Essentially the house system allows the creation of diverse cohorts, and these diverse cohorts provide students with opportunities to learn to work together and encourage one another in their academic pursuits.

A third way in which Fenway works to develop small learning communities is the advisory program. In this program, each teacher serves as an advisor to approximately twenty-five students in their assigned house, and advisory groups meet as a class three times per week. While students remain in the same advisory group throughout their high school experience, different teachers in their house serve as their advisor at each grade level. This allows students to get to know their teachers better, and it allows teachers to become highly proficient in the advisory curriculum that they teach in their assigned grade level. The advisory program is specifically focused on helping students develop the following college and life readiness skills and behaviors: study skills and time management, presentation skills, decision-making skills, violence prevention, and planning and preparation for academic deadlines. Helping students develop these skills and behaviors takes place in a variety of ways, including class assignments, guest speakers, and electronic media.

A Challenging Core Curriculum Provides Opportunities for All Students to Become College Ready

All students at Fenway High School take the same college preparatory curriculum that develops the following learning strategies: perspective, evidence, relevance, connection, and supposition. The school's documentation indicates that these are a part of Fenway vocabulary and the pedagogical approach used at the school. In addition, students are expected to understand them and employ them across the curriculum. The core curriculum, taught within each house, has four years of math, four years of humanities, four years of science, and Spanish I and II. These courses constitute graduation requirements for all students. In addition, students take physical education, and seniors can elect to take a psychology course, Dynamics of the Self, which seeks to help students develop their communication skills, understand their own behavior, and improve their imagination and stress management skills, emphasizing responsibility for oneself. Overall, the core curriculum and other course opportunities provide students with opportunities to develop the key cognitive strategies and learn the key content they will need to be successful in the college learning environment.

To gauge student competency within the core curriculum areas, Fenway employs a unique set of advanced assessment practices, including portfolios and exhibitions. All students must complete the Fenway junior review process before they proceed to their senior year. The junior review includes a student-created portfolio that is representative of each student's best work in all core content areas during his or her first three years of high school. In addition to examples of work completed, the portfolio usually includes a résumé and an essay by the student that outlines his or her strengths and weaknesses, future plans, and what the student intends to do to make the most of twelfth grade. Each student then formally presents the portfolio to a panel of house teachers. The panel comments on the presentation and discusses the student's upcoming senior year. The junior review provides students with the opportunity to demonstrate competency in key content areas, as well as develop the important overarching academic skill of presenting to an audience.

After successfully completing the junior review process, students move on to the Senior Institute. In preparation for college and life after high school, students in the three houses are mixed into three new cohort groups, and they study with new teachers in the core content areas of math, science, and humanities. However, students remain in the same advisory groups so that they can support each other through the college application process and the completion of senior graduation requirements. All seniors write a senior position paper, and they complete additional portfolios in all key content areas (math, science, and humanities).

In addition to the practice of using portfolios to assess student progress in the junior and senior years, the most important form of assessment at Fenway is an exhibition. Generally exhibitions require that students demonstrate an understanding of what they have studied, research that they have conducted, or problems that they have solved. Often exhibitions involve student presentations to panels of Fenway staff, colleagues, and other community partners. Exhibitions commonly take place at grade-level science fairs, which culminate in a student-designed senior project that is exhibited at the Boston Museum of Science. Advisory groups provide students with opportunities to prepare for the exhibitions, and the cross-curricular focus on this form of assessment allows students to develop their academic behaviors, such as time management, and overarching academic skills, such as presenting, that they will need to be successful college students.

A Local College and Community Partners Provide Transitional Learning Opportunities

In order to help students develop their college readiness skills and behaviors, Fenway High School has a dual-credit program with Emmanuel College, a four-year college that is a ten-minute walk from the Fenway campus. Both juniors and seniors may meet with their advisor or another teacher to discuss the possibility of dual enrollment in subjects of their interest, and if Fenway has a similar course, students can receive both high school and college credit. In order to participate in the dual-credit program, students must demonstrate competency in the subject area, be able to manage an increased academic workload, and be able to handle a college-like schedule. Overall the dual-credit program provides students the opportunity to experience a college classroom along with the support of a high school environment.

In addition to the optional dual-credit program, juniors and seniors are required to participate in the Fenway High School Ventures Program, which is designed to help students develop their communication and entrepreneurial skills. Once a week in the second half of their junior year, students participate in "The Pitch," which focuses on the development of initiative, resourcefulness, communication, problem-solving skills, respect for others, self-discipline, and self-confidence. This portion of the Ventures Program culminates with a presentation of a business proposal to a panel of judges. During the beginning of the senior year, students in the Ventures Program learn about personal finance, living on a budget, insurance issues, interviewing skills, résumé writing, and how to get and keep a job.

At the end of the senior year, all students complete a six-week unpaid internship, which is required for graduation. The requirements for the internship are working at least thirty hours each week at the internship site; returning to school on Mondays for an early afternoon seminar; working on a large project at the internship site, assigned by the student's internship supervisor; maintaining a weekly hours log, which has to be signed by the internship supervisor; and completing a senior portfolio that contains work done during the internship. By completing an internship, students gain firsthand experience with the concept that certain jobs require certain skills, and those skills are developed in the college-learning environment.

COMPREHENSIVE HIGH SCHOOL: CHERRY CREEK HIGH SCHOOL, GREENWOOD VILLAGE, COLORADO

Year established:	1955	**Enrollment:**	3,791
Locale:	Urban fringe of a large city	**Asian:**	6.4%
		African American:	3.4%
Free/ reduced meals:	5.1%	**Hispanic/Latino:**	5.0%
		Native American:	0.3%
Attendance rate:	93.2%	**White:**	84.9%
AP/IB participation:	24%		

A college going culture has to be very planned, and it requires a lot of time to get there. I think you can lose it in a second. So you have to pay attention to it every single day. But I think it is possible and can be implemented in every school.

CHERRY CREEK COUNSELOR

Cherry Creek High School is a comprehensive public high school serving over thirty-seven hundred students in Greenwood Village, Colorado. The school has a long-standing reputation for successfully preparing students for college success. At Cherry Creek, graduation and college attendance are the norm, which is evidenced by the 95 percent graduation rate and the 95 percent college enrollment rate. Students are strongly encouraged to take at least one of the twenty-nine AP classes offered, and 87 percent of students who take AP exams earn a passing score. Participation rates in the SAT and ACT exams are also high, with approximately 70 percent and 94 percent of seniors participating in each exam, respectively. Eighty-five percent of students at the school are white, and approximately 5 percent qualify for free or reduced-price lunches. Cherry Creek's success in preparing its students for enrollment and success in college can be attributed to a school culture that embeds a college focus at every level and specific instructional, administrative, and counseling practices that promote college readiness.

State and Local Context

Greenwood Village is an affluent suburb of Denver where 72 percent of the population has earned a bachelor's or advanced degree, and most people are employed in management/professional occupations (64 percent). The local school district's goal is for all students to be prepared to succeed in higher education, regardless of whether they choose to continue their education immediately after high school. The local school district's curriculum standards were developed in collaboration with Cherry Creek High School and are aligned to college readiness standards. There has been pressure in recent years to realign district curriculum standards with Colorado's achievement test, which has met resistance from both the district and Cherry Creek High School, because the test is not aligned to college readiness standards.

As in many other parts of the United States, Greenwood Village has experienced significant demographic changes that have affected school enrollment. Between 2000 and 2006, both the foreign-born and Hispanic/Latino populations in Arapahoe County increased more than 50 percent. During this same period, the percentage of families living in poverty there doubled. Cherry Creek High School is a school of choice that accepts students from outside the school boundary, and given the recent demographic changes, the school is challenged to develop and implement strategies that prepare increasing numbers of minority, low-income, and ELL students for college.

School Culture Revolves Around College Preparation from Day One

Students, teachers, and administrators agree: at Cherry Creek, it is not a question whether students will go to college but where. In order to graduate, students must apply and be accepted to college. Beginning freshman year, students are on a college preparatory track. Special attention is given to freshman schedules, and a freshman transition program and seminar program ensure students experience a successful transition into the high school learning environment and have the opportunity to meet with a counselor early to develop their four-year course plan.

Students find that expectations are universally high. The Cherry Creek mission states, "Excellence is not merely a goal at Cherry Creek High School; it is the standard." The minimum goal for students is to take biology, chemistry, and physics, and everyone is encouraged to take as rigorous a schedule as possible every semester. In addition, throughout high school, students are required to take at least four core subjects each term, and the principal personally reviews each senior's schedule for rigor. Students who make the honor roll are recognized for their achievement with an academic letter for their letterman's jacket.

Key Cognitive Strategies and Academic Behaviors Are Emphasized

A primary goal of the school is for students to become independent thinkers, and this manifests itself in a focus on helping students develop the skills they will need to become independent decision makers. The open campus provides students with a level of freedom that simulates college life and provides students with ample opportunities to make good decisions independently. Student schedules include free periods for study, research, and extra teacher contact.

The district and school have extensively promoted the use of key cognitive strategies in every classroom and with every teacher. Teachers and administrators alike have a solid understanding of the kind of thinking skills students will need to succeed in college and share in a college preparatory vision. Core subject department heads align curricula with ACT and College Board requirements, and classes across subjects focus on reading, writing, thinking skills, and oral presentations.

Cherry Creek's curriculum places a particularly strong emphasis on research. The required tenth-grade research paper is designed to develop content knowledge and engage students in key cognitive strategies and the development of the academic behaviors necessary for college success. Ninth and tenth graders use the Cornell note-taking system, a systematic method for capturing the main ideas of lectures with short phrases, symbols and abbreviations, relevant questions and keywords, and a short summary that has been in use for over fifty years. All students are issued a planner, which includes timekeepers, in order to help them learn time management, self-monitoring, and responsibility.

Students who are struggling or need additional help are expected to access the extensive support resources on their own. Students who are having difficulty with writing and research take a social science research course their sophomore year. In addition, Cherry Creek offers an AP summer program designed to assist underperforming students in becoming more proficient in the skills necessary for college success.

The School Campus Resembles a Postsecondary Institution

Cherry Creek's college preparatory culture is apparent throughout the physical configuration of the school. A large main building is the literal and figurative center of campus, and it closely resembles a university student union. Here, students (and parents) can visit the postgraduate center to see a counselor and obtain information about applying to college, study in the library (which has ample room for study groups), or purchase books, snacks, and school apparel in the bookstore, which is modeled after that of a university. In these ways, the school's design and atmosphere parallel that of a small liberal arts college, and students conduct themselves accordingly.

The school resembles a university in a number of other ways as well. Many of the systems in place have been modeled after university practices. The freshman orientation program is continuously revised with input from alumni and their parents so as to more closely parallel college student orientations. Beginning their sophomore year, students choose their own classes and teachers. The online system students use to register mimics that of a university registration system, and the guide students follow to register outlines exactly what colleges look for in a precollegiate curriculum.

Administrators Set a Tone of Professionalism and Evaluation

Cherry Creek's college-going culture is embedded in every programming decision, instructional practice, and component of building design, and much of this can be attributed to the school administrators, who require all teachers and counselors to support and adhere to a college readiness vision. The same high expectations that apply to students also apply to teachers, many of whom hold advanced degrees (80 percent have earned a master's degree, and nine possess doctoral degrees). Teachers are hired with the understanding that they have one year to demonstrate their ability to adhere and commit to the vision of the school. At three months, they are evaluated and subsequently groomed and mentored for further service—or told they will likely not be retained. Teachers at Cherry Creek are also learners with a genuine love of school and learning. Teachers are duty free, meaning they have no bus or lunch duties. This ensures that they can be available to meet with students during free periods. Those who teach AP classes teach regular classes as well as a means of integrating the college preparatory instructors at all levels.

Cherry Creek administrators have cultivated a culture of self-evaluation in which every teacher is evaluated. In an environment where students are rigorously evaluated, it does not seem out of place that teachers are thoroughly evaluated as well. Administrators conduct regular classroom walkthroughs in order to collect data to monitor the use of instructional strategies that promote the learning and use of key cognitive strategies. Data are shared individually with teachers, and in aggregated form schoolwide, in order to improve instructional practices.

Counselors Provide Continuity and Contextual Skills

Students are assigned a counselor who remains with them throughout all four years of high school. Counselors are charged with ensuring that their advisees receive college readiness, preparation, and application messages consistently and early in their high school careers. Students meet with their counselors at least once each year to review their four-year course plan, and seniors have mandatory conferences with their counselors to address issues related to the college application process. Alumni are encouraged to return and share their college experiences with students.

In addition to the one-on-one counseling with students, Cherry Creek counselors organize assemblies for students to provide information on course selection and the college application process. Counselors are in regular contact with teachers to encourage integration of college knowledge into their daily lesson plans. Five-minute college knowledge lessons are sent to teachers by e-mail, and all teachers are asked to spend a small amount of time each day discussing a college readiness issue.

CHARTER SCHOOL: MINNESOTA NEW COUNTRY SCHOOL, HENDERSON, MINNESOTA

Year established:	1983	**Enrollment:**	109
Locale:	Rural, outside core-based statistical area	**Asian:**	2.0%
		African American:	2.0%
		Hispanic/Latino:	6.0%
Free/ reduced meals:	32.0%	**Other:**	0.0%
Attendance rate:	94.0%	**White:**	90.0%
ELL students:	0.0%		

We want students to be prepared to handle critical assessment in postsecondary education. We want to prepare them for critical analysis of their work and to be able to work to other people's expectations.

New Country School teacher-advisor

Minnesota New Country School (MNCS), which opened in 1994, is a public charter school in Henderson, Minnesota, that became the prototype for the EdVisions educational model, which relies on project-based learning in small, democratic learning communities. Given its focus on small learning communities, MNCS has a student enrollment of only 109 students in sixth through twelfth grades. Ninety percent of the students who attend MNCS are white, and 32 percent are eligible for free or reduced-price lunch. Between the 2006–2007 and 2007–2008 academic years, the special education population grew from 28 to 39 percent, and the school staff is working to accommodate and support this growing subpopulation of students. MNCS has an overall attendance rate of 94 percent, and 90 percent of its graduates apply to two-year and four-year colleges and universities. The college acceptance rate for graduates is 100 percent. Furthermore, in 2006, the U.S. Department of Education recognized MNCS as one of the top eight charter schools in the nation. The school's success at preparing students for college, and life after high school in general, can be attributed to the project-based learning model, integration of technology into the student-driven curriculum, meaningful staff-student relationships, and a focus on helping students develop a sense of responsibility for their learning process.

State and Local Context

In 1991, Minnesota was one of the first states to create legislated public charter schools, which are independent public schools that are allowed to establish different and innovative learning environments and employ unconventional teaching methodologies. Legislated public charter schools in Minnesota operate under a charter from the local school board or state, and they are exempt from most state and local educational laws. However, in order to renew their charter, schools must demonstrate that students are learning the agreed-on educational skills. In order for MNCS students to earn their diplomas, they must demonstrate proficiency in all required Minnesota state academic standards.

Minnesota New Country School opened its doors just three years after the Minnesota state legislature created public charter schools, and although the designers of MNCS experienced initial resistance to the establishment of a charter school in rural Henderson, the educational model used at MNCS became the launching point for the EdVisions Schools, an organization that is managed as a cooperative by teachers with the goal of empowering teachers as owner and operators of the schools in which they teach. EdVisions Schools require the implementation of two unique organizational components: (1) a student-driven project-based learning model and (2) a democratically governed environment that provides opportunities for teacher ownership in decisions made about the school. Since 2000, the Bill & Melinda Gates Foundation has provided EdVisions Schools with the resources to establish forty schools in rural, suburban, and urban environments, and existing schools are also contracting with EdVisions for assistance in implementing the EdVisions model. Although this model is unconventional, research demonstrates that students in EdVisions Schools are reaching academic achievement levels that are commensurate to or exceed that of their peers in traditional education environments.

Project-Based Learning Helps Students Become Ready for Life After High School

Project-based learning "is based upon the idea that students will be most engaged in the learning process when they have a personal interest in what they are learning." Instead of using a teacher-driven model for curriculum organization and delivery, project-based learning relies on student interests and requires that students pursue those interests in the form of proposed and approved projects. Therefore, direct teacher-driven instruction takes place only in mathematics. Although direct instruction is limited, MNCS students, like all other students in Minnesota, are required to earn ten credits each year in order to receive their high school diploma. Students earn the majority of these credits by proposing projects at a team meeting and subsequently completing those projects. During the meeting, students propose an idea for a project that includes the amount of credit they think they should receive, the state standards the project addresses, and the rubric by which the project will be evaluated. Students revise their proposed projects based on proposal team feedback until the proposal team approves the project.

Generally students receive one credit for every 100 hours they spend on a project. However, the proposal team evaluates student projects on both quantity and quality, and some students may spend 150 hours on a project, although they receive only one credit. Students are required to log all of the time they spend on each project, and at its completion, the student receives the appropriate amount of credit rather than a grade. In addition, all MNCS seniors are required to complete an advanced project of their choice, which requires a minimum of 300 hours of logged time, multiple senior proposal team meetings, and a 25-minute presentation in a community venue.

The project-based learning model emphasizes inquisitiveness, intellectual openness, analysis, and interpretation of multiple types of information. All students also are required to make two project-related presentations each year to incorporate a minimum of three outside sources in their projects. One of those sources must be in the format of an interview, and students are required to reference their sources appropriately. Furthermore, in order to engage in project-based learning successfully, students must learn to manage their time, create to-do lists, request help when needed, and persist through difficulty. All of these skills and behaviors are necessary for success in the college environment and life after high school.

Integration of Technology Prepares Students for Twenty-First-Century Living and Learning

All MNCS students have their own computer workstation, which they are allowed to personalize, enabled with Internet access. This allows students to conduct research for their projects at a self-directed pace, and individual computers also simulate the twenty-first-century work environment. The integration of technology into the educational environment at MNCS is foundational to its success at preparing students for college, as it is consistent with the way in which people today find information and conduct business. Students at MNCS, with or without computer and Internet access at home, develop their research skills and explore potential project ideas through their school computers.

Advisory Groups Facilitate Students' Learning and Development

Student engagement in project-based learning takes place within the structure of advisory groups. Each teacher-advisor has fifteen to seventeen students assigned to his or her advisory group, and the purpose of the groups, and the advisor-student relationship, is to help students make a plan for each of the seven blocks that constitute the academic year. The advisory relationship also provides support for student development of self-directed learning skills and offers students a way in which to progress through the tasks required to complete each project. Through the advisory group, students develop self-awareness, self-control, and time management skills, and they are given the opportunity to work on their communication with adults and peers. If students find that their advisory group is not working for them, they may request to be moved to another group.

Students Develop a Strong Sense of Responsibility

In order for MNCS students to be successful within the project-based learning model, they are required to take responsibility for their learning process. This requirement is simply built into the student-driven process. In addition to taking responsibility for their academic learning process, two practices at MNCS help students develop a sense of responsibility in the area of personal choices and conduct. First, all activities at MNCS are coordinated and managed by the staff and students, which means there is no additional office or custodial support. Therefore, staff and students do all of the cleaning in the school, and they make and pass all rules in the school's congress. Due to the fact that staff and students have equal ownership in the school, there are few student behavior or vandalism problems.

Second, if there is a problem with misconduct, the necessary individuals participate in a justice circle. A justice circle involves the student and the necessary staff members, and the student who demonstrated misconduct has part ownership in determining the consequences of his or her actions. Through helping to determine their own consequences for misconduct, students learn to take responsibility for their personal choices within the small learning community environment. One of the teacher-advisors at MNCS stated, "Responsibility is big. I'm big on the idea that you make choices and need to follow through on these to reach your goals. You may have to do things you don't want to do to attain goals. You have to take responsibility for where you end up in life." Clearly the concept of taking responsibility for learning and personal choices is a cornerstone of the educational practice at MNCS.

EARLY COLLEGE HIGH SCHOOL: MANHATTAN HUNTER SCIENCE HIGH SCHOOL, NEW YORK, NEW YORK

Year established:	2003	Enrollment:	406
Locale:	Large city	Asian:	25.9%
Free/ reduced meals:	69.0%	African American:	21.9%
		Hispanic/Latino:	36.2%
Attendance rate:	95.0%	Multiracial:	1.7%
ELL students:	2.5%	Native American:	0.1%
		White:	13.3%

As a whole school, our mission is to get students into college and to keep them there.

MANHATTAN HUNTER TEACHER

Manhattan Hunter Science High School, which opened in 2003 in partnership with Hunter College, is an early college high school in New York City known for its science-focused and college preparatory curriculum. Eighty-seven percent of the 406 students who attend Manhattan Hunter are from minority backgrounds, and more than half of the student body is eligible for free or reduced-price lunch. Furthermore, approximately 80 percent of students admitted to Manhattan Hunter scored at or below grade level on their eighth-grade state math and reading assessments. The graduation rate for the first class of seniors to earn their diplomas at Manhattan Hunter, the class of 2007, was 100 percent. In addition, Manhattan Hunter has a 95 percent attendance rate, and 100 percent of the class of 2007 took the SAT. Of the seventy-seven seniors who graduated in 2007, 100 percent of them were accepted by a college or university and intended to enroll. Approximately 87 percent of the seniors planned to attend a four-year institution, and approximately 53 percent intended to remain in New York State. This school's evident success at preparing students for college can be attributed to a rigorous college preparatory curriculum, unique academic support programs, intensive guidance counseling practices, and a focus on helping students develop a sense of responsibility for their learning process.

State and Local Context

New York City Public Schools are located within the five boroughs of New York City (Bronx, Brooklyn, Manhattan, Queens, Staten Island), and students have more than six hundred high school programs from which they can choose. To assist students and parents in learning about these program options, the Department of Education conducts workshops and fairs. To gain entrance to one of the high school programs, a student must be a resident of one of the five New York City boroughs, meet eighth- or ninth-grade promotional standards, and complete an application by the deadline. Equity and choice are the cornerstone principles of the admissions process, and students are allowed to rank up to twelve programs on their high school application.

In the admissions process, Manhattan Hunter Science High School specifically seeks applicants across the five boroughs who have not necessarily excelled in middle school but have an interest in studying science in high school. Hunter College, its early college partner institution, "has a distinguished reputation for nurturing talented minority scientists and meeting the challenge of providing high-quality science education in the 21st century." Hunter College, located in Manhattan just a short distance from Manhattan Hunter Science High School, is one of the oldest public postsecondary institutions in the country. With a student enrollment of twenty-one thousand undergraduate and graduate students, it is the largest college in the City University of New York system.

A Rigorous College Preparatory Curriculum Facilitates a Successful Transition into Postsecondary Education

All enrolled students participate in the same college preparatory curriculum, and therefore all students attending Manhattan Hunter Science High School meet the requirements of a rigorous high school academic program and develop the academic skills and behaviors necessary for success in the collegiate environment. The specific programmatic components that form the foundation for the college preparatory program of study are an integrated curriculum, dual-credit courses, and the early college year on the Hunter College campus.

The curriculum at Manhattan Hunter is integrated in that the academic content of the courses offered was developed through the joint efforts of Hunter College faculty and Manhattan Hunter teachers. In this way, students are provided with the opportunity to learn the state standards necessary for performing well on the required New York Regents exams, as well as prepare for entry-level college course work. The principal indicated that one of the schoolwide goals at Manhattan Hunter is to have all students graduate with an Advanced Regents Diploma, which means that students pass a larger number of New York Regents exams at a higher level than many other New York City high school graduates.

In addition to an integrated curriculum, Manhattan Hunter assists students in transitioning successfully into higher education through dual-credit courses, taught on the Manhattan Hunter campus. On successful completion of these courses, students earn both high school and college credit. All students enroll in dual-credit courses at Manhattan Hunter and may start taking these courses as early as their sophomore year. There are no prerequisites for the courses.

One of the interim goals at Manhattan Hunter is to ensure that all students have accumulated enough high school credits to spend their entire senior year taking courses at Hunter College. Students take entry-level college math and science courses taught by Hunter College faculty, and they also take English and social studies courses on the Hunter College campus, although these courses are taught by Manhattan Hunter teachers. In the process of the transition to senior year on the Hunter College campus, students work with Manhattan Hunter teachers who serve as advisors and are also required to work in study groups. Furthermore, students are encouraged to use Hunter College's academic support services, including an early college high school liaison. The senior year was designed to be a year of transition, where students can learn to be successful college students through the process of making mistakes in a somewhat controlled environment. Through the early college program and dual-credit courses, students may earn a maximum of twenty-two college credits before graduating from high school.

Unique Academic Support Programs Promote Student Achievement

Three programs of academic support to students have been implemented: Homework Room, Lunch and Learn, and Spotlight on Success. All promote student achievement and are built into the structure of the school day.

The Homework Room is an after-school program staffed by the administrators that allows students to work on their homework before they go home. This optional program directly supports students who find it difficult, for various reasons, to complete their homework once they leave the school building.

Lunch and Learn is a tutoring program that takes place during the lunch period. All students at Manhattan Hunter have the same lunch period, and teachers are expected to be in their classrooms to provide academic support to students who are struggling in their course work, as well as to students who self-select to participate. The Lunch and Learn period is considered teachers' duty period.

Spotlight on Success is an enrichment program that runs for forty-five minutes every Tuesday, Wednesday, and Thursday. This optional tutoring program takes place at the end of the day, during an additional eighth period. Although students who are selected for this program are not required to participate, it is printed on their schedules.

Intensive Guidance Counseling Practices Build College Knowledge

The four Manhattan Hunter Science High School guidance counselors and schoolwide guidance counseling practices are important to Manhattan Hunter's administration, and they are a large component of the school's success at preparing students for college. Manhattan Hunter relies on one guidance-counseling program and four guidance-counseling practices to assist students in developing their contextual skills and awareness. The program at Manhattan Hunter is a required junior advisory class. In this class, all students receive free SAT preparation and learn about the college application, financial aid, and acceptance processes. Students are also offered access to a Kaplan SAT preparation course that takes place after the eighth-period Spotlight on Success on the Manhattan Hunter campus. Although students must pay a fee of one hundred dollars for this course, it is made more accessible to students by providing the sessions on the high school campus.

The four guidance-counseling practices that help students develop their college knowledge are a required e-mail account, assistance with college applications, assistance with financial aid applications, and parental support. First, students who enroll at Manhattan Hunter are required to open a new e-mail account that demonstrates professionalism. All students have a gmail account that adheres to the following format: lastname.firstname@gmail.com. The school's guidance counselors, administrators, and teachers will not communicate with seniors using any other e-mail account; this helps prevent students from using an inappropriate e-mail address during the college application and admissions process.

While the required e-mail account assists students with appropriate electronic communication, the guidance counselors also practice providing students with detailed information about, and assistance with, the college application and financial aid processes. They also assist students in choosing three types of schools to apply to: safe schools, match schools, and reach schools. Students receive help with their college application essays, and sometimes the guidance counselors mail the applications directly from the school for the student. In addition, they provide students with a letter to put in their application that describes Manhattan Hunter Science High School. Students receive intensive assistance with the financial aid process. Guidance counselors often have students bring their parents' tax information to school in order to ensure that the form is filled out correctly. When students receive acceptance letters, the guidance counselors help students understand what kind of financial aid they will receive at that particular school.

In addition to helping students understand and successfully complete the college application and financial aid processes from start to finish, the guidance counselors at Manhattan Hunter have a practice of making themselves available to assist parents with this process as well. Parents may use the computers in the guidance counseling office to perform college searches based on Web sites that the counselors provide; the counselors are also readily available to take phone calls from parents. These outreach efforts demonstrate the school's commitment to helping both students and parents build their contextual skills and awareness.

Students Develop a Sense of Responsibility for Their Learning

The Manhattan Hunter Science High School teachers, administrators, and guidance counselors are committed to helping students develop a sense of responsibility for their learning process and personal choices. This commitment is evident across the curriculum and throughout the school's programs and practices. It is another way in which this school assists students in becoming college ready. Specifically, students are taught to ask for help when they need it. They are encouraged to ask for a teacher who explains concepts in a way that the student is able to understand, and the school emphasizes self-advocacy when students are struggling. The school staff teaches students that asking for help is necessary in both high school and college. Students are taught to be accountable to the syllabus in high school and in college, and they are encouraged to take personal responsibility for turning in their assignments on time.

MAGNET HIGH SCHOOL: GARLAND HIGH SCHOOL, GARLAND, TEXAS

Year established:	1898	Enrollment:	2,464
Locale:	Urban fringe of large city	Asian:	5.6%
		African American:	17.5%
Free/reduced meals:	44.9%	Hispanic/Latino:	44.3%
Attendance rate:	94.3%	Native American:	0.4%
ELL students:	11.6%	White:	32.2%
AP participation:	26.3%		
IB participation:	27.8%		

We do teach content, definitely, but we also teach the skills on what you're going to have to do to be successful.

GARLAND HIGH SCHOOL DEPARTMENT CHAIR

Garland High School is a magnet public high school located in Garland, Texas, with a student population of over twenty-four hundred. More than 67 percent of students are from minority backgrounds, and nearly 45 percent qualify for the free or reduced-price lunch program. Garland High School celebrates a 93.8 percent graduation rate and has been selected as one of *Newsweek*'s top U.S. high schools for five out of the past six years, reaching a rank of 178 in 2005. Garland's success can be attributed to its focus on key cognitive skills and college content, opportunities provided to Hispanic/Latino students to encourage college attendance, teacher collaboration, and developing academic behaviors and professional skills.

State and Local Context

Located fifteen miles northeast of downtown Dallas, Garland is a large suburb on the urban fringe of this large city. As of 2007, it had a population of more than 230,832 residents, with 28.4 percent born outside the United States. Garland High School is the Gifted and Talented magnet in the school district and offers the International Baccalaureate Programme (IB), the Advanced Placement Program (AP), and the Performing Arts Endorsement. Students can enter the Gifted and Talented program in elementary or middle school by completing a formal application and receiving standardized achievement test scores in the ninetieth percentile in both reading and math. Both the AP and IB programs have a strong presence at Garland High School.

Garland Independent School District (GISD) has an open freedom-of-choice enrollment policy. In most school districts, enrollment is determined by location of the student's residence; in this school district, parents can choose the school that their child attends with very few restrictions. Although the normal busing zone creates some limitations, GISD boasts that only 2 to 3 percent of students do not receive admission to their first-choice school.

In 2003, the Texas legislature passed the Texas Success Initiative, which is designed to measure competency in reading, writing, and mathematics and provide developmental studies in areas of identified deficiencies. In compliance with the Texas Success Initiative, students must take an approved placement test prior to enrolling in any Texas public college or university unless they have received an exemption or waiver. A student who enrolls without test scores may be subject to remediation.

Texas is among a handful of states that have passed state legislation regarding dual credit. Dual credit programs are one of the ways Texas encourages more students to engage in postsecondary-level educational experiences while still in high school. Students may pay tuition and fees for dual credit, but in many cases, it can be very low cost or even free. Enrollment in dual-credit courses overall in Texas grew from 11,921 in 1999 to 64,910 in 2007.

The Program Focuses on Key Cognitive Strategies and College Content

Garland High School enables students to prepare for the rigors and demands of postsecondary educational institutions by focusing on the development of key cognitive strategies throughout the curriculum. The school seeks to instill a desire to learn within its students by creating lessons that will nurture and encourage passion, excitement, and curiosity.

In order to cultivate interpretation skills, Garland High School requires all juniors and seniors to complete a critical analysis paper. Students read a novel of their choice (selected from a list) and interpret critical viewpoints using examples that support their point of view. Teachers place a noteworthy emphasis on learning to write, analyzing data or documents, constructing an argument, and drawing appropriate conclusions based on research. The language arts department promotes precision and accuracy skills by requiring students to undertake independent writing assignments, with multiple drafts and revisions expected in order to receive credit for the assignment.

Garland High School emphasizes reasoning skills, in particular math and science courses. In the algebra II honors class, students participate in class discussions where they describe their processes and solutions and defend their answers. In science courses, students write lab reports that include sections on measurements, observations, data, analysis, and conclusions.

Hispanic/Latino ELL Students Are Encouraged to Attend College

Garland High School provides multiple opportunities targeted toward assisting the ELL student population. In addition to its traditional college fair each year, the school holds a Hispanic/Latino job and college fair. Visits to college campuses are coordinated so that a Spanish translator accompanies students. To accommodate the student population that has Spanish-speaking parents, the school arranges for interpreters to be present at all college and financial aid information nights. While targeted primarily to ELL students, a voluntary Saturday session of classes is offered for all students who need help passing the state assessment. The students who attend Saturday sessions are also taken to the local community college admissions office to receive assistance with college-related paperwork.

Teachers Collaborate to Align Curriculum Vertically

Both Garland High School and Garland Independent School District offer opportunities for teacher collaboration and vertical alignment. The school district provides district-wide professional learning communities to assist teachers in collaborating.

At content-specific meetings, all teachers within the same subject area meet weekly to share what they are teaching and their respective approaches. These meetings facilitate coplanning among the teachers within content areas. In addition, IB teachers have common planning meetings after school that meet by subject and grade-level areas.

The IB social studies department also facilitates vertical alignment. Its expectations begin with every ninth grader being able to write a thesis and introductory paragraph. Starting in tenth grade, students learn to analyze documents and write a thesis based on those documents. For eleventh grade, students are expected to start writing analysis papers, and twelfth graders are then challenged to demonstrate in-depth analysis.

Academic Behaviors and College Knowledge Are Emphasized

Garland High School incorporates a variety of methods to facilitate the development of academic behaviors and college knowledge. In many courses, collaboration and self-awareness skills are taught, along with an array of test-taking strategies.

Students in their freshman year are required to take a leadership course that teaches fundamental academic behaviors. Included in this course are resources and information on organization, time management, note taking, how to read a textbook, study skills, test-taking strategies, and how to request needed help. This course encourages students to use a planner and organize color-coded notes in a three-ring binder. Students are also taught how to create a study plan, apply reading and study techniques, and understand their individual learning style.

Garland High School's online grade book, available to students and parents, enables grade checking and progress tracking. Parents can also get involved through Garland Independent School District's online Parent Communication Center. Using this Web site, parents go to Garland High School and select the teacher and appropriate course to find more information on their student's classes. Syllabi are also available to students and parents so that they can view due dates for various assignments and plan accordingly.

Garland High School offers career exploration opportunities and methods for students to develop professional skills. The vocational program offers career and technical classes for interested students, requiring students to fill out applications, participate in interviews, and receive parental approval. Through the vocational program, students are given opportunities to work, job shadow, or participate in internships.

MAGNET SCHOOL: POLYTECH HIGH SCHOOL, WOODSIDE, DELAWARE

Year established:	1991	**Enrollment:**	1,150
Locale:	Urban fringe of midsize city	**Asian:**	1.9%
		African American:	21.9%
Free/reduced meals:	17.5%	**Hispanic/Latino:**	4.2%
Attendance rate:	95%	**Native American:**	0.5%
ELL students:	0.2%	**White:**	71.4%
AP/IB participation:	5.9%		

I stand in front of the faculty each fall to identify the good, the bad, and the ugly, to put it out front and to let them know where we need to improve.

Polytech principal

Polytech High School is a magnet career technical high school with a college preparatory curriculum where all students are expected to perform at high levels. The graduation rate for African American students is 96 percent, the best in the state of Delaware, and the overall graduation rate in 2006 was also 96 percent. Sixty percent of graduating seniors go directly into postsecondary education, and 40 percent choose to go directly to work. Most of the students graduating from Polytech and enrolling in a college or university on high school completion are first-generation college students. The school's successful integration of academic course work with technical specialties provides students with marketable skills, and many graduates choose to utilize these skills to support themselves through college.

State and Local Context

Polytech High School is located in Woodside, Delaware, a small town just south of Dover located within Kent County. Woodside has a population of fewer than 200, but Kent County has a total population of nearly 127,000. The school population of more than 1,100 students is 74 percent white and 21 percent African American. These demographics are comparable to those of the Kent County population. The school draws students from throughout the county, which includes five school districts and a mix of rural communities, small towns, and small cities.

Initially, Polytech was a half-day vocational program that catered primarily to students struggling academically. During the 1990s, the school underwent a restructuring using the "High Schools That Work" model, a program sponsored by the Southern Regional Education Board that is designed to promote research-based solutions to improving secondary schools, and in 1991 it became a full-time technical high school, which resulted in shifts in external perception and name change. Today demand for admission is high, and some students travel up to ninety minutes each way to attend the school. The school admits an equal number of students from each of the five local school districts on a first-come, first-served basis.

The State of Delaware requires twenty-two credits for graduation from high school, which is comparable to other states. Students who maintain at least a B average qualify for funding to attend a community college. Many students use this program to acquire a community college degree and then transfer to a four-year institution. Only 45 percent of the students at the University of Delaware come from the state, and some individuals suggest that this reflects a clear preference for out-of-state tuition dollars.

The Polytech Curriculum and Academy Structure Integrate the Academic and the Technical

The integration of academic course work with technical specialties helps students realize the practical applications of their skills and knowledge, and it also provides them with marketable skills, which encourages students to take their work seriously. At Polytech, the expectations of all students are high, as demonstrated by the rigorous curriculum required of all students. The school graduation requirements meet the State of Delaware curriculum standards, with additional required credits in a technical concentration area. Consequently, Polytech has the highest number of required credits in the state (twenty-seven minimum), and seniors graduate with an average of thirty-one credits.

Polytech is composed of five academies: the Educational Foundations Academy for freshmen and four career academies with industrial, modern technology, professional services, and health and medical themes. The freshman orientation process acclimates students to the academy structure, as well as the expectations, which are enforced through a strict discipline policy. The freshman Educational Foundations Academy courses include college-preparatory English, science, social studies, and math. During their first year, students explore each of the twenty-one technical concentrations and eventually select a concentration within one of the four career academies. Once students have chosen a technical area, they go through a formal interview process for admission to the program. Ninety percent are accepted into their first- or second-choice technical area. Over the next three years, students follow a prescribed course plan. By graduation, they have gained skills in a high-demand career area, and in some cases, students also have earned a professional certification; Automotive Service Excellence (ASE) automotive, cosmetology, Certified Nursing Assistant (CAN), and pilot certifications are all possible certification areas.

Even with a Strong Technical Program, the School Maintains a Focus on College Preparation

Polytech has a marked focus on college preparation, which makes it stand out from many other career and technical schools. Every student in the school takes a similar college preparatory academic curriculum in addition to career academy classes. It is the only technical school in Delaware to offer AP courses, and given the current demand, the school hopes to offer more AP courses in the future. Writing, critical reading, research, study skills, and oral communication are integrated across subject areas.

Students are encouraged to take risks and take advantage of the opportunities to enroll in classes at local colleges. Students begin writing papers their freshman year, using APA style, and their paper length and quality requirements increase each year. Seniors complete a rigorous project that includes a research paper, a tangible product, and an oral presentation. These projects prepare students for college-level independent writing, research, expectations, communication, and presentations. All Polytech students also develop a portfolio that contains their résumé, references, cover letters, report cards, and examples of their best academic work.

PASS Program Provides Systemic Support

All Polytech students benefit from the Polytech Advisement and Support System (PASS). Teachers and administrators act as advisors in the PASS program, and each teacher and administrator mentors eight to ten students. The advisors function as caring, committed adults in the lives of the students, and they are matched with students on the basis of student interests and needs to the extent possible. Administrators advise freshmen, and once freshmen have selected a technical concentration, they are transferred to an advisor within their chosen academy. Students meet with their advisors at least four times each year to discuss their four-year high school plan and their two-year post–high school plan (known as the 4+2 plan). Advisors regularly review student grades and make sure students stay on track to meet their goals. Each spring, students and their parents meet with their PASS advisors to discuss course selections for the upcoming year as well as the six-year plan.

The PASS program is administered by the school's guidance counselor office and high school administration. Guidance counselors train the teachers, help students select colleges to apply to, and provide information to students about other postsecondary options. This effective low-cost program has won the State of Delaware's Superstars in Education Award. In addition to providing students with strong support, the PASS program increases cohesion across the staff. In order to advise students effectively, teachers need to understand the requirements across departments.

Staff Communication Leads to Articulation of Standards

Teachers and administrators at Polytech interact frequently and in meaningful ways. Excellent communication promotes the dissemination of data to and among teachers and administrators, which in turn drives instruction. Administrators expect close ties between the technical and academic programs, and they also expect that all teachers share the school's philosophy of high expectations for all students. Students who perform below state standards are enrolled in multiple English and mathematics courses. Teachers within content areas such as math or social studies subjects meet twice weekly to collaborate and integrate state standards across the academies. Within each academy, academic and technical faculty also come together for weekly meetings. The principal meets with lead teachers each week to ensure teachers are on the right track and improve the curriculum. Teachers at Polytech are given the freedom to take instructional risks, and the administration is supportive of funding teacher-determined professional development opportunities. The principal meets monthly with all students (by class) at "town meetings" to hear student concerns, honor students who have garnered awards, highlight key upcoming events, and emphasize the importance of attendance.

PRIVATE SCHOOL: CRISTO REY JESUIT HIGH SCHOOL, CHICAGO, ILLINOIS

Year established:	1996	**Enrollment:**	535
Locale:	Large city	**Asian:**	0%
Free/ reduced meals:	86.4%	**African American:**	0%
		Hispanic/Latino:	100%
Attendance rate:	98.5%	**Native American:**	0%
ELL students:	0.3%	**White:**	0%

The school works with us from the very beginning and helps us achieve the goal of attending college right after graduation.

CRISTO REY JESUIT HIGH SCHOOL SENIOR

Cristo Rey Jesuit High School is a private Catholic high school that serves low-income, at-risk immigrant students primarily from the Pilson and Little Village neighborhoods of Chicago, Illinois. Recognized by President George W. Bush in 2008 as a successful and innovative school model, Cristo Rey is structured around a four-year internship program that provides students the means to finance their private education. The school's vision is to provide its five hundred students with a safe and challenging learning environment in which they can maximize their potential to assume leadership roles in their civic, religious, cultural, and professional lives. This is supported by a dual-language college preparatory curriculum and the expectation that all students will apply to and attend a four-year college or university.

To be admitted to Cristo Rey, students and parents must participate in a comprehensive application process. All new students attend an intensive three-week summer orientation to learn relevant job, study, technology, and time management skills. The student body is 100 percent Hispanic/Latino. The attendance rate is 98.5 percent, and the graduation rate is 99 percent. Ninety-nine percent of students are accepted into a two-year or four-year institution. The school's success at preparing students for college and the working world can be attributed to its unique structure, bilingual curriculum and culture, and comprehensive student support services.

State and Local Context

With more than 400,000 students, Chicago Public Schools is the third largest school district in the nation. Eighty-five percent of its students are considered low income, and 92 percent are from minority backgrounds. Approximately half of the city's freshmen graduate within five years of entering high school. District officials have undergone targeted efforts over the past decade to steadily improve academic performance and graduation rates, including new programs created in partnership with city officials, nonprofit organizations, philanthropists, and communities.

Nearly fifteen years ago, Jesuit priests dedicated themselves to helping low-income immigrant families living in Chicago's near-southwest side. By surveying the community, they found that families in Pilson and Little Village sought a small college preparatory high school but were unable to afford private education. In response, the Jesuits developed a work-study program to generate income for the school and provide students with valuable work experience. Through Cristo Rey's Corporate Internship Program (CIP), Chicago businesses and firms hire students to work as interns; all income the students earn through CIP is applied to their tuition and fees. In addition, the high school partners with the University of Chicago School of Social Work, DePaul University, Chicago School of Professional Psychology, and Loyola University. The school's overall success has led to the establishment of nineteen Cristo Rey Jesuit High Schools around the country.

While Cristo Rey has achieved a high graduation rate (99 percent), student retention, at 70 percent, is below target. Administrators are committed to improving retention and highlight three main reasons students are asked to leave the school: failing a class and refusing to complete summer school, being suspected of gang activity, or being fired from an internship and deemed to be unemployable. These three scenarios, which make up the majority of cases, reflect strict policies to ensure student safety and the financial sustainability of the school. Students and parents support these policies and report that Cristo Rey is one of the few places in their community where they feel safe and valued.

Corporate Internship Program Builds Community Connections and Contextual Skills

The Corporate Internship Program (CIP) was designed to make private education affordable to at-risk youth living in economically challenged areas of Chicago. The program combines job sharing and employee leasing. The school contracts with private companies that pay the school twenty-eight thousand dollars per academic year for each full-time, entry-level position filled by Cristo Rey students. Four students share each position. Students spend four extended days at school and one at work each week. As part of freshman orientation, the school provides comprehensive training to prepare students for the experience. Topics include everything from professional attire to operating office equipment, Microsoft Office skills, team building, and relevant terminology.

All five hundred students participate in the program, and fewer than 2 percent have their internships terminated during the year. When this occurs, students must complete a reemployment process during which they read *The Seven Habits of Highly Effective Teens* (1999, by Sean Covey and Debra Harris), and complete a report and PowerPoint presentation on its concepts. They must also write a letter to their parents, the school, and the employer to describe the circumstances that led to their dismissal and how the situation could be prevented in the future. Additional technology training may also be required. This process helps students develop self-awareness as well as resilience. All students and their sponsoring companies complete an exit survey at the end of the year to determine which students will return to the same location; 20 percent of students stay with the same company all four years.

Overall, the CIP program cultivates independence, self-advocacy, strong communication, and time management skills, as well as the ability to relate to people from outside their immediate community. Students learn that to become a professional, they must do well in high school and earn a college degree.

Bilingual Students and Staff Enhance Culture and Parental Involvement

The dual-language curriculum at Cristo Rey Jesuit High School is an integral part of the school's culture. Students must demonstrate ability in both English and Spanish to be admitted to the school. The vast majority of teachers and administrators are fluent in Spanish in order to communicate fully with students and parents; teachers who are not bilingual may be hired for some positions, but administrators acknowledge that this creates unwanted barriers inside the community. All students are required to take Spanish courses, which helps them develop advanced writing and reading skills in their first language. Grammar, writing, and presentation skills in both languages are incorporated into English and social studies courses. This complete integration of English and Spanish into the school curriculum and culture works to help students appreciate, improve, and ultimately apply their language skills in college and the workplace.

Since nearly everyone at the school is bilingual, parents feel more connected to their children's education. The ability to discuss issues in Spanish encourages closer relationships among parents, teachers, and administrators and builds a stronger community for students. A Spanish-speaking culture also allows parents to fully participate in important college-related classes, known as *Escuela Para Padres*, which cover topics such as completing the FAFSA, financial aid, and cultural transitions from high school to college. Students report that these classes have been valuable in helping families understand why students want to attend college, as well as the value of a college education.

Curriculum and Assessments Are Designed Collaboratively

To accommodate CIP work schedules, the curriculum for freshmen and sophomores is fixed so that students in each grade take the same courses; juniors and seniors have more freedom to select electives. Teachers work collaboratively to design and assess the college preparatory curriculum through benchmarking, goal setting, and soliciting feedback from alumni currently enrolled in college. Instructional objectives and learning outcomes are evaluated against college entrance requirements, accreditation requirements, Illinois state standards, ACT standards, AP standards, and Jesuit education standards. Interdepartmental goal setting helps to strengthen the curriculum and reinforce student academic knowledge and skills, such as reading and critical thinking skills. Departments work to increase students' reading skills by incorporating into most classrooms active reading strategies, such as underlining and the use of graphic organizers to enhance notes and reading comprehension. Similarly, the history, Spanish, and English departments collaborated to increase activities that promote higher-level thinking skills, such as interpretation and reasoning, across courses. Alumni feedback has also helped teachers determine how closely the curriculum is aligned to college course work and to identify how it should be modified. This multilayered and collaborative approach enables teachers to evaluate and improve the curriculum in order to consistently prepare students for college.

Personalized College Counseling Supports College Readiness

College counseling at Cristo Rey Jesuit High School begins during freshman orientation when counselors meet individually with students to establish the expectation that all students will apply to and attend college. The school hosts two college fairs each year, and students across all grades are invited to learn about specific colleges and the application process. The college counseling program intensifies in the junior year with college visits, retreats, and individual sessions with counselors. Juniors are required to take the ACT and PSAT and engage in career exploration activities through IllinoisMentor.com. Seniors are invited to attend a three-week summer institute to work individually with counselors on writing personal statements and completing applications. Some students submit all of their applications during this time. Roughly half of the seniors complete the institute, while the others attend an after-school workshop held three days a week once the school year begins. College counselors also send information about scholarship opportunities and summer writing programs offered at the local colleges to students and parents by e-mail. Cristo Rey's comprehensive and personalized college counseling program reinforces the school's expectations and offers students important contextual skills for college success.

Homework Center Cultivates Academic Behaviors

A few years after the school opened, Cristo Rey Jesuit High School instituted an after-school homework center to provide students with additional academic support. Students struggling to meet academic standards or complete homework on time are required to attend, but roughly half of the students in attendance on any given day are there by choice. Up to four teachers from different departments and additional peer tutors are available for assistance. Students can also arrange to meet teachers who are not scheduled to work in the center for additional help. The center includes space to work on group projects and computers to complete research. This structured yet flexible study environment promotes accountability, focus, self-management, and time management skills. It also helps students develop persistence by understanding that mistakes or initial failure should not cause one to give up. Administrators indicated that the central purpose of the homework center is to help students develop the ability to seek out help and take the necessary steps to correct mistakes. Such behaviors will lead students to succeed in high school, the workplace, and college.

CHAPTER 6

Putting It All Together

Up to this point, this book has laid out an expanded conception of college readiness and presented a series of strategies and practices that schools might adopt to improve their ability to prepare students for postsecondary learning. But those who work in schools know how difficult it is to shift to a new focus and then to implement myriad strategies and programs needed to support it. Schools can be easily overwhelmed when confronted by too many things to do or to change at once. This often leads to analysis paralysis: everyone knows a problem exists and may even be aware of potential solutions, but cannot reach agreement on action because taking that first step seems too intimidating. When an undertaking appears too daunting, the response is often to avoid tackling it altogether.

This is the situation in which many high school faculty and administrators may find themselves as they consider the changes their school or district program must undergo to prepare all students for college and careers. Even educators whose schools have done a good job preparing a subset of students for college can find themselves challenged, by their state policymakers, business community leaders, parents, and even students, to retool and upgrade their expectations so that more of their graduates are ready for postsecondary learning opportunities. This challenge often means getting more students from groups that have not pursued postsecondary education previously to the level of college and career readiness by the end of high school.

How should schools proceed if they wish to improve their programs systematically in ways that lead toward higher levels of preparation for postsecondary learning? A detailed accounting of the process of systemic change in a school is beyond the reach of this chapter, but it may still be useful to consider a potential sequence of activities that can yield an action plan for improvements designed for and adapted to the needs, context, and culture of each school. The specific activities and programs a school would undertake would be influenced by the nature of that school, but the major elements of the process set out in this chapter could be followed by most schools.

The process begins by developing a profile of the school's current capacity to enable students to become college ready, including analysis of which types of students have the opportunity to reach readiness levels. Next, the school identifies and commits to outcome measures of success that provide a clear target against which progress can be measured. This is followed by a consideration of the gap between current practice and desired outcomes along with a determination of the capacity the school has to close the gap and meet the targets. The four dimensions of college readiness provided in this book define the action framework and suggest specific changes that should occur. At this point, outside partners become more important to help leverage internal change and also to assist in concrete ways with programmatic support and linkages. The focus of the process then shifts to the necessary professional development designed to ensure that all staff have the knowledge, skills, and techniques necessary for the school to achieve its stated goals. Throughout all of this, special attention is paid to changing the overall culture of the school, not just implementing programs. Interim measures of progress provide feedback to the school community, creating opportunities for celebration of accomplishments as well as identifying places where mid-course corrections are necessary. The net result is a school that is intentionally and systemically focused on enabling as many students as possible to be fully ready for the opportunities available to them in learning settings beyond high school.

DEVELOP A PROFILE OF THE SCHOOL'S COLLEGE READINESS CAPACITY

All high schools without exception can benefit from taking a long, hard look at the strengths, weaknesses, and gaps in their approaches to postsecondary preparation for all students. Interestingly, it's often the schools that are already doing the best job of preparing students that pay the most attention to making changes and improvements in this area. Another group of schools—those that successfully prepare a moderate proportion of their population for college—may feel less pressure to increase the pool of postsecondary-ready students. Change in these schools can be particularly challenging because few perceive a problem to exist. At the other extreme, high schools in which students do not seem interested in college often have strong belief systems that make it difficult to entertain the notion that large numbers of students at the school could eventually become college and career ready. Their challenge is overcoming the perception that "these kids aren't really college material" and that the gap is too large to close in any event.

A productive first step for all of these schools is to generate a school profile that provides some insight into current practices in each of the four dimensions of college readiness. If this is too ambitious, the goal can be to capture all available information related to college preparation and participation by students and recent graduates. Either of these steps requires an awareness and acceptance of the fact that all schools have room for improvement and a willingness to entertain the possibility that even students currently being accepted for postsecondary study could be prepared better in one or more of the four readiness dimensions.

One of the first things a school should determine is its capacity to prepare students for postsecondary learning opportunities. That capacity is determined by a host of factors. The number of students who enter as ninth graders prepared to take the mathematics sequence necessary to apply to a four-year institution of higher education is an example of a limiting factor. For example, the number of students who fail algebra is a choke point that tends to reduce the ability of students to take the required three years of math courses to meet college entrance requirements. In science, part of the problem may be the number of spaces available in courses such as biology, chemistry, and physics. These also restrict the number of students who can achieve eligibility for postsecondary institutions that require multiple years of high school science, including lab sciences, and can affect student preparation for career programs that have science emphases to them.

Other examples include the number of spaces in Advanced Placement (AP) courses, the procedures and policies that govern access to such courses, the capacity of the counseling office or career center to provide support to students to apply to college and for financial aid, the number and type of parents who participate in workshops on college admission and financial requirements, and the number of students who take admissions tests such as the SAT and ACT. The list is long. Students who miss even one of these crucial steps can effectively be blocked from pursuing postsecondary learning directly from high school. Each of these limits the number of students who will be ready for college. In some cases, the limitations are structural and determine who will even be able to apply to college or a certificate program in an area leading to a career. In other cases, they are quality related and will affect the ability of students to succeed once they are admitted. In all cases, these factors accumulate to determine the opportunity the school's students will have to be college ready.

Very few high schools are explicitly aware of these structural impediments, although faculty and administrators may acknowledge them tacitly. An unspoken awareness of these limitations may exist behind an uneasy silence. Even fewer schools have quantified them and then calculated the absolute maximum percentage of students the school's instructional program could ever make college eligible. Add to that the schools that have attempted to determine the proportion of their students likely to succeed in college, and the need for more systematic data gathering, analysis, and reflection becomes more readily apparent.

Identifying the limitations of a high school's program is not much use in and of itself. However, this information may help create an environment within which adoption of a redefined definition of college readiness becomes more feasible. Removing the structural barriers once they are identified is unlikely to appear feasible or even useful unless such actions are paired with more fundamental changes. The first of these is to take a closer look at how the school's instructional program measures up against all four essential dimensions of college readiness: key cognitive strategies, key content knowledge, academic behaviors, and college knowledge. Such a diagnosis is the key to gaining a perspective on the current state of expectations and opportunities present in the school and the areas that should be given priority to bring about the greatest improvements.

This type of self-reflection helps create a clearer sense of the gap between what is and what ought to be, a critical precursor to any action.

 For more information on the methods and strategies presented in this chapter, go to http://CollegeCareerReady.org.

This brief overview overlooks and understates the importance of the political dynamics that play out whenever data of any sort are collected and shared within an organizational context. Getting staff agreement on the importance of reflective analysis is essential, and this is where skilled leadership becomes critical. It may take time to lay the groundwork for this type of analysis to occur, or it may be possible to use the momentum or pressure from some external event, such as a new state policy or a public report, to spark interest and build support for a serious self-examination of practices related to college and career readiness.

IDENTIFY OUTCOME MEASURES OF SUCCESS

Once a diagnosis has been conducted, a key next step is to specify outcome measures toward which the school will aim its efforts—in other words, the ways in which success will be judged. Establishing a limited number of goals, between three and six, for example, allows focused effort to implement specific interventions, at least one of which should be designed to yield some successful results relatively quickly.

Some of the potential outcome measures are readily apparent. Others may be less so. For example, a simple count of the number of students applying to college and the colleges to which they are applying is a metric that can be influenced relatively quickly by implementing activities that get as many students as possible to apply to postsecondary education. This type of outcome measure is good in that the school can achieve demonstrable success in a relatively short period of time, it is easily calculated, and it is a measure of something directly connected to postsecondary participation. However, it has its limitations, and those limitations reflect the fact that some of the more important measures are difficult to achieve and even to gauge.

Applying to college is not the same as being accepted, and being accepted is not the same as succeeding. This suggests two other measures, acceptance rates and performance in first-year courses, that are important but more difficult to collect and for which a greater time lag exists. Combining all three of these basic measures provides some insight into the access and success equation along one important dimension: postsecondary participation.

Measures related to high school course-taking patterns are important. How many sections of courses tied closely to college and career prep does the school offer? How well do students do in these courses? Does the school have gate-keeper courses where large numbers of students fail regularly and thereby don't progress through a sequence of more challenging courses in the subject area? These measures can be calculated and tracked with existing data systems. Getting more students to take courses required by two- and four-year colleges will help make more students eligible for college. It is worth noting that many two-year certificate programs that are more career oriented do have course prerequisites that students can meet while in high school, thereby saving the time of having to fulfill those requirements at the two-year institution.

Other similar measures are relatively straightforward to monitor. Information on participation in AP courses, grades received in these courses, participation in AP exams, and scores on the exams are available to high schools from the College Board. Student scores on admissions tests such as the SAT and ACT are also easy to gather and examine for trends. These data can be compared to those of other schools to get a better picture of the value-added of the school's college prep program in relation to similar schools. Admissions tests have their limitations as absolute or comparative measures, however, and they should only be used as one measure among many. They serve best to get an overall picture of who is taking the tests and generally how students at the school are faring on them. They are less useful as means to redesign curriculum and instruction.

Other measures are targeted at deeper levels of preparation and may therefore be somewhat more challenging to gauge or more difficult to influence because they require changes in teacher behaviors. One of these key metrics is the degree to which teachers are teaching in ways that cause students to become familiar and competent with a full range of cognitive strategies. How often do students solve complex problems, interpret disparate findings, conduct original research, debate controversial issues, defend a point of view with evidence, or consider alternative explanations for phenomena? Do students complete research reports, conduct investigations, revise essays, and work on problems without obvious solutions?

Information on teaching practices can be gathered through a combination of measures such as teacher self-reports, classroom observation, and document analysis (e.g., syllabi, assignments, tests). However difficult it may be to gather data in this area, teacher instructional methodology and proficiency is much more important in the long run to preparing students to succeed in postsecondary learning environments than are special programs or add-ons.

Ideally the school will select a set of measures that range from easy to collect and monitor to difficult to collect and monitor and from relatively straightforward to influence positively to much more complex to influence. Such a range of measures will likely address the full set of issues associated with improving college readiness, from institutional capacity to classroom practice to student performance. In this way, any goals based on the data will be significant and comprehensive but also sensitive enough to register improvements when they are made, both short term and long term. Charting progress over time is essential and helps avoid one-time quick fixes to what in most cases are systemic problems.

ASSESS THE DISTRICT CAPACITY TO SUPPORT IMPROVEMENTS

The vast majority of high schools exist within a governance structure that exercises some degree of control over the school but also provides, at least in theory, services and support. For charter schools, this may be a charter management organization. Networks of new schools may have a coordinating authority that provides specified services. Small school districts with only one high school often are members of a regional service provider. In larger public school districts, particularly in urban areas, each high school is governed by a central office that may have staff dedicated to providing support in the areas of curriculum, instruction, assessment, and professional development. In each of these cases, the capacity of a resource agency to support improvements is an important variable in any process to increase college and career readiness within a school. Schools need external help to make the changes necessary to focus on college and career readiness.

Organizational help for a high school may take a variety of forms, including curriculum developers, staff trainers, coaches, data systems, and even political support and cover. External agencies can allocate targeted resources to help schools conduct analyses to align curriculum or institute programs that support first-generation college attendees. Staff in these agencies can often help broker partnerships with local and national experts and organizations, local postsecondary institutions, and organizations of like-minded schools that can share ideas and resources.

At the very least, the resource agency can provide a form of moral support and legitimacy to initiatives designed to enhance the challenge and rigor level of the curriculum to help all students become college ready. It is difficult in today's system of locally determined courses and grades for one high school or one district to increase the challenge level of its curriculum without seemingly placing its students at a disadvantage in relation to other schools that grade more leniently and expect less of students.

While it is worth noting that students generally respond well to such increases in expectation, schools must be prepared to cope with negative reactions from some segments of their communities if they make changes designed to increase the proportion of students going on to college and careers. Opening enrollment to AP courses has proven unpopular at times in communities where particular groups have previously had exclusive access to those courses. Getting more students to take the SAT or ACT will likely lower the school's average score on these exams, at least initially. Even partnering with one postsecondary institution can cause resentment among other local colleges. Schools benefit from having political support and cover necessary from another agency in order to enact significant curriculum alignment and redesign efforts.

Assuming some level of centralized resources is available, the next step is to constitute a task force charged with prioritizing actions based on the analysis of data and then developing a detailed implementation plan. The task force should include a broad range of participants: teachers from most subject areas, the agency providing support for the effort, local postsecondary institutions, parents, and community members. The task force should be charged with reviewing the data already gathered from a variety of sources and then considering a range of possible changes to existing practice along with new programs and materials.

The task force's plan should address all four dimensions of college and career readiness and not be limited to only one or two, such as more workshops on financial aid or perhaps greater access to AP courses or a requirement that all students take a college admissions test. The plan should be multiyear in nature, acknowledging that some of the changes, particularly increasing the emphasis on developing the key cognitive strategies in more students, will take more time and be more difficult to implement.

INSTITUTE SPECIFIC PROGRAMS TO ADDRESS THE FOUR DIMENSIONS OF COLLEGE AND CAREER READINESS

Once a task force has completed its work, under the sponsorship and with the support of a sponsoring agency, a plan for improvement can be presented to the school for adoption and implementation. The plan should begin by setting concrete goals that state the increases to be achieved in the number and type of students going on to postsecondary education and succeeding in their entry-level courses. The goals should be specific enough to address increases in select categories, such as participation in community college certificate programs, apprenticeships, regional skill centers, or proprietary schools that offer industry skill certification programs in addition to enrollment in two-year transfer programs and four-year baccalaureate-granting institutions.

The specifics of any plan will be influenced by the nature of the school. However, in general, all plans will contain some mix of small, incremental changes and larger, more systemic changes. Ideally, the task force will be able to develop an implementation plan that capitalizes on the degree of readiness and willingness of the staff to adopt some smaller and less complex changes initially. The idea is to achieve identifiable small successes in order to build on them before undertaking larger issues that must ultimately be addressed. One of the dangers of adopting this approach is that the plan will proceed no further than the small, incremental changes. Therefore, even when the task force is recommending small changes, it should select carefully so that even if those projects are the only ones undertaken successfully, the school will still be better positioned to help all students become college ready. These small projects should help open the door for the larger, deeper changes that will require teacher retraining or new methods of learning and assessment, such as expanding the number of teachers who teach AP courses or experimenting on a small scale with classroom-based performance tasks that measure key cognitive strategies schoolwide.

Make Small, Incremental Changes

Even small changes are difficult to implement in large, complex organizations, but incremental changes have the advantage of not necessarily requiring significant retraining, resource reallocation, or rethinking of values and beliefs. A brief example from an earlier chapter of a recommendation that might be considered a small, incremental change would be to have all students record all assignments in an agenda planner and expect all teachers to monitor these planners, at least informally, to verify that students are doing so. The school might provide the agenda planners to all students (or at least all students who cannot afford one). Teachers would need to agree to distribute them and go over how to use them, but this is an activity that does not require training or new skills. It does require all teachers to agree to expect students to use the agenda planners and to enforce this expectation consistently for all students.

This degree of agreement and cooperation would be an important first step toward creating a college-going culture within a school. Students would encounter the same expectation for their behavior in all classes. Teachers would have to agree on a common practice, a small step in the direction of larger, more substantive cooperation in areas such as curriculum alignment. If a school could not get teachers to implement this practice, it would be good evidence that more work around awareness needed to be done, which could require gathering more data, discussing the issues in greater depth, reexamining school goals, and perhaps agreeing at least symbolically to the importance of making changes at the school to enhance college and career readiness before attempting to adopt another incremental change.

Another example of an incremental change, this one in the dimension of college knowledge, would be a requirement that all students attend workshops on applying to college and becoming eligible for financial aid. While organizing the logistics of this would be more complex than what is required to purchase and distribute agenda planners, this activity does not require any specific change on the part of teachers or in teaching practices. In that sense, it is a small, incremental change. Admittedly, in some schools this would seem like a big change, but only by recognizing that changes of this type are in fact small and incremental can a faculty come to a realization of the scope and challenge posed in transforming a high school by addressing all four dimensions of readiness, not just the college knowledge portion.

The two remaining dimensions of college readiness, key cognitive strategies and key content knowledge, tend to require changes that are larger and potentially more controversial, but that does not mean that change is not possible in these areas. Perhaps an initial activity to undertake here that is less threatening is to have teachers discuss curricular expectations within their department. What does the mathematics department, for example, expect of students from grade to grade and course to course, and how does this align with college and career readiness? Certainly these are thought-provoking questions, but they stop short of leading to action. In that sense, they represent smaller, more incremental approaches to the systems redesign that is most often needed in the areas of content knowledge and cognitive strategies.

It might also be possible to arrange for such conversations to occur between the high school and postsecondary staff at local colleges. The conversations could focus simply on the areas where entering students in general do well and where they struggle. Although such conversations can be complex to organize, they have the advantage of helping teachers see the gap between where their students are and where they need to be. That information begins to suggest how each institution might need to adapt to help students make the difficult transition from high school to postsecondary learning.

Make Larger Systemic Changes

What then of the larger systemic changes, which are more difficult to manage? How can they be introduced and implemented successfully? In general, teachers must see the reason for and importance of making such changes. That means that some of the smaller changes should help lead teachers to reach such a realization. If this is not practical, then more time may need to be spent getting teachers involved in reviewing, analyzing, and discussing data from a variety of sources. The goal of such involvement is to help build a greater sense of the need to make substantive changes in practices in key areas such as curriculum, assessment, and instruction.

Almost no high school will be able to undergo a review of its practices and not find a need to make substantial changes in core areas in order to be better aligned with expectations for students in postsecondary education. Perhaps the most important thing to remember is that change needs to penetrate to the classroom. If activities do not affect teaching and learning directly, they will not achieve the changes in educational practice that will ultimately be necessary to tighten the alignment between high school and college.

The most important and most needed changes are in the area of key cognitive strategy development. High school students generally do not have extensive opportunities to practice and use a wide enough range of thinking and metacognitive strategies and techniques of the type necessary for success in college and careers. Addressing this pressing need requires curriculum redesign, new methods of assessment, and modifications to current instructional methods.

The most natural starting point is deep curricular alignment across grade levels, working backward from senior-year courses tightly aligned with college readiness standards. The vertical alignment is complemented by horizontal alignment across all courses in a department, which results in certain key cognitive strategies being emphasized and developed in all courses. This type of process almost inevitably leads to course redesign. Generally in such a process, teachers naturally tend to focus on content coverage, which is important, and ideally seek to eliminate redundancies and address areas of omission. However, any alignment process must stay focused on the cognitive strategies as the overall organizers for the school's program of study.

Systemic changes to strengthen student mastery of key cognitive strategies include greater use of assignments and tasks that require students to make more decisions about how to complete them. Assignments in aligned courses should take longer to complete and be fewer in number than is currently the case. This is accomplished by building courses around key tasks, large and small, and projects of varying scale and scope. These do not replace content instruction but serve to integrate and apply content knowledge to deepen understanding and retention and, most important, develop the key cognitive strategies.

Assessments in an aligned system require more writing and more analysis of data. Readings include more original source material in addition to or in place of textbooks. Teaching methods emphasize more interpretation, explanation, and investigation of the big issues and key concepts of the subject area being studied. Factual information is used as the basis for achieving these understandings, not as an end in itself.

Students are expected to take more responsibility for their own learning and to be more actively engaged in learning. This deeper engagement requires considerable feedback to students on the decisions they are making in the learning process, combined with a broader set of learning strategies that accommodate success with more complex materials and assignments. As explained in more detail in previous chapters, this can be accomplished through judicious use of advisory periods or class-based reflection times, student goal setting, and journals where students record their academic development.

These learning capabilities need to be developed systematically and in a sustained fashion over all four years of high school, and not simply introduced in the senior year, in order to achieve coordination among all faculty members. This process can be threatening to teachers who do not already possess at least some of the skills necessary to teach the key cognitive strategies. In this case, the process will need to move slowly, and teachers will need to see how they will be supported to acquire the new instructional techniques and skills. In short, changes of this magnitude cannot occur without large-scale planning, support, coordination, and a sustained effort that spans multiple school years.

Because these changes take longer and progress may be difficult to gauge, the baseline conditions that exist before the change is initiated need to be carefully documented so that any growth or improvement can be noted, along with lack of progress as well. Information on teaching practices, for example, will need to be collected annually, at the least using a self-report process that may be augmented by walk-throughs in which instructional methods being used are noted and by reviews of key course assignments, tests, and grading practices. By consistently measuring the same set of practices, a school or district can gauge the degree to which large-scale change is taking hold across the school or system and to make midcourse adjustments as necessary to support continued adoption and implementation of systemic changes.

Most systemic changes are subject to the phenomenon of a tipping point: a level of implementation that when it is reached, the system basically switches over in a very short period of time to the new way of doing business after perhaps resisting change vigorously for some period of time. The specifics of getting an organization to that tipping point are beyond the scope of this chapter. The essential element is to sustain efforts in the face of attempts to remake the change into something less threatening and to continue to achieve a series of small victories that in the end set the stage for the larger conversion to a new way of doing business.

In the case of college readiness, these small victories can come in a variety of areas, including getting students to develop the academic behaviors necessary for college and career and ensuring that they and their parents have the college knowledge to enable successful enrollment in postsecondary education. As more of these incremental changes accumulate, the school culture may begin to tilt in a direction that makes it more feasible to introduce changes in how key cognitive strategies are developed in students and the nature of the content that is taught in order to do so.

Engage Outside Partners

An additional lever to help bring about change in the direction of college and career readiness within a school is to engage a range of partners from the community beyond the school. Key, but not sole, partners will be faculty members from local postsecondary institutions. These institutions have not always been viewed as potential partners with high schools, but this perspective is beginning to shift as the emphasis on the high school–college connection receives increased emphasis at the state and national levels. Secondary educators and administrators can take advantage of this newly emerging sense of interdependence between high schools and colleges by reaching out to local postsecondary institutions to become fuller partners in the process of ensuring that more students are ready to succeed in college.

In the context of a comprehensive improvement plan, the local partnership is a tool to help make real and concrete the reasons for specific changes that need to take place. While the emphasis is on change at both levels, high school and college, the postsecondary partnership can be used to motivate change within a high school by focusing on the precise, mutually agreed-on areas that will maximize student success in college.

In most cases, central office or school building administrators are responsible for initiating partnership relationships with local colleges, although teachers on some occasions have been successful on a case-by-case basis. The exact nature of a partnership will vary greatly depending on the state, the local student population, and the history of relations between high schools and colleges locally and in the state. Nevertheless, all partnerships have certain key elements that serve as the foundation: a clear focus on an area or set of issues of mutual interest or concern, a commitment to meet or interact regularly and on a sustained basis, a willingness to consider programmatic change to accommodate program goals, and cooperation in sharing information across levels in ways that help each accommodate student need better.

Partnerships work best when they exist within a larger state policy context that supports local action. States can create the conditions that motivate local secondary and postsecondary institutions to convene in order to consider specific issues mandated by the state as well as locally identified concerns and priorities. This approach helps create a "top-down, bottom-up" dynamic that supports alignment and coordination across system boundaries through local solutions that address statewide priorities to increase the number of students succeeding in college.

Once the basics of a partnership have been established, the interactions among members of the partnership quickly need to become substantive in nature. Many partnerships become consumed by procedural matters involved in specifying the relationship of the institutions. Although these are important, they are not a substitute for a full investigation of the practices and assumptions that most directly affect student success at each level. If nothing tangible results from the partnership fairly rapidly, key participants will lose interest and cease to be a part of the process.

The partnership can be used to enforce a form of mutual accountability on each partner to achieve certain results. The partnership's goals should be measured in an annual evaluation that assesses progress on set, clear, quantifiable targets that members of each organization can then break into the tasks each is accountable to achieve.

One measure of success is the number of new relationships being formed among members of each institution. In essence, a constituency is created in each institution that reinforces stronger connections. This constituency is more likely to support incremental and systemic changes of the type described previously. For example, high school teachers and instructors may be more willing to exchange examples of student work to get a sense of each other's expectations. More opportunities for dual-credit programs may arise. Greater insight into placement testing and ways to reduce remediation can be explored. Specific feedback on students' performance in entry-level postsecondary courses can help high school educators focus content instruction but also emphasize and develop key self-management skills, for example.

Partnerships with community and business organizations can lead to opportunities for internships, mentorships, and other experiences where more students can gain a better understanding of the knowledge and skills they need to attain to pursue a particular career. When the high school's program provides opportunities for students to build these career-readiness skills, they are more motivated to participate and make the efforts necessary to succeed.

INSTITUTE PROFESSIONAL DEVELOPMENT TO SUPPORT COLLEGE READINESS

All of the preceding steps lead up to and have to be supported by a program of professional development designed so that the school can ensure that all students will be given the opportunity to develop the knowledge and skills necessary for college and career success. Much has been written about the importance of professional development in any school change strategy. For the purposes of college and career readiness, professional development must equip teachers with a knowledge and skill set specifically attuned to preparing all students for postsecondary education.

Help Teachers Strengthen Content Knowledge, Instructional Strategies, and Awareness of College Knowledge

Professional development needs to focus on three critical areas: teacher content knowledge within the subject area; instructional strategies necessary to ensure all students are developing a broad set of cognitive strategies; and teacher knowledge of postsecondary requirements, expectations, and culture. The teaching staff of the school needs to be highly proficient in these three areas as a foundation for the establishment of high expectations for all students and the resulting programs, supports, and requirements needed to make high expectations a reality. If teachers are not knowledgeable in their content areas at a high level, do not have mastery over a set of instructional strategies that cause students to develop key cognitive strategies, and have little or no knowledge of college requirements and expectations, it may still be possible to get more students to enroll in a postsecondary program using other means, but the proportion of those students who succeed is unlikely to increase. No amount of change in other areas of the school can substitute for a strong foundation of teacher knowledge and skill in these areas.

Of the three areas, content knowledge is perhaps the most important initially because teachers who do not know their content area deeply cannot effectively integrate the key cognitive strategies into instruction in their content area. Students will not have the opportunity to develop an understanding of the structure of knowledge in a discipline or subject area if the teacher lacks a deep understanding and conceptualization of the discipline and what makes it distinctive from other forms of knowledge.

Each discipline represents a way of thinking about what is known about a subject and simultaneously how to know a subject. In other words, the structure of knowledge for a subject is intimately intertwined with the way in which an understanding of the subject is developed. Both what is known and the ways of knowing it must be taken into account in learning a new subject. In the absence of this understanding by teachers, a subject is taught as a series of essentially disconnected facts, algorithms, or topics. Students not only fail to make connections among the information they are presented, they do not develop any insight into the structure of knowledge in the subject and how and why that structure is most appropriate for that subject.

When teachers have a deep understanding of their subject matter, they can help students develop a broader range of cognitive strategies to master the subject matter and understand the subject area or discipline. Developing a cognitive strategy requires repetition of that strategy over time in a variety of situations. Problem solving, for example, cannot be taught as a unit in which students learn six steps for solving all problems. The strategy is developed by attempting a range of increasingly complex problems over time in differing settings and formats. In fact, problem solving is a series of strategies and techniques, and the key skill a student must possess is knowing when to exercise each strategy, recognizing when a strategy is not working, and knowing which strategy to employ next.

Helping teachers learn to do this is not simple and requires persistence. A program of professional development designed to help teachers become highly proficient in teaching a wider range of cognitive strategies requires multiple opportunities for teachers to practice the strategies themselves so that they intuitively understand the cognitive process in which a learner engages to use the strategies successfully. This sort of professional development does not lend itself particularly well to one-shot workshops or prepackaged programs. Much of the learning is embedded in the lessons that teachers must try out on their own to discern effects. They must be ready to learn and adapt while simultaneously expanding their repertoire of techniques. In essence, the teacher becomes a life-long learner who reaches progressively greater understanding of the cognitive strategies he or she teaches.

The final area, awareness of college knowledge, probably is most amenable to straightforward training models because much of this is information that can be simply dispensed to teachers and made available centrally through a number of convenient sources that teachers can tap as needed or to which they can refer students and parents directly. Because researchers have found that teachers can be an important source of information on topics such as college course require-ments and financial aid, teachers need to be prepared to dispense accurately at least basic information in these areas. Examples include the entrance require-ments of local public universities, placement exams for community colleges and four-year institutions, a general sense of what is required in an entry-level col-lege course in the teacher's subject area, and where to locate information about applying to college and researching financial aid options.

Use the Power of Professional Learning Communities

Professional learning communities have been recognized as an increasingly important element in the improvement of educational practice. They are also crucial to the transformation of school culture. A professional learning commu-nity structure in which teachers are reinforced for holding higher expectations for students will help sustain teachers through the difficulties they experience as they seek to modify their practice. The professional learning community can be a source of ideas and inspiration, as well as a vehicle to vent frustration in a safe environment. The professional learning community helps to inculcate the belief that everyone is working together, an important notion in schools where teach-ers spend most of their time alone in classrooms surrounded by students who have their own agendas distinct from those of the educators.

Schools and school districts can help organize and facilitate professional learning communities for the purpose of studying lessons, analyzing data about student performance, developing new curriculum or acquiring new content knowledge in order to understand a field of study more deeply, or simply reflect-ing on what works with the students in their charge. The communities need to exist within a larger structure and culture that supports them and allows them some leeway to investigate issues of concern to their members and generate solutions that members accept as valid. They are not a substitute for a targeted program of training and development, which can complement professional learning community activities where appropriate.

Professional learning communities can also be environments where secondary and postsecondary faculty can interact as peers. This is particularly true when the community focuses is on the key topics and issues of the subject area. This sort of a community is more complex to organize, but its inherent interest level is higher and its focus more clearly on what it takes to get students ready for postsecondary success. As secondary teachers come to see themselves as more tightly connected to a community of scholars who study a particular subject area and engage in the consideration of important questions about that area, they transmit more of this to their students in the form of higher, clearer expectations and in a better articulation of the conceptual framework of the subject area itself.

Much of this sort of change in expectations is subtle and beyond the reach of any specific training activity. The cumulative effect of having all the teachers in a school more engaged with the academic content and methods of their discipline is a learning environment in which it is not possible to compromise on the big ideas and enduring understandings of the subject, and where students must go into greater depth to master the course content. In this fashion, expectations for all students increase in a way consistent with college readiness.

RECOGNIZE THE IMPORTANCE OF CULTURE AND CHANGE CULTURE

As overly simple as it may sound, nothing is more important than the beliefs teachers hold about what students are able to do. Research on cognition and brain functioning has been leading to the conclusion that intelligence is much more malleable than assumed previously. To state this in a slightly oversimplified way, students can be taught to be smarter. Schools can make a difference, but this can occur only if teachers believe it can happen and are willing to challenge students to do more than the students themselves think they can do.

The causes for the differential in the results achieved at high- and low-performing high schools are complex, but expectations for students are one important explanatory factor. Such assumptions, when they are about what students cannot be expected to do and are not capable of doing, are often accepted unquestioned or taken as common wisdom and not subjected to systematic review that could lead to a modification of the assumption. The result is a series of self-fulfilling prophecies that reinforce the dominant belief system in the school. Over time, teachers' beliefs influence student self-perceptions and estimations of capabilities. These two variables then interact in a sort of death spiral, each dragging the other downward.

The most striking difference at every school we have studied that outperforms the predicted level of student college preparation is a pervasive culture that assumes students can achieve high levels of performance consistently. Although this is not the only difference, it is perhaps the most distinctive one. Educators can control the culture in a school and, in doing so, achieve real changes in the performance of students.

Changing Behaviors to Change Beliefs

At the heart of culture change are teacher beliefs. It's not easy to change someone's beliefs through discussion alone. The in-service that tells teachers that students can do better is quickly challenged or dismissed because teachers "know better." Witnessing something happen that they did not predict can have a more dramatic effect. In other words, changes in behavior can precede changes in beliefs. Stated differently, if it is possible to get people to change their behavior and they experience new and unexpected results as a consequence, their belief systems may begin to change in response to the evidence. In essence, getting people to do something different, even if they do not entirely believe in it, can be a highly productive strategy, provided that the change in behavior leads to positive results that support or enable a subsequent change in beliefs.

The most important single belief about students from low-income families, first-generation college attendees, or members of groups historically underrepresented in college is that they should not be encouraged too strongly to aspire to a postsecondary education because they might be "disappointed" if they did so and failed to achieve that goal. Not only might the child fail academically, the belief goes, but the parents might not support the student attending in the first place, financial constraints might be too severe, or the culture shock might be too great. Might it therefore not be a better goal to prepare the student to find a good job after high school graduation first and worry about college later? Goodness knows it's enough of a challenge many times to get them to graduate, educators often state.

Test scores often play a large part in shaping beliefs about who is college material and who isn't. While scores are certainly important in understanding how to tailor instruction to help students learn more effectively, data are not destiny. A student who is reading at the fifth-grade level is not a fifth grader. This student does not benefit from a lesson devoid of cognitively engaging material in the mistaken belief that the best way to support student success is to gear the challenge level to the chronological age range identified by a test.

Teachers need the skill set to challenge all students with tasks at high cognitive levels and then to provide all-important scaffolding to students whose basic skills are emerging and developing at a slower rate than those of their peers. These students are not incapable of discussing the symbolism in a piece of poetry or analyzing the etymology of a word. They can develop and express opinions regarding public issues and support their opinions with evidence. They can, with proper scaffolding, solve a range of complex problems that require logic and even intuition. They can become confident in their capabilities even as they continue to remedy basic skill deficits they carried with them to high school.

Scaffolding is achieved by providing different levels of assistance and structure to different groups of students based on their demonstrated needs. This assistance can be in the form of study guides, vocabulary lists, sample topics, a set of starter sources for a research project, closer monitoring and a more step-by-step approach to problem solving, requirements to write more preliminary drafts or versions of progressively greater complexity before a final product is submitted, team approaches to study, mentors, access to online resources for self-guided instruction, and a host of other forms of assistance that make it possible for these students to succeed on tasks that might be beyond their reach without such support.

Scaffolding requires teacher skill and judgment to implement well, particularly in determining the degree of scaffolding that any individual student is allowed to access. Here is where data on reading skills can be more useful if the information is in a diagnostic format and is descriptive of literacy fluency, not simply a grade-level equivalency for the student. The score ranges can define the amount of scaffolding that any given student should receive. The degree of scaffolding can also limit the highest score a student can obtain on a project or assignment so that some motivation remains for students not to use scaffolding inappropriately. With high degrees of scaffolding, the highest attainable grade might be a B, for example. The student would be encouraged to remove enough scaffolding eventually to be eligible for an A.

Scaffolding should not be used to lower the challenge level for some students or to allow students to give less than their full effort. This is where teacher knowledge of individual students and a clear external reference point by which student performance is judged become critically important. Scaffolding can easily devolve into doing the work for students if it is not properly managed. Used properly, it is an important tool to help teachers stretch all students so that they are developing key cognitive strategies.

By building a rich, challenging curriculum that pushes students to their limits as thinkers, a school's culture becomes focused on supporting the learning process, not on sorting students. As a result, students become more motivated to want to read better, write with greater precision and depth, and acquire control over a wider range of mathematical tools to help them explore new and interesting problems. In short, they have to be given a reason to learn. And on occasion, they have to be allowed to fail—but in a controlled fashion, where they learn from their failure and emerge motivated to try harder the next time with new insight into what it takes to succeed.

On a practical level, changes in expectations are best undertaken as a whole school, not by individual teachers. Students need to receive a consistent message, not a fractured one, from all educators in a building. It is of little benefit for one teacher to challenge all students while the next teacher sends the message to them that they are too fragile for a postsecondary learning environment.

Schools can establish these higher expectations in a number of ways, but only if all educators are on board. Examples of such changes are schoolwide grading policies tied to high, consistent standards; common grading rubrics for writing and problem solving; a well-aligned curriculum with core content infused into all courses; a range of support services available to struggling students; examples of students who have succeeded and what it took for them to do so; and an activist counseling or career center that reaches out to students, teachers, and parents constantly in myriad ways.

Culture is changed when a variety of factors align. Many of the schools we visited were able to hire teachers who subscribed to their vision, something that helped them build and reinforce a sense of common purpose. Large, comprehensive high schools will be challenged to duplicate such a strong mission-driven ethos, but it is not impossible for large schools to insist that all new teachers demonstrate a belief that all students can be made college and career ready and a commitment to adopting practices consistent with the belief.

Symbolic Changes

The manipulation of symbols is a potent means of expressing cultural beliefs. Schools can make use of symbols in a variety of ways, through both activities and behaviors that signify core values of the school. Symbolic change is attractive in part because leaders can control it more easily than many other variables. For example, hallway signs, bulletin boards, newsletters, assemblies, and parent nights are all opportunities for symbols and symbolic behavior.

Many schools we studied employed a wide range of symbolic behaviors from very simple (all teachers agree to wear apparel related to the college from which they graduated and then discuss their college briefly in class) to more elaborate (encourage all students to apply to college). Many more examples exist of largely symbolic activities, from posting college acceptance letters on school bulletin boards or hanging college banners in classrooms, to announcing all scholarship winners at graduation and acknowledging the postsecondary plans of graduates. College visitations are largely symbolic events, but they can be used to emphasize inclusiveness and opportunity by allowing all students to participate and by visiting more than one type of postsecondary institution.

The attractiveness of symbolic actions is clear. The challenge is to use the symbolic activities as a springboard into in-depth change that affects what is taught and how it is taught. The symbolic statements can be thought of as an important first step when taken in tandem with a wider range of programs and strategies designed to ensure that students develop necessary knowledge and skill in all four of the dimensions of college and career readiness.

GAUGE THE PROGRESS OF CHANGES IN THE HIGH SCHOOL

Because the process of converting a school to a clearer, more consistent focus on college and career readiness is complex and multidimensional, regular measures of progress are critically important. This is all the more true if the school has adopted the strategy of undertaking a combination of activities designed to pursue incremental and systemic changes simultaneously. In this type of multilevel change model, feedback on progress at all levels is important to sustaining efforts and momentum.

Most schools lack data systems necessary to track many aspects of student performance in the four dimensions of college readiness. Nevertheless, many states, with support from the federal government, are initiating new data systems and considering new assessments that may lead to greater availability of information on content knowledge mastery related to college and career readiness. But even with the existing limitations, schools can collect a great deal of information to gauge their progress in moving toward a program centered on college readiness.

The area of college knowledge, as noted earlier, may be the easiest to track progress. For example, a school can count how many students participate in new activities designed to increase college awareness, such as more intensive, focused campus visits or college fairs with greater participation by colleges that welcome and support first-generation college attendees. Special attention needs to be paid to the types of students who are participating in these new activities or increase participation in existing activities. Measures of teacher knowledge of local college requirements and the number of times and ways that they share that knowledge with students is an example of an indicator of the degree to which teachers are advising students on the basic requirements for college eligibility.

The area of academic behaviors easily lends itself to a wide range of measures that can provide snapshots of progress in student self-management. Have study groups been implemented? If so, how many students are participating, and what types of students? Are students keeping track of their assignments in agenda planners, and what proportion of assignments are being submitted late? Do all students have a four-year plan for their high school studies that they update annually? Are students setting goals and then comparing their goals to their program of study? Does this result in their making changes in their program of study? Are students choosing to take more challenging courses? Are they able to handle more complex assignments that require a modicum of independent work? Are teachers providing more candid feedback to students, and are students more capable of accepting such feedback and then making changes in their academic strategies accordingly?

The school's progress in developing a curriculum aligned with key content knowledge can be ascertained through a number of strategies, although this is more difficult area to gauge. A number of options exist for conducting curriculum audits including tools created by the Educational Policy Improvement Center that can be reviewed by accessing the Web site listed following.

 For more information on the methods and strategies presented in this chapter, go to http://CollegeCareerReady.org.

Another way to gauge the content that is being taught is to analyze or review the content of course syllabi. This approach is useful only if the school has previously undergone a syllabus revision process as part of larger content alignment process. Once all teachers have quality syllabi that detail what they are teaching and update them regularly, content analysis can be used to track the content of courses and the overall structure of the school's curriculum.

A less comprehensive but still useful means of gathering information on what is being taught is systematic classroom observations. Through a consistent year-long program of classroom visitations that is kept separate from any observations required for teacher evaluation purposes, administrators or teacher coaches can discern a great deal about the content of courses and the instructional methods being employed. This firsthand information, episodic as it may be, can be combined with results from other measures to paint a more comprehensive picture of the content of the curriculum and the teaching strategies, information that is crucial to gauging progress aligning courses to key content knowledge necessary to be college and career ready.

Finally, the key cognitive strategies, although the most important, can be more difficult to observe in practice. However, several good strategies can be employed. Classroom assignments, tests, and grading systems can be analyzed to determine whether and to what degree they require or measure the use of key cognitive strategies. Observations of instruction yield a great deal of information about the ways in which students are being engaged and asked to process information.

A common assignment, such as a research paper for all tenth graders, scored against common criteria, can generate a schoolwide profile of how well students are developing thinking skills in a number of key areas.

DOCUMENT THE EFFECTS ON STUDENT PERFORMANCE IN COLLEGE

Most of the indicators described previously are measures of process, not outcomes. The ultimate success criterion is how many students make the transition to college successfully. Progress toward this goal can be determined in a number of ways. Beyond counting the number of students who apply to college, are accepted, and then actually attend college, it is important to note how well they do in their all-important first year. How they score on placement tests and the subsequent rate at which they are placed into remedial course work is one important and relatively straightforward piece of information to gather and track. Perhaps even more interesting are the courses students choose to take during their first year in college. Although many factors influence course choice, students often avoid subjects initially that they feel they are not well prepared to take on, so first-year course selection can be an indirect indication of students' perceived strengths and weaknesses. When the grades students receive in these courses are added to the mix, an even better picture of preparedness emerges. Here is another place where a partnership with a postsecondary institution is critical in order to access this information from the college's institutional research office.

Directly polling students also yields rich information on how well their high school program of study prepared them for college. A number of commercial services locate and survey recent high school graduates regarding their experiences in high school and college. More high schools are employing Facebook as a means to remain in contact with graduates and gather information from them. Such strategies allow greater insight into a wider range of student behaviors and strategies, which helps paint a fuller picture of the reasons for successes and failures. Information of this type can be particularly compelling to high school faculty members as they consider how to modify programs and practices to support college and career readiness.

In the final analysis, gauging student progress on the four key dimensions of college readiness is perhaps the best strategy for determining the success of any improvement effort. Focusing solely on processes conducted and programs implemented is not enough, but it is important information to collect and share. The ultimate goal is to gauge the effect on student transitions to postsecondary education and their performance during the freshman year or in a certificate program, and then to celebrate resulting successes and learn about areas in need of continuing refinement.

Part Two

Steps on the Road to Readiness

CHAPTER 7

Steps High Schools Are Taking to Make More Students College and Career Ready

Many commentators are painting a bleak picture of the American high school and its future. Nevertheless, it is worthwhile to step back and examine some of the efforts that are already underway to redesign high school education in ways that could help get more students ready for college and careers. As this book emphasizes, a great deal more needs to be done for high schools to become focused on postsecondary readiness and enhanced student success beyond high school. However, this does not mean that nothing is being done or that these efforts are not worthwhile steps on the road to improved college and career readiness.

High schools around the nation have been investigating a range of strategies to engage students more fully and enable more students to graduate from high school. The focus is on changing the structure and content of a secondary education. Examples of these strategies that address structural changes include converting large, comprehensive high schools into smaller schools, creating theme high schools within large high schools, designing networks of independent schools, offering students the choice of career academies, and developing early college high schools in partnership with postsecondary institutions. Other strategies that are more content and instruction oriented in nature include addition of Advanced Placement (AP) courses or an International Baccalaureate (IB) program, and dual-credit courses.

SMALL SCHOOLS AND HIGH SCHOOL CONVERSIONS

The small schools movement has resulted in the creation of numerous high schools of five hundred or fewer students that focus on a particular area. Literally thousands of these schools have been created in the past ten years, many of them in the nation's urban areas and inner cities. Although their primary purpose has been to counteract the impersonality of large factory-like high schools created between the 1920s and the 1970s, an equally important organizing principle of these schools has been to challenge all students to achieve at higher levels and enable more urban students to pursue an education beyond high school, preferably in college. Evaluations of the small high school have been mixed, with some showing decreases in dropouts and increases in student engagement in learning. However, they continue to be promising beacons in many districts that have had little success getting students to graduate from high school.

While the small school model does not appear to be a panacea to all the ills that confront high schools, many of these schools have established a stellar track record of getting students into college. Those that have been successful adopt college readiness as their primary or sole focus. Often located in school districts where fewer than half of the students graduate from high school, some of these schools have managed to graduate over 90 percent of their students, get most of them to apply to a postsecondary program of some sort, and see essentially all of these students continue their education beyond high school.

This is one of the advantages of personalizing the educational program. Teachers are able to have higher expectations for all students and communicate those expectations to their students. Counselors are able to assist students in preparing college applications and seeking financial aid. Students cannot simply pass through high school unnoticed and disengaged. They must think about what they are going to do after high school and must use high school as a means to prepare for that future. These small schools can provide particularly good support in the college knowledge area, ensuring that students navigate the complexities of college preparation and application, do not fall through the cracks, and do what it takes to get into a college program.

Many small, independent start-up high schools, some operating in quasi-charter fashion within large districts and some members of independent networks, have been able to break free from the culture and conventions of traditional high schools and the bureaucracy of large districts. These schools have a strong entrepreneurial spirit, and their challenge is to transmit this enthusiasm beyond the founding generation of the school and institutionalize it as the school's core values and culture.

Some of these schools get more students to apply for college by sending a clear message to all students of the importance of being college ready. Some do not innovate much in their instructional programs beyond sending this message, but others strive to create courses that engage students in challenging material and in tasks consistent with what they will experience beyond high school. Whether the school actually modifies its curriculum and instruction to focus on college and careers, the measure of success continues to be the proportion of students accepted to college, not necessarily by the success their students experience once they arrive in college.

The other major strategy for creating small schools—converting large high schools into smaller schools on the same site—has been less successful on the whole. Problems include management issues (Who is in charge overall when multiple schools exist on the same campus?), competition for common resources (Who gets to use the gym when?), inefficiencies resulting from redundant course offerings to retain distinctiveness (Which school offers which AP courses, and how do students from other schools access them?), and a sense that one school is more desirable than the others. It is this school that often becomes focused on college readiness while others offer career or job preparation or are focused primarily on credit recovery and high school graduation. Many conversions also experience the inverse problem: a tendency to drift back toward a larger and larger common core of courses, which then weakens the distinctiveness of each school.

This tendency for an informal hierarchy to arise among the schools is an important issue when viewed through the lens of improving college and career readiness for all students. Parents in particular may want to know which school is the "best," by which they mean which school gets the most students into college. Teachers and counselors may inadvertently steer students toward one small school over the others based on the assumption that the school would be a better fit for the student in question. The problem arises when this steering leads to overconcentration of certain racial, ethnic, or income groups in one small school.

The danger with small schools in general is that they will become vehicles for sorting students based on preconceived expectations of student interests or abilities. Some schools then will be geared to academically oriented students and others for students going on to work. Unfortunately, this steering of students toward different futures, however well intentioned, often leads to exactly the type of grouping and sorting that plagues the current high school model. College and career readiness is unlikely to increase if this type of sorting becomes reinstituted because postsecondary readiness requires high, common expectations for all students. This does not take place when students are cordoned off based on the assumptions well-intentioned adults make about what students are able to do or the future toward which each student should aspire.

A small school can be particularly well suited to preparing more students for college and career success if it has a clear focus on readiness, develops an intellectually coherent program geared to college and career expectations, creates a culture focused on the expectation that all students continue their education beyond high school, uses the personal relationships between teachers and students to engage students more fully in learning and challenge them at higher cognitive levels, and develops close relationships with one or more postsecondary institution. Nothing in the structure of small schools guarantees this outcome. Instead, the structure presents a set of possibilities that can be realized through a program deliberately designed to achieve the aim of postsecondary readiness for all students.

CAREER ACADEMIES

Career academies focus on a set of potential occupations within a larger career cluster. Ideally the set of occupations covers the full range of academic preparation within the cluster. For example, an academy that focuses on health occupations or future careers in business would equip students to pursue a variety of pathways within these area, not simply secure an entry-level job. Students are encouraged to think in terms of a career pathway that will require additional education beyond high school. This helps motivate students to develop a wider range of academic skills and knowledge than if they were preparing only for high school graduation leading to an entry-level job. The student may aspire initially only to the lowest-level occupations in the career cluster, but the program illustrates for the student that the path to advancement within the cluster requires a wider range of knowledge and skills and additional academic preparation eventually. In this model, students at various skill levels can find a successful niche within a career cluster and focus on preparing for that niche initially while simultaneously developing higher aspirations to pursue eventual advancement toward high skill roles in the cluster.

Career academies have a relatively long history as a successful reform strategy, particularly in urban high schools. Studies suggest that these programs retain students better and help more students to graduate. Their record as a means to prepare more students for college and more knowledge-intensive careers is nowhere near as clear. In many cases, they have been seen as a way to keep students from dropping out of high school, not as a bridge to postsecondary readiness.

The challenge with the career academy model is similar to that of the small schools model of reform. It is very easy for particular groups of students to be aimed toward identified futures and for academies to be organized around career options that reflect assumptions about student capabilities. In an attempt to be comprehensive in nature, schools or districts may offer a range of career academies without enough attention to the specific connections between the academies and postsecondary readiness. This lack of attention to the connections and transition can doom these programs to becoming a home for students without postsecondary aspirations, which can rapidly turn into a self-fulfilling prophecy.

Low-achieving students and those from low-income backgrounds or racial or ethnic minority groups may inadvertently receive the message that they should aspire only to jobs that do not require college courses, or the students themselves may make shortsighted decisions about which program seems likely to lead to the most money in the shortest amount of time, thereby cutting off the path to greater rewards down the road. They may end up being prepared for a job without really being prepared for a career. It can be quite challenging to get all students to aim high and understand that being able to progress in most careers requires significant additional amounts of training and formal education. Well-designed career academies do not allow any bad choices down dead-end paths. They send a consistent message that careers are lifelong endeavors; they require a full set of academic knowledge and skills if students are to be able to continue beyond the entry level in the career.

ADVANCED PLACEMENT AND INTERNATIONAL BACCALAUREATE PROGRAMS

Approximately sixteen thousand high schools currently offer AP courses, which are designed to be college-level classes taught in high schools by high school teachers. The program is organized by the College Board, the makers of the SAT and other college admissions tests, and consists of exams in thirty-three distinct courses. Advanced Placement does not have a required curriculum for the courses, although each course must conform to the curricular requirements developed by advisory groups consisting of college and high school faculty in the subject area. In addition, each instructor must submit a syllabus that is reviewed and approved (audited) to verify that the course is consistent with the curricular requirements in the subject area.

Students can take an AP exam without taking an AP course, but this is not a common practice. Students can also take an AP course without taking an AP exam, a practice that has become much more common as colleges have come to give additional weighting to the grade from an AP course regardless of whether the student takes the AP exam. Recent research seems to confirm that participation in AP courses is beneficial to college success independent of the AP exam, although the positive effect is more pronounced for students who take the exam and do well on it. Benefits of AP seem to be greatest for students from groups historically underrepresented in higher education.

The distinctive feature of AP is that it serves as something of a national standard in a subject area—in most cases, the only national standard for the subject area in question. The exams are the closest thing to national assessments that exist in the United States, although AP will never be a true national exam because so few students take them. Approximately 15 percent of high school students take an AP exam and receive a score of 3 or higher, what would be considered a passing score. More and more students are taking the exams each year. The number of test takers has nearly quadrupled in the past fifteen years, and the average number of tests each student takes has also continued to increase. Where it was unusual twenty years ago for college applicants to have more than one AP course on their high school transcripts, increasingly students applying to selective colleges and universities have three or four AP courses. Although the average AP course taker still completes only one exam, a quarter of all AP students take two, and nearly 20 percent take three or more exams.

Advanced Placement has also turned out to be a powerful form of professional development for teachers. A national network of AP teachers promotes discussion of the subject area and how best to teach it. AP teachers can participate in a range of professional development activities, including being trained to score the constructed response portion of the AP exam in their subject area, an excellent way to learn more about what to expect from their own students and how to prepare them better for the exam. In this way, the AP community develops and perpetuates common understandings of what it means to challenge high school students at a college level.

In many schools, AP has become the new college preparatory curriculum in large measure because postsecondary institutions value the exams. Many offer college credit for specified scores, and many college admissions offices increase, or weight, the value of a grade earned in an AP course when calculating a student's high school grade point average. Parents in particular may press high schools to offer an expanded program of AP courses, often in the hope of decreasing the cost of college by having their children earn college credit while in high school.

The program's explosive growth and ability of students to take the course without taking the exam has led to a perception in some higher education institutions that AP courses may not always be at the college level. The College Board has instituted the AP Course Audit to review the content of all AP course syllabi to ensure they are consistent with the curricular requirements for the subject area. But individual course quality will always be a function of how well monitored the course is at the high school where it is offered because it is impractical to have external oversight of each of the over 150,000 AP courses taught annually.

Principals and teachers in the end are responsible for ensuring that each AP course is at the college level and is preparing its students across all of the multiple dimensions of college readiness. However, student scores on AP exams each year provide high school teachers with insight into how challenging their course is and how many of their students are reaching a college level of performance in the course. This standards-based feedback potentially allows a teacher to adjust the challenge level to a point where students are passing the exam, which then indicates the AP course is in fact at a college level.

The College Board is beginning a redesign process for AP courses, with the goal of updating the courses based on current trends in college teaching and evidence of the key content taught and best instructional practices in college courses students who pass AP exams are most likely to take. In addition, the redesigned AP courses and exams attempt to gauge student mastery of the kinds of key cognitive strategies contained in the four-dimensional college readiness model presented in this book. Over time, AP courses and exams are likely to become less of a survey of everything that is taught in every possible college environment and more of a representation of what is found in high-quality college courses and is most important generally to succeed in rigorous entry-level college courses.

The IB Programme consists of two years' worth of specified courses in the eleventh and twelfth grades, culminating in a series of examinations and requirements calibrated against challenging college courses. In contrast to AP, the IB has a prescribed and relatively detailed curriculum framework that all IB teachers are expected to abide by. Whereas students may take any number of AP courses in any sequence, students in an IB program have their junior and senior years mapped out for them and take a common set of courses, although a few variations are possible. This combination of specified courses and specified curriculum tied to specified exams creates a much more coherent program of instruction that is highly intentional and focused in its goal of preparing students systematically for college.

Another distinction that may be less important in practice is that the IB courses, in contrast to AP, are not specifically identified as being college level, although students who score on the upper levels of IB exams are performing at a level equivalent to students in college courses. Many colleges offer credit to students who reach higher score levels on IB exams. For this reason, many parents support IB for the potential economic benefit of college credit for high school courses. While every high school can offer an AP exam if the syllabus is approved, no school can offer an IB program without going through a formal certification process.

These two programs suggest different high school structures to support them properly and to ensure students are prepared during the ninth and tenth grades, particularly to be ready for college-level or college-like experiences in these courses. However, in practice, high schools do not necessarily adapt their programs so that they culminate in AP courses or the IB curriculum. In fact, many schools have both programs in place without regard to the difference in these two approaches to college readiness. Getting the most out of these courses and exams requires a carefully aligned program of secondary instruction from sixth grade on, something that is lacking in most schools offering AP or IB.

The unfortunate reality is that AP courses and the IB program have been grafted onto existing middle and high school programs without concomitant redesigns of the prerequisite courses necessary for students to take full advantage of higher challenges programs of this nature offer. Rather than a design-down model that begins with AP and IB and then considers everything that occurs beforehand in terms of what it takes to be ready for courses in these programs, most high schools have added AP courses one or two at a time without any clear plan for preparing students to succeed in them. While the process that schools must undergo to be approved to offer an IB program is more prescribed, just as often the IB program is simply added on to the existing structure of a comprehensive high school as one more choice for students, without necessarily designing the lower-division high school program to ensure that essentially all students have the option of participating in the program.

 For more information on the methods and strategies presented in this chapter, go to http://CollegeCareerReady.org.

The result is that students who already have the upper hand are able to get into AP courses or an IB program more easily than others. The assumption that only an elite subset of students is really AP or IB "material" shaped school policies related to AP and IB participation, including, in some cases, the imposition of entrance requirements or even exams to get into an AP course or an IB program. The policies are simpler to institute than a redesign of the courses preceding AP and IB so that more students had experiences preparing them for advanced courses.

A few high schools have taken up this challenge, but they remain the exception and not the rule. This may begin to change as more schools seek to integrate AP and IB into a coherent sequence of course work that provides essentially all students the opportunity to reach the level necessary to participate in these programs. A few high schools and school districts have even gone as far as to require or expect that all students enroll in at least one AP course before they graduate. The number of low-income and minority students taking AP exams and scoring well on them is on the upswing, although these groups continue to remain a small proportion of the total number of test takers. The important point is that as schools change their assumptions about what students can accomplish and provide the means for more students to access more challenging academic programs, more students seem to be able to do so successfully.

EARLY COLLEGE HIGH SCHOOLS

Early college high schools have as their central focus college readiness and the high school–college transition. The model that early college high schools most often follow is to have students begin to participate in college courses during their last two years of high school while remaining enrolled in the high school program. The number of college courses that students in these programs take varies, but all early college high schools expose students to significant amounts of postsecondary participation before they graduate from high school.

This is accomplished in most cases by situating the early college high school near or on a college campus. This facilitates the physical movement of students into college courses in an efficient fashion and also helps connect the high school with the culture of college. Many early college high schools appeal to students who are not interested in the traditional social aspects of high school and wish to (or need to) complete their secondary schooling as quickly and efficiently as possible. These students may be the children of recent immigrants to the country, for example, or other students not interested in the social rituals of the traditional high school, who are motivated by moving beyond high school as soon as they can.

Another strength of the early college high school model is that these schools are constituted in close partnership with a postsecondary institution, most often a community college. This connection between the two schools helps facilitate the planning and coordination necessary to smooth student participation in college courses. The relationship can also help high school teachers and college instructors connect more directly in order to coordinate their expectations for students and the content of their programs. While this sort of close-order coordination is still the exception, even in early college high schools, promising practices are emerging at many of these partnership sites that demonstrate how a secondary and postsecondary program can be aligned and coordinated.

Creating well-aligned programs is challenging, even for the early college high schools. The foundational step is to understand well the difference between a high school class and a college course and then to design the high school courses so that they gradually prepare students for the college courses. Early college high schools employ a wide variety of strategies to help students make the transition, including offering special seminars on the nature of college teaching and learning, providing scaffolding in the form of tutoring, carefully limiting the initial college course into which the students can enroll, monitoring student progress and intervening when problems arise, and facilitating communication between high school students and their postsecondary instructors. The faculty at early college high schools are learning well the issues that need to be addressed and all the problems that can arise as students attempt to make the transition from high school to college. These programs can serve as laboratories for more traditional schools interested in offering more opportunities to students who are ready for postsecondary opportunities before they fully complete high school requirements.

DUAL CREDIT

Dual credit goes by a number of labels, including *postsecondary options, dual enrollment,* and *concurrent enrollment.* The basic design is to have students enroll simultaneously in high school and at least one college course and receive both high school and college credit for the college course taken. Dual-credit programs fall into three basic categories: courses taught at a college by a college instructor, courses taught at a high school by a college instructor, and courses taught at a high school by a high school instructor.

Dual credit has some obvious advantages in theory and practice, the most important of which is that high school students are given a chance to experience college-level expectations while still in high school. This type of experience can be motivating to students for whom high school instruction moves too slowly or for whom the offerings available do not address any of their interests or needs. These courses have another obvious advantage: the more college credits students earn in high school, the more rapidly and economically they can proceed through college.

Dual credit has been highly successful and well regarded in the states that have encouraged it. Greatest success has been achieved where students are double-counted for financial purposes. That is, both the high school and the college can claim the student as enrolled and receive reimbursement from the state for that student's participation. The colleges generally do not have to provide any specialized services for these students (although some do), and colleges may be able to restrict admission to courses where space is available, meaning that the marginal costs of enrolling participating high school students are minimal.

With all of this, what is there to complain about dual credit? In fact, some issues do exist with this strategy. First and foremost is the issue of what constitutes a college class. What makes a class a college class? Is it the textbook used? Many introductory college courses use a text similar to their high school counterparts, so perhaps the text alone is not the discriminator. Is it the amount of time the course meets? College courses typically meet for fewer hours in a week and over the course of a semester than do high school classes, so this may not be a good measure. Is it the instructor's qualifications? A strong argument can be made for this as an important distinction, but it does not account for situations where the qualifications of the high school teacher equal or exceed those of an equivalent college instructor for the course. Is it the location of the course, given that many colleges insist that being on campus is a key dimension of the college experience? Perhaps, except that many colleges allow their dual-credit courses to be taught off-campus.

What about the course syllabus? Here is one place a case can be made for the need for careful coordination and consistency between high school and college practices. The content of the course, its pacing and workload, the assignments and assessments, the standards and criteria for grading, the intellectual level at which material is pitched, the expectations for student independent work—in short, to use a popular term to describe all of this, the rigor of the course: this is what is most important and most clearly makes the course a college course. A well-constructed college syllabus is much different from a typical high school syllabus, and the syllabus for a dual-credit course taught at a high school by a high school teacher looks much more like a college course syllabus and has been developed with careful reference to an equivalent college course.

Dual credit, then, is a viable strategy for introducing college-level expectations and experiences to high school students, but this approach requires some level of management, particularly in thinking about what a college class taught at a high school by a high school teacher looks like and the standards to which such a course is held. Dual-credit programs also require careful sequencing and coordination regarding the courses available to high school students, the type of preparation high schools provide to help students succeed in college courses, and the support a college provides to its dual-credit students once significant numbers of these students are on campus.

LEARNING FROM THE NEW MODELS

The new models of high school reform and redesign that could potentially improve postsecondary readiness have much to recommend them. They help humanize education and create much stronger connections between adults and youth. They make education more relevant and offer opportunities for students to explore careers. They can challenge students to reach higher levels of achievement. They can connect more closely with postsecondary institutions and ease the transition from high school to college.

All of these innovations and adaptations face a common challenge: How do they calibrate their expectations so that students in the program are ready to continue to learn beyond high school? Schools that are redesigning their programs of study, whether through reconfiguration into a small schools model, through the addition of career academies, through the addition of AP or IB programs, or by using an early college or dual-credit model, need to ensure they are developing and implementing the new practices with careful attention to the ways in which students are being prepared for college and careers. How can all students in the school be held to high expectations? How can programs be made inclusionary and not exclusionary? How can the programs be used as means to build better alignment and connections between secondary and postsecondary education? How can the quality of the programs be maintained to ensure they are appropriately challenging?

Many of these new methods and models have been around for a while, and we know quite a bit about implementing them successfully. As educators and administrators increase their emphasis on readying more students in their high schools for college and career, they need to plan carefully and comprehensively how to utilize existing practices, programs, and structures with the capability of getting more students ready for college and careers in addition to other more fundamental change strategies. The quality and thoughtfulness of the implementation of familiar programs will be as important as the program or structure being implemented.

CHAPTER 8

Steps States Are Taking to Make More Students College and Career Ready

Local schools and individual postsecondary institutions cannot increase the proportion of students going on to college ready to succeed without help from their state. States are the primary level of governance that controls or influences the public secondary and postsecondary systems. Although the federal role continues to increase in these areas, states still have at their disposal the most effective policy levers to create stronger connections between secondary and postsecondary education.

In short, states need to assume the role of the guiding force behind systems alignment. This new relationship has a number of dimensions. For example, states have the ability to trigger the reconsideration of placement policies and procedures, admission requirements and decisions, dual-credit and Advanced Placement–type programs, senior year requirements, state accountability testing and exit exams, credit by proficiency, and other methods by which high school and college can be better aligned by creating continuous and consistent challenge expectations for all students. States, through their state education boards and legislative actions, control high school graduation requirements, exit exams, accountability systems, school improvement processes, textbook adoptions, and a host of other policies that can be used to align high school and postsecondary education and put more students on a path to college and careers. Finally, teacher education program criteria can be refocused to help ensure that the next generation of teachers is fully capable of enabling more students to be college and career ready, and teacher licensure requirements can be designed to pay more attention to teacher content knowledge and skill necessary to promote college and career readiness.

State governors who have the authority can appoint new members to K–12 and postsecondary governing boards and work with legislatures to create policy guidelines that encourage or mandate cooperation and coordination across system boundaries. Governors and legislators can allocate funds for cross-segmental activities that cause high schools and colleges to engage in alignment activities without squabbling over the budget from which the funds for such activities would come. State education boards and higher education governance boards can adopt policies that standardize important elements of each system necessary for consistency in preparing students to succeed, and these boards can meet jointly on a regular basis to conduct substantive business. In some cases, these boards can be merged so that policy for both secondary and postsecondary education emanates from one body.

Greater alignment through state-level policy will result in changes in high schools and colleges. States can help signal the importance of these changes and provide resources to enable planning and redesign work that illustrates the new relationships to be developed at each level. Educators can become more accustomed to receiving consistent policy messages that outline the ways that continuity between high school and college is to be achieved.

STATE ACTIONS TO DATE

The vast majority of states have been increasing academic expectations since the mid-1980s through tougher graduation requirements coupled with state-level standards, assessment, and accountability systems. Unfortunately, none of these reforms was designed specifically to align secondary education more closely with postsecondary readiness. This assertion may seem a bit harsh, in part because many state leaders have expressed the goal of increasing college readiness for more students; these leaders have assumed that if course requirements, standards, and assessment were made more rigorous, K–12 educational systems would then be well aligned with postsecondary readiness.

The truth of the matter is that while state standards and assessments have revealed the remarkable weaknesses in student basic knowledge and skill and have encouraged schools to address them, they have not necessarily improved college and career readiness for the majority of students. All evidence suggests that state reforms vary tremendously in terms of the challenge level at which they are set and the degree to which they address development of key postsecondary readiness skills.

This means that high school teachers and students are expending considerable time and energy preparing for tests that may or may not help students succeed in college. To solve this politically vexing problem, state education leaders have adopted a range of strategies. Some simply declare that their standards and testing requirements are aligned with college readiness and move on. Others convene task forces that analyze the existing high school content standards and deem them as appropriate for college preparation. A few administer an existing admissions test such as the ACT or SAT statewide. An increasing number are developing and adopting college readiness definitions, sometimes in the form of course requirements, occasionally stated as desired knowledge and skills, and, where possible, linked to end-of-course examinations aligned with postsecondary readiness.

The unfortunate result for many of the most vulnerable students is that they may believe that by getting good grades or passing the state test they are on a path to be ready for college when, in fact, this is a questionable assumption in many cases. The correlations that do exist between state test scores and performance in first-year college courses do not represent particularly strong evidence of a causal relationship between the two. Often they are a reflection of other correlates, such as family income or parental education, more than of the effects of state tests or new course-taking requirements. State standards may be potential precursors of college readiness in many cases, but the relationship has not been well established for the most part because few states have adopted college readiness standards in forms that parallel state academic content standards. Once states do so, it becomes possible to compare the two sets of standards to determine how well they are aligned with one another.

The development of a national set of college and career readiness standards may help states achieve this alignment in a relatively straightforward way. By comparing a state's standards to the national standards, it will be possible to ascertain any gap that may exist. Are state standards at too low of a challenge level? Are they too diffuse, covering everything but not engaging students in deeper understandings of key content? Do they take into account development of key cognitive strategies along with content mastery? In short, the national college and career readiness standards can serve as a benchmark against which state standards can be measured and states can achieve a modicum of certainty that their standards are aligned with postsecondary readiness.

Another indicator of the mismatch between state education reforms and college and career readiness is the fact that even as states have ratcheted up the high school graduation requirements, the number of students who end up in remedial courses once they enter college is showing no signs of abating. Adding to this challenge for states that seek to lower remediation rates is the fact that the demographic profile of the next generation of children entering school in the United States is increasingly composed of more children of immigrants and others who will be the first in their family to go on to postsecondary education. Not only must state standards and assessments be geared toward seeing that these students acquire basic literacy and numeracy skills, they must help to ensure that fewer of these students end up in remedial education. Secondary and postsecondary education will need to connect much more systematically and in ways that enable these students to be prepared for the challenges of entry-level college courses. Postsecondary access will be a cruel hoax for students who can pass high school courses and exams but then find out that success in college is beyond their reach.

States will have the primary responsibility to set the policies that trigger necessary changes. A poorly prepared and poorly educated workforce and citizenry has an immediate, visible effect that policymakers understand when states are competing with one another for new industries and investments. States therefore have a clear, strong incentive to take the initiative to create policies that encourage, support, and compel better alignment between high school and college in order to improve college and career readiness for a wider range of students.

EXAMPLES OF STATE ACTIONS

While many states have been slow to act in the arena of college readiness, some are beginning to enact significant policy measures that go beyond the goal of improving basic skills for all students to creating an aligned system that prepares more students for postsecondary success. These efforts can be grouped into several categories. The most widespread involve making the course requirements for a high school diploma the same as those for admission to state universities. Increasingly popular are efforts to create more postsecondary options for high school students. Dual-credit programs are perhaps the best example of this, but state-sponsored efforts to increase the number of Advanced Placement (AP) courses and International Baccalaureate (IB) programs are prominent in a subset of states as well. Finally, a few states are engaged in what might be characterized as systemic efforts that are designed to increase the pool of high school students who are college ready and simultaneously decrease the structural barriers to making a successful transition to college. These efforts involve changes in high school standards and assessments and concomitant changes in college placement testing and the support students receive on entry into college.

Many of these efforts are in the early stages, but they serve as important examples of how the delicate balance between local control and state education goals that characterizes American education is being adjusted to provide students with a coherent, carefully sequenced and aligned educational system that prepares them for success in college while still leaving local schools the discretion to provide programs tailored to the needs of their students. Given the tendency of state policymakers to look to one another for answers, state initiatives bear closer scrutiny for evidence of which strategies are most effective in enabling more students to be college ready.

Efforts to Increase the Value of State High School Exams and of the High School Diploma

Perhaps the initiative that best personifies state attempts to increase the value of a high school diploma is the American Diploma Project organized by Achieve, Inc. In 2008, thirty-three states were members of Achieve. States that sign on to the Achieve agenda agree in principle to these action points: they will align their high school standards with college and career expectations, require all high school students to take challenging courses that prepare them for learning after high school, streamline their assessment systems so that any state test that high school students take connects with college and work, hold high schools accountable for ensuring that their graduates are ready for college and work, and hold postsecondary institutions accountable for the success of admitted students.

Achieve's efforts have been important for a number of reasons. Governors are the officials in each state who agree to have their state join Achieve. This is important because governors can theoretically exert influence across all branches of public education in a state. The governor, through the power of budget development, control over executive agencies, executive decree, and the ability to appoint members of state boards, can bring the varying governance systems together and can expect or mandate that they cooperate in important ways to align their expectations for students. While these powers do not automatically lead to successful creation of K–16 educational systems, they can compel participation in a series of activities that begin to break down the walls between high schools and colleges—and between different branches of the postsecondary system, for that matter.

Achieve asserts that in 2009, thirty-two states had aligned their high school standards with college and career expectations in one form or another, and an additional thirteen states were in the planning stages to do so. This type of alignment is an important first step because state high school exams are built off state standards in almost all cases. If the high school standards can be made to align with college readiness, then teachers will not need to offer one curriculum for those preparing for the high school exam and another for those going on to college. At the very least, these efforts will bring issues of alignment to the state level for closer scrutiny by all of the principal policy players, an important step in formulating new policy responses and solutions to a problem.

State Efforts to Align High School and College

A number of states have undertaken programs that begin to address more directly the issue of alignment between high school and college. These efforts have been episodic, and they vary significantly from state to state. They fall into two general categories: those largely focused on repurposing existing measures or data to provide more information on college readiness and those that are seeking to adopt entirely new methods and systems to connect high school and college.

Universal Admissions Testing Requirements or Opportunities

A relatively simple and straightforward way to make stronger connections between high school and college readiness without upsetting the applecart of existing state standards and assessments is simply to overlay an additional test onto the state assessment system—one that is specifically designed for college admission purposes. This strategy has the advantage of not even pretending that the state test is an appropriate measure of college readiness and therefore avoids using results for that purpose. The ACT and SAT are perfectly good indicators of college readiness in general terms, although they have only recently begun to try to provide substantive diagnostic feedback about what students should be taught to be better prepared for college based on their scores. These tests are relatively affordable for a state, straightforward to administer, and have a long history. They are accepted by all postsecondary institutions (although not required by all) and can be used for a variety of purposes, including financial aid determinations.

Although these tests have several potential drawbacks, primary among which is the fact that they may not align well with the state content standards, they can nevertheless be a useful source of information about overall college preparedness statewide. Policymakers have also argued that administering the test to all students results in some proportion of test takers who might not otherwise think of themselves as college material finding out that they score at a level that would qualify them for college admission and suggests they might be college ready. These students would then be more likely to apply for college, the theory goes.

Six states in 2009 had provisions for all students to take either the ACT or SAT, and a number of other states are considering variations by which all students would receive some form of encouragement and support if they wished to take one or the other test. All students in Michigan, Colorado, Illinois, Kentucky, and Wyoming take the ACT. One state, Maine, has combined the SAT with its state assessment to meet federal NCLB testing requirements for high school students. Several other states offer the opportunity to any student who wishes to take one of these tests.

The preliminary evidence in states that have instituted such a requirement suggests that taking the test may have some positive effects for students who did not perceive themselves as potential college material, but that the requirement itself has not necessarily resulted in significant changes in school practice. The results have been used to identify students who have scores indicating they could succeed in college but are underperforming academically in high school. This test information is rarely used to change instruction in high schools, but it is believed to be a useful means to motivate more students to perform up to their potential while still in high school. The admissions tests used in this fashion essentially report on the status quo but do not appear to be much of a lever for substantive change at the high school or state level.

This is not to say that individual high schools or districts have no reaction at all to data suggesting their students are not performing well on the admissions tests and that they do not make any changes at all to help improve performance on those tests. The point is that administering the SAT and ACT to all students does not automatically lead to a better-aligned system of secondary and postsecondary education. These tests can yield valuable information that can serve as a starting point to improve alignment, but only if this initiative is seen as part of a larger state strategy that expects secondary and postsecondary systems to address a broader range of issues necessary to improve alignment and student success.

Connecting High School Exams to College Readiness and Placement

Some states are moving to determine a cut score on the state high school exam that corresponds to college readiness. Ideally, knowing if one's score is below the college readiness cut score would motivate students to take concrete steps to be better prepared for college, perhaps by taking more challenging courses in areas where they need improvement. But if the college readiness score is higher than that needed to pass the test for graduation purposes, students will have little motivation to take the test again to see if they did in fact reach college readiness levels at a later point.

If states can develop exams that truly set the skill level necessary for high school completion in line with college readiness, then it will be possible to use high school exam scores as a means to signal students whether they would be placed into a remedial course in college. Such information is even more concrete than a general indication of college readiness such as an SAT or ACT score, and the consequences are more significant.

But would high schools be prepared to help students take the necessary steps to meet placement standards? Do most high school teachers understand what is required to place into a credit-bearing college course in their subject area? Do most colleges, for their part, pay any attention to high school standards and tests? And perhaps more important, is any state willing to say that its high school graduates are prepared at a level that enables them to pursue postsecondary learning, or, if they are not, that they know what they need to do to be ready if they do choose to go on at some point?

California is one of a very few states attempting to use the state high school exam score in a way that signals college readiness and places the student into college courses. The way the state accomplishes this is by including on its California Standards Test additional, optional items in English and mathematics developed by California State University (CSU) faculty as a means to determine how the high school students who complete the questions would place into CSU entry-level English and math courses. In 2007, nearly 350,000 California high school juniors completed the voluntary questions and received scores indicating how well prepared they were to meet CSU standards. This simple test augmentation is an example of how a very general determination about college readiness can be made by means of the state testing process, although the two systems, high school and college, continue under this approach to have two separate tests rather than an integrated version. Early results suggest that remediation rates have decreased at one campus where the effects of the Early Assessment Program (EAP) have been tracked since the augmented test has been implemented.

STATE COLLEGE READINESS STANDARDS: THE EXAMPLE OF TEXAS

Another approach that a few states have attempted is to develop state-level college readiness standards. These standards can then be compared to the state high school standards and assessments as a means to determine how well the two are aligned. The college readiness standards can also be used by high school teachers to align their course expectations more directly with college readiness. This is particularly important for high school courses that are beyond the level of the state high school exam or in areas not tested by the exam that have no explicit reference point for what they should contain or how challenging they should be.

The most obvious problem with the college readiness standards is their relationship to the existing state standards. While there is no one obvious or simple answer to this issue, the experiences in Texas can be informative. It is worth bearing in mind that most state standards systems do not extend to twelfth grade currently, ending at tenth or sometimes eleventh grade, so it is not unreasonable or necessarily in conflict with state policy for a district or high school to adopt its own set of college readiness standards against which to align its program. It is likely that more states will adapt state standards to align with national college and career readiness standards, but in the interim, the Texas standards are at the least an interesting case study for educators and policymakers considering how to align state standards with college and career readiness.

These Texas standards are particularly interesting and potentially valuable because they were developed at the state level and were designed specifically to connect a state's K–12 standards with college readiness. Teams of Texas high school and postsecondary educators developed the standards, which helps to strengthen their validity. Furthermore, they are the only set of college and career readiness standards that have been carefully validated against practices in entry-level college courses to confirm they are in fact the right things for students to be learning in high school.

The Educational Policy Improvement Center (EPIC) conducted a study on behalf of the Texas Higher Education Coordinating Board in which course documents were collected from college instructors of 913 courses in twenty subjects that students most commonly take during their freshman year in college. Instructors also provided detailed information on their expectations and practices. The results confirm that the Texas College and Career Readiness Standards (TCCRS) are highly aligned with the content and requirements of entry-level college courses. These standards, then, serve as one of the best examples of a comprehensive set of expectations toward which all students who are contemplating learning beyond high school should strive. The standards offer a framework for high school educators to use to judge the alignment of their instructional program with college readiness.

Texas has one of the most highly developed and long-standing standards and test-based high school accountability systems in the nation, one that high school teachers and students take seriously. In effect since the early 1990s, the system has influenced instruction in Texas and resulted in more of a focus on basic skills instruction for students with deficiencies in these areas, particularly students from low-income families and from ethnic minority groups that have not historically performed well on state exams. However, little evidence existed to suggest that this system had led to an increase in the proportion of Texas students who were ready for college and careers. This was a real issue in a state that has seen and will continue to experience a dramatic increase in the proportion of its school-going population that will be first-generation college attendees. If the system could not prepare more of these students for college success, the state's economy and social structure would be affected dramatically.

With the passage in 2006 of House Bill 1, the state created a framework wherein a number of activities designed to improve college readiness for more students would take place. The centerpiece was a set of college readiness standards to be developed by vertical teams comprising Texas secondary and postsecondary educators in core academic subject areas. The teams were also charged with examining the high school curricular requirements to determine if they were sufficient to prepare students for college, identifying instructional strategies that would result in students being ready for college-level work, and developing standards for curriculum materials for students who need additional assistance preparing for college.

The legislation went on to specify that the State Board of Education align the Texas Essential Knowledge and Skills (TEKS), the state K–12 content standards, with the college readiness standards, a daunting proposition in a state where an established set of high school standards had long held sway with high school teachers. At around the same time, the Texas legislature authorized a transition from standards-based tests to end-of-course exams. The legislation specified that any such end-of-course exam be designed to the extent practicable to yield data that could be used for placement purposes into an entry-level college course in the same subject area.

In January 2008, the Texas Higher Education Coordinating Board adopted college readiness standards in four subject areas as developed by vertical teams of Texas educators. The standards in English, mathematics, science, and social studies define the content knowledge necessary for college success, along with the key cognitive strategies and cross-disciplinary skills students must possess to be college ready. They serve as a reference point against which the high school program of study can be gauged and toward which student progress can be measured.

The TCCRS do not specify what students must master to graduate from high school; rather, they set out what students need to know in order to have a reasonable probability of success in their introductory college courses at two- and four-year institutions. Research suggests that success in these courses is a critical predictor of who will eventually graduate from college. The TCCRS exist to help ensure that students are prepared for the demands of entry-level courses and are able to avoid remedial placements.

High school courses rightly provide a broad-ranging set of core knowledge and skills meant to lay a foundation in literacy and numeracy and to introduce students to a variety of subject areas. But even a high-quality college preparatory curriculum is not likely to equip students to embark on a specific major in college. The high school preparation for college can only help students develop the foundational skills on which success in the literally hundreds of majors can be achieved eventually. The

TCCRS are designed to specify the all-important foundational knowledge that students should seek to learn in order to begin a postsecondary program of study and succeed in their general education courses, which serve as gateways to the majors, or in courses in two-year certificate programs that lead to a career pathway.

The TCCRS as developed by the vertical teams are designed to represent the full range of knowledge and skills that students need to strive toward to be fully ready to succeed in entry-level general education and two-year certificate courses and proceed into a wide range of majors and career pathways. They also delineate many of the key cognitive strategies that students will be expected to use in postsecondary learning environments.

Organization of the Texas College and Career Readiness Standards

The structure of the TCCRS reflects the ways that English/language arts, mathematics, science, and social science are approached in higher education. Rather than a simple, one-level checklist of things to memorize or facts to master, the standards consist of a multilevel hierarchical framework that presents what is important to know and understand conceptually within a subject area and how each subject area is organized overall.

This is critical because one of the most important results of studying a subject in postsecondary education is for students to understand the structure of that subject and, by extension, the ways of knowing and thinking about the phenomena that the subject presents. Without an adequate understanding of the structure of the discipline, students will have difficulty succeeding in upper-division courses in that discipline. Therefore, the TCCRS introduce the disciplinary structures at the entry level in order to help familiarize students with key concepts and content in each of four subject areas and in a set of cross-disciplinary standards.

The TCCRS should not be thought of as a checklist. However, as a general rule, the more standards a student can demonstrate successfully, the more likely it is that the student will be college and career ready. More important, that student will be prepared to succeed in most subject areas offered in college. Students will benefit by mastering the TCCRS in depth rather than by passing over each in a superficial fashion.

While analyses find high degrees of alignment between the TEKS and the TCCRS, this does not mean they are the same or that knowledge specified in each is necessarily taught the same way or learned for the same purpose. It is possible, and even desirable, for students to be introduced to a topic in high school and then have it reinforced once they reach college. However, this sort of repetition should always be done intentionally and with purpose. Therefore, standards that appear in both a state's standards and a set of college readiness standards should be examined carefully to ensure they are being taught in a complementary, not redundant, fashion at each level.

The TCCRS are somewhat unique as a set of standards because, in addition to specification of necessary content knowledge, they also contain statements of cross-disciplinary, foundational skills that should be considered as important as any particular piece of content knowledge. Some of these skills, such as problem solving or writing, are also stated in standards within specific subject areas, but they are given additional emphasis as skills that cut across all subject areas by their inclusion in a separate cross-disciplinary standards section.

Structure of the Texas College and Career Readiness Standards

The TCCRS are organized in four nested levels of specificity. Roman numerals indicate the overarching or keystone ideas within a subject area or discipline. Capital letters specify the organizing components in a subject area that are the broad headers for key knowledge and skills. The numbered headings delineate the performance expectations that offer students greater specificity regarding expected knowledge and skills and also suggest the challenge level of the standard. The lowercase letters present indicators of ways in which students would demonstrate performance in each area. An explanation follows.

I. Key Content: overarching or keystone ideas of a discipline that reverberate as themes throughout the curriculum. Designated by roman numerals.

  A. Organizing components: Knowledge and subject areas that organize a discipline around what students should retain, be able to transfer, and apply to new knowledge and skills. Designated by capital letters.

  1. Performance expectations: Knowledge and skills that represent the important ideas of the current understanding of each organizing concept as well as the multiple contexts in which each organizing concept can be manifest. Designated by numbers.

  a. Performance indicators: Examples of how to assess and measure performance expectations.

For more information on the methods and strategies presented in this chapter, go to http://CollegeCareerReady.org.

No school or school district wants to undertake the development of a comprehensive set of college readiness standards. And while national college and career readiness standards may well become an accepted reference point, the TCCRS presented here are a model that can help a district or school determine how well aligned its program is with college and career readiness. The Texas standards have little in them specific to Texas and align well with the national college and career readiness standards and with most state high school standards. The English/language arts and mathematics standards are presented here to illustrate the way the structure of knowledge in these subject areas is organized.

English as a Way of Knowing

Listening, speaking, writing, and reading are vehicles for communication. They enable people to express their thoughts and demonstrate what they have learned. In the past, students were taught specific lessons under the rubric of language, and the skills were practiced, reinforced, and analyzed throughout the day in geography, history, science, and other subjects. Today the teaching of language arts is often considered the exclusive responsibility of English teachers. However, the complex role of language in education makes it clear that the language arts cannot be left entirely to the English class. Improvement in the language arts requires students to read and write frequently in all disciplines and to receive ample feedback. Following these standards, the language arts should be viewed as being fundamental to pedagogy in any subject.

Texas College and Career Readiness Standards in English/Language Arts

I. Writing

    A. Compose a variety of texts that demonstrate clear focus, the logical development of ideas in well-organized paragraphs, and the use of appropriate language that advances the author's purpose.

        1. Determine effective approaches, forms, and rhetorical techniques that demonstrate understanding of the writer's purpose and audience.

2. Generate ideas and gather information relevant to the topic and purpose, keeping careful records of outside sources.

3. Evaluate relevance, quality, sufficiency, and depth of preliminary ideas and information, organize material generated, and formulate a thesis.

4. Recognize the importance of revision as the key to effective writing. Each draft should refine key ideas and organize them more logically and fluidly, use language more precisely and effectively, and draw the reader to the author's purpose.

5. Edit writing for proper voice, tense, and syntax, assuring that it conforms to standard English, when appropriate.

II. Reading

A. Locate explicit textual information, draw complex inferences, and analyze and evaluate the information within and across texts of varying lengths.

1. Use effective reading strategies to determine a written work's purpose and intended audience.

2. Use text features and graphics to form an overview of informational texts and to determine where to locate information.

3. Identify explicit and implicit textual information including main ideas and author's purpose.

4. Draw and support complex inferences from text to summarize, draw conclusions, and distinguish facts from simple assertions and opinions.

5. Analyze the presentation of information and the strength and quality of evidence used by the author, and judge the coherence and logic of the presentation and the credibility of an argument.

6. Analyze imagery in literary texts.

7. Evaluate the use of both literal and figurative language to inform and shape the perceptions of readers.

8. Compare and analyze how generic features are used across texts.

9. Identify and analyze the audience, purpose, and message of an informational or persuasive text.

10. Identify and analyze how an author's use of language appeals to the senses, creates imagery, and suggests mood.

11. Identify, analyze, and evaluate similarities and differences in how multiple texts present information, argue a position, or relate a theme.

B. Understand new vocabulary and concepts and use them accurately in reading, speaking, and writing.

  1. Identify new words and concepts acquired through study of their relationships to other words and concepts.

  2. Apply knowledge of roots and affixes to infer the meanings of new words.

  3. Use reference guides to confirm the meanings of new words or concepts.

C. Describe, analyze, and evaluate information within and across literary and other texts from a variety of cultures and historical periods.

  1. Read a wide variety of texts from American, European, and world literatures.

  2. Analyze themes, structures, and elements of myths, traditional narratives, and classical and contemporary literature.

  3. Analyze works of literature for what they suggest about the historical period and cultural contexts in which they were written.

  4. Analyze and compare the use of language in literary works from a variety of world cultures.

D. Explain how literary and other texts evoke personal experience and reveal character in particular historical circumstances.

  1. Describe insights gained about oneself, others, or the world from reading specific texts.

  2. Analyze the influence of myths, folktales, fables, and classical literature from a variety of world cultures on later literature and film.

III. Speaking

A. Understand the elements of communication both in informal group discussions and formal presentations (e.g., accuracy, relevance, rhetorical features, organization of information).

1. Understand how style and content of spoken language varies in different contexts and influences the listener's understanding.

2. Adjust presentation (delivery, vocabulary, length) to particular audiences and purposes.

B. Develop effective speaking styles for both group and one-on-one situations.

   1. Participate actively and effectively in one-on-one oral communication situations.

   2. Participate actively and effectively in group discussions.

   3. Plan and deliver focused and coherent presentations that convey clear and distinct perspectives and demonstrate solid reasoning.

IV. Listening

   A. Apply listening skills as an individual and as a member of a group in a variety of settings (e.g., lectures, discussions, conversations, team projects, presentations, interviews).

      1. Analyze and evaluate the effectiveness of a public presentation.

      2. Interpret a speaker's message; identify the position taken and the evidence in support of that position.

      3. Use a variety of strategies to enhance listening comprehension (e.g., focus attention on message, monitor message for clarity and understanding, provide verbal and nonverbal feedback, note cues such as change of pace or particular words that indicate a new point is about to be made, select and organize key information).

   B. Listen effectively in informal and formal situations.

      1. Listen critically and respond appropriately to presentations.

      2. Listen actively and effectively in one-on-one communication situations.

      3. Listen actively and effectively in group discussions.

V. Research

   A. Formulate topic and questions.

      1. Formulate research questions.

      2. Explore a research topic.

      3. Refine research topic and devise a timeline for completing work.

B. Select information from a variety of sources.

   1. Gather relevant sources.

   2. Evaluate the validity and reliability of sources.

   3. Synthesize and organize information effectively.

   4. Use source material ethically.

C. Produce and design a document.

   1. Design and present an effective product.

   2. Use source material ethically.

Mathematics as a Way of Knowing

Mathematics knowledge is essential to becoming a productive citizen in today's society. Many factors have increased the level of understanding of mathematics that the average adult needs. Our ever-changing world has become increasingly quantitative in nature. For example, in the physical and social studies and in the business world, a widening array of phenomena is explained with numerical data presented visually in the form of charts and graphs that require interpretation. Mathematical reasoning is key to solving problems, formulating logical arguments, understanding quantitative features of various disciplines, critically analyzing media sources, and searching for patterns. Through mathematics, people become better able to make well-informed decisions by formulating conjectures and testing hypotheses. Mathematics cannot be viewed solely as a series of stand-alone courses or a set of specific skills. It must also be considered as a source of cross-disciplinary knowledge that is essential for success in numerous areas of study.

Texas College and Career Readiness Standards in Mathematics

I. Numeric Reasoning

  A. Number representation

    1. Compare real numbers.

    2. Define and give examples of complex numbers.

  B. Number operations

    1. Perform computations with real and complex numbers.

c. Number sense and number concepts

    1. Use estimation to check for errors and reasonableness of solutions.

II. Algebraic Reasoning

  A. Expressions and equations

    1. Explain and differentiate between expressions and equations using words such as "solve," "evaluate," and "simplify."

  B. Manipulating expressions

    1. Recognize and use algebraic (field) properties, concepts, procedures, and algorithms to combine, transform, and evaluate expressions (e.g., polynomials, radicals, rational expressions).

  C. Solving equations, inequalities, and systems of equations

    1. Recognize and use algebraic (field) properties, concepts, procedures, and algorithms to solve equations, inequalities, and systems of linear equations.

    2. Explain the difference between the solution set of an equation and the solution set of an inequality.

  D. Representations

    1. Interpret multiple representations of equations and relationships.

    2. Translate among multiple representations of equations and relationships.

III. Geometric Reasoning

  A. Figures and their properties

    1. Identify and represent the features of plane and space figures.

    2. Make, test, and use conjectures about one-, two-, and three-dimensional figures and their properties.

    3. Recognize and apply right triangle relationships including basic trigonometry.

  B. Transformations and symmetry

    1. Identify and apply transformations to figures.

    2. Identify the symmetries of a plane figure.

3. Use congruence transformations and dilations to investigate congruence, similarity, and symmetries of plane figures.

C. Connections between geometry and other mathematical content strands

1. Make connections between geometry and algebra.

2. Make connections among geometry, statistics, and probability.

3. Make connections between geometry and measurement.

D. Logic and reasoning in geometry

1. Make and validate geometric conjectures.

2. Understand that Euclidean geometry is an axiomatic system.

IV. Measurement Reasoning

A. Measurement involving physical and natural attributes

1. Select or use the appropriate type of unit for the attribute being measured.

B. Systems of measurement

1. Convert from one measurement system to another.

2. Convert within a single measurement system.

C. Measurement involving geometry and algebra

1. Find the perimeter and area of two-dimensional figures.

2. Determine the surface area and volume of three-dimensional figures.

3. Determine indirect measurements of figures using scale drawings, similar figures, the Pythagorean Theorem, and basic trigonometry.

D. Measurement involving statistics and probability

1. Compute and use measures of center and spread to describe data.

2. Apply probabilistic measures to practical situations to make an informed decision.

V. Probabilistic Reasoning

A. Counting principles

1. Determine the nature and the number of elements in a finite sample space.

B. Computation and interpretation of probabilities

    1. Compute and interpret the probability of an event and its complement.

    2. Compute and interpret the probability of conditional and compound events.

VI. Statistical Reasoning

  A. Data collection

    1. Plan a study.

  B. Describe data

    1. Determine types of data.

    2. Select and apply appropriate visual representations of data.

    3. Compute and describe summary statistics of data.

    4. Describe patterns and departure from patterns in a set of data.

  C. Read, analyze, interpret, and draw conclusions from data

    1. Make predictions and draw inferences using summary statistics.

    2. Analyze data sets using graphs and summary statistics.

    3. Analyze relationships between paired data using spreadsheets, graphing calculators, or statistical software.

    4. Recognize reliability of statistical results.

VII. Functions

  A. Recognition and representation of functions

    1. Recognize whether a relation is a function.

    2. Recognize and distinguish between different types of functions.

  B. Analysis of functions

    1. Understand and analyze features of a function.

    2. Algebraically construct and analyze new functions.

  C. Model real world situations with functions

    1. Apply known function models.

    2. Develop a function to model a situation.

VIII. Problem Solving and Reasoning

    A. Mathematical problem solving

        1. Analyze given information.

        2. Formulate a plan or strategy.

        3. Determine a solution.

        4. Justify the solution.

        5. Evaluate the problem-solving process.

    B. Logical reasoning

        1. Develop and evaluate convincing arguments.

        2. Use various types of reasoning.

    C. Real world problem solving

        1. Formulate a solution to a real world situation based on the solution to a mathematical problem.

        2. Use a function to model a real world situation.

        3. Evaluate the problem-solving process.

IX. Communication and Representation

    A. Language, terms, and symbols of mathematics

        1. Use mathematical symbols, terminology, and notation to represent given and unknown information in a problem.

        2. Use mathematical language to represent and communicate the mathematical concepts in a problem.

        3. Use mathematics as a language for reasoning, problem solving, making connections, and generalizing.

    B. Interpretation of mathematical work

        1. Model and interpret mathematical ideas and concepts using multiple representations.

        2. Summarize and interpret mathematical information provided orally, visually, or in written form within the given context.

    c. Presentation and representation of mathematical work

        1. Communicate mathematical ideas, reasoning, and their implications using symbols, diagrams, graphs, and words.

        2. Create and use representations to organize, record, and communicate real world situations, and everyday life mathematical ideas.

        3. Explain, display, or justify mathematical ideas and arguments using precise mathematical language in written or oral communications.

X. Connections

    A. Connections among the strands of mathematics

        1. Connect and use multiple strands of mathematics in situations and problems.

        2. Connect mathematics to the study of other disciplines.

    B. Connections of mathematics to nature, real world situations, and everyday life

        1. Use multiple representations to demonstrate links between mathematical and real world situations.

        2. Understand and use appropriate oral communications.

        3. Know and understand the use of mathematics in a variety of careers and mathematics professions.

Cross-Disciplinary Skills: Foundations of Learning and Knowing

Although the TCCRS are organized into four distinct disciplinary areas (English/language arts, mathematics, science, and social studies), some elements cut across one or more disciplines. In fact, some skill areas span all four subject areas. It is important to identify the cross-cutting knowledge and skills that underlie and connect the four disciplinary areas. This important need has been addressed through the addition of a section that identifies cross-disciplinary standards.

Think of cross-disciplinary standards as tools that college instructors in all areas use to challenge, engage, and evaluate students in each specific subject area. They include key cognitive strategies, such as reasoning, problem solving, and conducting research, as well as foundational skills, such as reading, writing, and data analysis.

Many of these skills are also taught within a single subject area. For example, while the primary responsibility for developing reading and writing skills in secondary school resides within English/language arts courses, first-year college students are expected to employ a range of subject-specific reading and writing strategies and techniques in all of their courses. They will write a lab report in a biology class or read primary source documents in a history class. They need to apply reading and writing skills across disciplines and develop different strategies for doing so that are specific to each discipline and its unique demands and conventions.

Academic and business leaders emphasize the importance of being able to apply these skills across a variety of contexts and subject matter areas. They describe work environments in which the cross-disciplinary skills are prerequisites to solving important problems and producing products. These problems and products increasingly require applying knowledge across disciplines and subject areas and the mastery of a base set of communication and analysis skills that span subject areas. Students, then, need not only to possess content knowledge but also be able to draw from an array of key cognitive strategies in order to complete successfully the academic tasks presented to them, most of which require much more than simple recall of factual knowledge. These cross-disciplinary standards enable students to engage in deeper levels of thinking across a wide range of subjects. They help high school students prepare for the transition from high school's primary focus on acquiring content knowledge to postsecondary and work environments in which complex cognitive skills are necessary to achieve success.

Texas College and Career Readiness Cross-disciplinary Standards

I. Key Cognitive Skills

    A. Intellectual curiosity

        1. Engage in scholarly inquiry and dialogue.

        2. Accept constructive criticism and revise personal views when valid evidence warrants.

    B. Reasoning

        1. Consider arguments and conclusions of self and others.

        2. Construct well-reasoned arguments to explain phenomena, validate conjectures, or support positions.

3. Gather evidence to support arguments, findings, or lines of reasoning.

4. Support or modify claims based on the results of an inquiry.

C. Problem solving

1. Analyze a situation to identify a problem to be solved.

2. Develop and apply multiple strategies to solve a problem.

3. Collect evidence and data systematically and directly relate to solving a problem.

D. Academic behaviors

1. Self-monitor learning needs and seek assistance when needed.

2. Use study habits necessary to manage academic pursuits and requirements.

3. Strive for accuracy and precision.

4. Persevere to complete and master tasks.

E. Work habits

1. Work independently.

2. Work collaboratively.

F. Academic integrity

1. Attribute ideas and information to source materials and people.

2. Evaluate sources for quality of content, validity, credibility, and relevance.

3. Include the ideas of others and the complexities of the debate, issue, or problem.

4. Understand and adhere to ethical codes of conduct.

II. Foundational Skills

A. Reading across the curriculum

1. Use effective prereading strategies.

2. Use a variety of strategies to understand the meanings of new words.

3. Identify the intended purpose and audience of the text.

4. Identify the key information and supporting details.

5. Analyze textual information critically.

6. Annotate, summarize, paraphrase, and outline texts when appropriate.

7. Adapt reading strategies according to structure of texts.

8. Connect reading to historical and current events and personal interest.

B. Writing across the curriculum

1. Write clearly and coherently using standard writing conventions.

2. Write in a variety of forms for various audiences and purposes.

3. Compose and revise drafts.

C. Research across the curriculum

1. Understand which topics or questions are to be investigated.

2. Explore a research topic.

3. Refine a research topic based on preliminary research and devise a timeline for completing work.

4. Evaluate the validity and reliability of sources.

5. Synthesize and organize information effectively.

6. Design and present an effective product.

7. Integrate source material.

8. Present final product.

D. Use of data

1. Identify patterns or departures from patterns among data.

2. Use statistical and probabilistic skills necessary for planning an investigation and collecting, analyzing, and interpreting data.

3. Present analyzed data and communicate findings in a variety of formats.

E. Technology

1. Use technology to gather information.

2. Use technology to organize, manage, and analyze information.

3. Use technology to communicate and display findings in a clear and coherent manner.

4. Use technology appropriately.

CLEAR MESSAGES STATES CAN SEND TO THE SECONDARY SYSTEM

State policy initiatives point the way for changes that high schools and colleges must undertake, but policy directives go only so far. Educators at both levels will need to change practices in ways that extend beyond complying with state policies and rules. States need to send consistent messages to secondary educators regarding what is important for their students to be learning, how student success will be measured, and the means by which high schools will be held accountable for achieving identified state goals related to college readiness. While such actions should fall short of specifying what is to be taught and how, high school educators will benefit from a clarity of purpose and expectations that allows them to design local solutions within a larger state policy context that better aligns secondary and postsecondary learning.

Focus High Schools More Clearly on College Readiness

The American high school is in the midst of an identity crisis, a topic explored in Chapter One. States can help high schools reduce the tension between preparation for postsecondary learning and for work by reviewing the state standards to demonstrate where and how they connect with college and career readiness and then to revise and expand the standards as necessary to make sure they have a strong connection with postsecondary preparation that leads to a baccalaureate or career pathway.

This does not mean that every standard must relate directly to postsecondary education, but the overall alignment should be clear and strong. This helps educators focus their curriculum and teaching in ways that are consistent with students continuing to develop understandings of material introduced in high school. Even more important is the development by students of a range of learning strategies that will serve them well in any of a range of situations where they might be called on to learn new material, including job training or retraining on career development programs.

A clear focus on postsecondary readiness does not mean abandoning courses oriented toward career and technical education. Quite the contrary, these courses help students develop key learning strategies, skills, and academic behaviors; apply concepts and knowledge learned elsewhere; and make connections among material from a variety of subject areas. States need to support new career technical education models in high schools and the training or retraining of teachers to offer these courses. Such courses should be academically rigorous even as they have a strong application focus to them. In this way, the high school can be the base of operations and the jumping-off point for students to engage in a much wider range of learning opportunities than can ever be offered in U.S. high schools currently, which will never be able to provide the programs needed for success in most careers that require expensive equipment, dedicated space, instructors with specialized skills, or extended periods of on-the-job training and supervision.

Many high schools offer high-quality career and technical education programs that are the gateway to advanced training in one or more areas already, so state policy needs to encourage this trend and help guide its development. Rather than standardizing these programs, high schools should be encouraged to adapt them to local circumstances—not as job training programs but as career pathway gateways that use local expertise and resources. Each high school could choose to focus on a few areas that are most locally relevant, for which local employers might provide support, and that could be revised, updated, and even replaced as the local economy evolves.

It is not necessary to impose on high school educators and students practices they find unfamiliar or distasteful, particularly when many high school educators already are taking many steps in the right direction on their own. It is necessary to help high schools as institutions make the transition from a shopping mall model to one focused on core learnings and proficiencies that are applied in a wide range of settings, all of which connect with additional learning, and in which applied learning programs are vehicles to develop and use core academic knowledge and skills.

Develop and Use More Comprehensive Measures of Student Readiness

State accountability measures and systems need to take into account to a much greater degree than they do now how successful each high school is in preparing a wide range of students for learning beyond high school. Graduation rates are a particularly poor means of determining high school success and tend to skew the system more toward moving students through and finding ways to keep them enrolled (or not counted on the high school's rosters) than on preparing them properly. In fact, connecting high school more closely with an assortment of college and career programs and allowing students to begin some postsecondary work while still in high school can be a stronger motivator for some students than is the offer of a high school diploma. High schools need to be encouraged to create a much more seamless zone of transition for students to move incrementally and by degrees from secondary to postsecondary learning as they are ready. Not all students will be able to take advantage of these opportunities, but many more students will continue their education if they are given opportunities of this nature and are not limited to taking only high school classes.

Pay Attention to the Needs of First-Generation College Attendees

It is much easier to prepare students for college if their parents, siblings, and extended family and community have experience with the demands and expectations of postsecondary education. It is far more difficult to do so for students and families who lack the cultural capital and access to the privileged knowledge that surrounds so much of the transition from high school to college. It has to be tempting to high schools to concentrate resources on the students who are most likely to be successful (and, by extension, to make the high school look successful). Although it is much more difficult to develop programs that address the needs of students who are more challenging to prepare, this is where the real value added of a high school education can become apparent.

Many high schools have taken it on themselves to offer support in the form of programs such as Advancement Via Individual Determination (AVID) and Gaining Early Awareness and Readiness for Undergraduate Programs (GEAR-UP), two structured approaches to getting more students from underrepresented groups on a track to college readiness. The AVID model is more consistent across schools, focusing on an advisory-type class (the AVID elective) that teaches more students the key academic behaviors and self-management skills, and provides them with necessary support. The GEAR-UP approach is a federal grant program to states and partnerships that implement a wider variety of strategies to support low-income students to become ready for college.

These are important starting points, and they can address well the needs of the students who are able to access them. What of all the students who do not have access to such programs? What of the high schools that have not chosen to adopt such programs? State policy needs to ensure that high schools are providing programs and resources aimed specifically at first-generation college attendees and at students from groups historically underrepresented in college.

Commit to Ensuring Teachers Have Necessary Content Knowledge and Instructional Skills

Increasing numbers of college graduates with an interest in teaching are avoiding preparation programs altogether in favor of options that allow them to go directly to the classroom with minimal formal training. Such approaches are attractive if they allow more individuals with deep content knowledge to get the opportunity to work with students. They are potentially problematic when the content knowledge level of these prospective teachers is not known. Regardless of the route to the classroom, all prospective teachers need to have superior content knowledge bases and an understanding of how to communicate to students the structure of knowledge in their subject area.

This issue is nowhere more pressing than in inner-city schools, where faculty turnover is high and many novice teachers are assigned. It has become almost a given that these new teachers will struggle with issues such as classroom management and lesson design initially, but often overlooked is the content proficiency of this cadre of teachers. Studies suggest that many secondary school teachers in the sciences in particular have not taken enough course work in the subject they teach to have acquired deep knowledge of it. They may meet state certification standards and still not have achieved deep content knowledge.

Teachers who do not possess the necessary content knowledge will never challenge their students at the level necessary for college readiness, even after they have learned to manage their classrooms and attend to lesson designs and teaching methods. Students quickly perceive when their teacher does not understand well what he or she is teaching, and they lose respect for that teacher. More important perhaps, the students come to believe that they themselves are not particularly capable of handling difficult content matter because their own teacher struggles to do so or avoids challenging topics altogether. Students who have teachers who possess deep content knowledge come to respect those teachers and value their own role in the learning process to a greater degree. They also have more opportunities to develop the key cognitive strategies necessary to delve deeply into the discipline.

State education agencies and teacher certification departments need to become serious about ensuring that all teachers have high levels of content knowledge in the subject areas they teach. Recent federal requirements that all teachers be "highly qualified" were a potential step in the right direction, but many state definitions of "highly qualified" significantly diluted the potential impact of the requirement. An important first step states could take toward creating a teacher force with uniformly high content knowledge expertise is to adopt clear, high criteria that all applicants for teaching positions must meet regarding their content knowledge in subjects they are being authorized to teach.

States can also help current teachers augment their content knowledge and keep up to date with new developments in their field of study by sponsoring opportunities for secondary and postsecondary faculty to interact within disciplinary-based structures. Many states already have the basis for such interactions in the form of statewide content organizations or networks. Some offer opportunities for the dissemination of new knowledge and techniques in the discipline. But in most cases, only a small fraction of a state's teachers participate, and the organization may take on many other issues in addition to content knowledge renewal.

States can help expand the scale of and participation in these subject-based networks while simultaneously encouraging them to focus on the knowledge and skills necessary to prepare students better for postsecondary success. In the process, teachers will take away a wide range of ancillary information and skills, but the key value added will be renewed and deepened content knowledge that will help secondary students prepare for postsecondary education.

The other important area where additional teacher skill is required is in developing the key cognitive strategies associated with college and career success. Many teachers lack a clear understanding of how to teach students to write a highly structured research paper, for example, and, as a result, are reluctant to make the writing of research papers an integral component of their courses. They need to know how to formulate challenging research assignments and then provide feedback to students on all aspects of a quality paper. Students need to complete multiple papers over the course of the term. In this way, they develop key cognitive strategies necessary to conduct research.

Learning to teach in a manner where the development of cognitive processes is the central goal is not an easy or familiar task for many high school teachers, particularly in cases where instruction has been focused on transmission of content matter contained on state tests. States have a responsibility, having introduced these tests in the first place, to help teachers learn how to transmit necessary and important content, but to do so in ways that require thinking, analysis, interpretation, and deep engagement with the material.

Knowing how to organize and conduct a good discussion, for example, seems like a relatively straightforward teaching skill that one might assume all teachers know how to do. In fact, it is a complex activity, requiring significant planning and anticipation of potential pitfalls if the discussion is to be kept from digressing or deteriorating into a superficial conversation that does not address the desired goals regarding the issue and content under consideration. How many teachers can question a student's assertions without making that student feel defensive? How many can get students to engage in deep discussions of conflicting explanations of an event without having the students seek simply to find out the "right" answer? How many can put forth a problem that does not have a simple, predictable solution and then lead students through a process that results in each individual's coming up with her or his own process to solve the problem? When all teachers in a school possess these types of skills, the likelihood that the school's students will be college and career ready on graduation increases dramatically.

The state's contribution here can be to develop materials that can be accessed online and to provide resources for workshops where teachers learn to integrate the materials into their existing courses. Many organizations have developed training programs in these areas. Teachers need to be given access to these programs and encouraged to use them. Local school districts need to follow through by developing expectations that teachers participate and implement what they are learning. Administrators need to be able to look for these practices in classrooms, reinforce and recognize teachers who are doing so successfully, and provide support and resources to those who are struggling.

Here, once again, collaborative efforts between secondary and postsecondary education can lead to the most productive outcomes. Even while new practices are being put into place in high school classrooms, secondary educators should not lose sight of the larger goal, which is to have greater continuity between the high school and college experiences so that the transition is not so difficult for students because they have already developed familiary and some facility in high school with the key cognitive strategies that are being developed further in entry-level college courses.

In short, states have at their disposal a variety of tools that can be used to send clearer messages to secondary school administrators and teachers regarding the importance of focusing the core of a high school education on preparing all students to be ready to learn beyond high school. Although the complexity of implementing the various strategies outlined in this section should not be underestimated nor can implementation issues be fully explored here, the activities themselves can be given a prominent place on a state's policy agenda even as the details for implementation are worked out. Laying out a comprehensive program that will lead to stronger ties between high schools and colleges will help nudge the system in that direction.

CLEAR MESSAGES STATES CAN SEND TO THEIR POSTSECONDARY SYSTEMS

As state policies help secondary education focus more clearly on college readiness, similar policies must also be implemented to guide the postsecondary system to engage in a series of activities to align admissions, placement, and the content of entry-level courses in particular with exit from the secondary system. Higher education has many other areas where practices might be improved to help support greater student success, but beginning by concentrating on the intake, placement, and initial success of incoming students is the highest value-added strategy currently available. Postsecondary institutions will realize tangible benefits by designing their programs to fit better with the needs of incoming students and to communicate more clearly and consistently what it takes to be able to succeed in a postsecondary program of study.

Align Exit-Level High School Courses and Entry-Level College Courses Better

For the most part, college faculty and administrators do not give serious consideration to the degree to which the content of any particular entry-level course relates to what was taught in its corresponding exit-level high school course. As noted previously, many entry-level college courses are built on the assumption that students know little or nothing about the subject, and the course proceeds from this assumption.

An alternative is to have entry-level college courses that align more deliberately with what is being taught in high school. This requires a commitment not just by college instructors but by their high school peers as well to give consideration to what each other is attempting to do. Alignment does not consist solely of continuity of content coverage, although this is an important element.

Equally important is the emphasis each places on the various thinking and meta-cognitive skills associated with the area of study, the ways in which learning is being assessed, and the kinds of academic behaviors necessary to succeed at each level.

States can promote this sort of alignment by sponsoring the development of what are called paired courses, which were described in greater detail in Chapter Two. The state of South Carolina is designing high school and college courses where the exit-level high school course pairs with the entry-level college course. These are being developed initially in English, math, and science with involvement by all of the postsecondary systems and campuses within the state. This effort was initiated and led by the postsecondary partners with active involvement by the state education department and school districts statewide. Participation was voluntary at both levels. Notably, participation by high school educators was more difficult to achieve because they tended to be focused exclusively on the state's high school standards and exams. However, once secondary school teachers did become involved, they were enthusiastic contributors to the design process and to course piloting.

Control the Quality of Entry-Level Courses

We noted earlier that many secondary educators argue that high schools should not attempt to align courses to a postsecondary system that engages in ineffective instructional practices in entry-level courses. They point to large lecture halls in which students doze or check their Facebook page while an instructor drones on in the front of the room with his back to the students, covering the chalkboard with indecipherable scribbles.

While this extreme stereotype can indeed be encountered in the world of postsecondary teaching, it is not the norm. More common is the dedicated, enthusiastic, knowledgeable instructor who imparts to students an interest in and excitement about an area of study heretofore unbeknown to the student. The tremendous diversity of the U.S. postsecondary system is both a strength and a weakness when it is paired with a highly decentralized secondary system. No one really knows what to expect from the other because the range of practices is so great at each level. The key missing element is some form of quality control across entry-level courses that can be achieved without standardizing these courses in a way that leads to enforced mediocrity.

It is not as unrealistic as it may seem to seek some form of agreed-on consistency in these entry-level general education courses. They are offered at nearly all postsecondary institutions, two year and four year, and are accepted broadly (although not universally) for transfer purposes among institutions. A number of states have already achieved consistency in the numbering of these courses and, in a very few states, even some rudimentary agreement on course content. After that, it is a relatively small step to creating some sort of quality assurance standard and process.

One strategy to set a quality standard that communicates within the postsecondary system and also to the secondary system is to create what we call reference courses for all key entry-level courses. A reference course is much like a model course for a subject area. It attempts to capture the best of current courses and to integrate and synthesize these best practices into an integrated whole that reflects what a course in the subject area should look like. This course is then analyzed against a set of college readiness standards to identify the content and strategies that high school students need to have mastered in order to be ready to succeed in the reference course once they reach college. In this fashion, the course signals to high school teachers and students the important learnings and skills on which to focus in order to be college and career ready.

Simultaneously, the reference course can be used in a postsecondary system to establish explicitly and with greater specificity what is actually being taught in entry-level courses. Currently a great deal is assumed about entry-level courses and what is occurring in them with scant data to confirm these assumptions. Often the title of the course alone is the only evidence of what is being taught. Understandably, courses of the same title get adapted considerably across postsecondary institutions based on the needs of students and the beliefs and interests of instructors. The net result is that just as in high schools, courses with the same title may not cover the same or similar content or have comparable challenge levels. This creates a problem when the courses are used for transfer purposes, among other things. It becomes very unclear within the postsecondary system if students at different institution types are receiving comparable educations in the foundational general education requirements. This is an important consideration if a baccalaureate is to represent a combination of common and specialized components in the form of general education courses and those in the major.

This lack of consistency is also an issue when attempting to communicate to secondary educators how they should be preparing students to be ready for college courses of a particular title. If it is not possible to make assumptions about what a student will encounter in College Composition, College Algebra, or Introduction to Biology, then any high school course is acceptable as preparation for these college courses. In the process, the opportunity to use the high school–level college preparatory course as a means to be ready for the entry-level course is largely lost. Having some clarity and a known target can help those high school educators who really want to align their courses with what their students will encounter in college and will allow them to do so knowing they are aligning with the best of college teaching, not the average or the outlier course of substandard quality.

 For more information on the methods and strategies presented in this chapter, go to http://CollegeCareerReady.org.

The reference course profile consists of a detailed syllabus in which a number of elements are explained in more detail than they would be in a typical syllabus. This facilitates greater insight into the intentions of the course and the methods used to teach the material and achieve the desired learnings. Assignments are included and explained along with grading criteria and examples of prototypical student work, where feasible. Annotations accompany the course documents where useful to help the reader understand the level of challenge in any particular activity or assignment and in the course as a whole.

This detailed exposition of intentions and actions results in a comprehensive picture of the course, how it is taught, and what students need to do to complete it successfully. This level of transparency allows faculty at postsecondary institutions to compare their expectations to the reference course and enables the high school teacher to discern the best ways to prepare students for this now-predictable challenge.

Use Better Diagnostic Information for Placement

The diagnostic information available to make decisions about incoming college students relative to course placement, skill development, and general readiness for college is extremely thin and general in nature. High school transcripts are essentially useless given the variance in the content of high school courses and the demonstrated grade inflation that has occurred over the past thirty or so years. Placement tests are not much better. They concentrate largely on high school–level material and function best to discern students who do not possess the basic skills necessary to do college-level work, but don't provide much useful information beyond that. Admissions tests are only very general yardsticks that are explicitly not designed to do more than place students on a scale relative to one another. The higher on the scale, the greater the likelihood the student is college ready, but there is no absolute line, and the tests do not provide subject-specific diagnostic information. Advanced Placement and International Baccalaureate test scores can be used for some placement decisions, but even here, colleges report considerable difficulty using the score as the sole means for waiving course requirements or accelerating a student in a course sequence.

What is needed is a much more detailed profile of a student's readiness for postsecondary studies. Such a profile takes into account all four dimensions of college readiness laid out in this book: key cognitive strategies, key content knowledge, academic behaviors, and college knowledge. The profile is developed throughout high school to help send clearer messages to students regarding their degree of college readiness and the specific actions they need to take to continue to prepare for the expectations of postsecondary education.

The first step in developing this profile is to generate more detailed information on the content students have been taught in high school. This element is achieved through a curriculum map that each high school teacher completes in which the course content is identified and the importance of each topic or element established. This makes it possible to see if certain pieces are given disproportional emphasis while others are not addressed at all. This map is compared to the college readiness standards to determine overall alignment of the high school content coverage with the college expectations.

After determining what has been covered in the course—in other words, what students have had the opportunity to learn—the next step is to gauge how well they have mastered the content they have been presented. This is somewhat more problematic, but a basic determination can be achieved through the use of rubrics specific to subject areas and to key college-ready content. The rubrics are not overly complex, indicating a holistic judgment about the overall skill level achieved in each topical area—high, medium, or low, for example. High school teachers are called on to make these general determinations regarding student mastery of all specific topics and skills in the subject area. This produces a knowledge profile consisting of what the student has an opportunity to learn cross-referenced against how well the student in fact learned what he or she is taught in each topical area. Keep in mind that this information is used for placement, not admission, decisions.

Next, student development of key cognitive strategies is assessed. As noted earlier, EPIC has developed a means to do so that generates scores on student performance on complex tasks, and other organizations, have programs underway in this area as well. The scores on the EPIC instrument indicate on a four-point scale how well a student has developed each of five key cognitive strategies: problem formulation, research, interpretation, communication, and precision and accuracy. Each score has three subcomponents. This amount of information is sufficient to make general determinations regarding the level of mastery of key cognitive strategies that the incoming student has achieved. This is added to the profile of the content mastery to paint a fuller picture of a student's readiness to undertake college-level course work at two-year and four-year institutions.

The profile also includes a breakdown of how well a student develops the important academic behaviors that support success in college studies. These include strategies discussed earlier in Chapter Three in areas such as time management; study skills; goal setting; persistence; handling new, novel, or nonroutine situations; resilience; and following directions. Many students who are otherwise well prepared academically stumble in college because they do not develop the capacity to cope with the level of independence they suddenly have and lack the necessary self-management skills. The profile helps identify potential problem areas as well as areas of strength that can be built on. Information for this component of the profile is gathered through a combination of student self-reported behaviors and teacher observations of student behaviors.

The final element of the profile captures information on the student's understanding of the context, culture, and expectations of the college environment, along with the specific knowledge about financial aid, advising, student support services, and other technical aspects. This information is gathered largely through surveys students complete each year in high school that cover the most important elements necessary to navigate the college environment.

When all of this information is combined, it yields a much broader picture of how ready for college-level work the student is. Instead of thinking in terms of assigning students to remedial or nonremedial course work as the primary means of accommodating differences in college readiness, colleges offer a range of services and course types and then work to fit students better to these options. In this model, the dichotomous light-switch notion of students being remedial or not remedial is replaced by a continuum in which students are ready in varying degrees and where essentially all students enter postsecondary education with identified areas of strength and improvement needs. The next section discusses the student support system in greater detail.

Create Integrated Student Support Programs

Most colleges have a number of programs devoted to supporting students—for example, academic advising centers or specialists, writing centers, student support groups, tutorial sessions, and various skill-building seminars. An increasing number also have specialized supports for students from groups underrepresented in college. The problem is that most students either don't access these services at all or don't do so until it is too late to be of much use. Colleges will be challenged to develop more comprehensive programs of student support that connect more directly with diagnosed student need and then expect students to use the services necessary to succeed in college.

The profile described above can be the bridging tool that helps match the student to the service but also helps the college identify the services from which its students will most benefit. The profiles, when aggregated across all incoming students, also paint a portrait of student need that clearly suggests the kinds of programmatic support that the institution needs to be offering to its students.

For example, at colleges with large populations of first-generation college attendees, the profile may reveal that these students are highly unlikely to use an academic advisor without prodding and support to do so. In such cases, mandatory visits with an advisor would be scheduled into the first semester of attendance for these students. These same students may never before have been part of a study group. Similarly, the college would make available access to study groups for these students, provide general guidance on how to participate successfully in a study group, and require students to report on their participation in such groups.

Although nearly all college students are adults legally and the goal would not be to compel behavior, the expectation that students will participate in a series of activities designed to help them succeed is not an unreasonable one, and student failure to do so could provide a reasonable starting point for charting out a program of improvement for students, many of whom are likely to end up on academic probation if they do not avail themselves of these resources. The institution at the least would be fulfilling its obligation to ensure that students accepted by the institution have some reasonable probability of succeeding if they conform to the program of readiness prescribed by the profile and supported by the institution's programs and services. Given the likely increase over the next decade in the proportion of incoming students who are not ready for college, an integrated program consisting of a profile and a set of linked institutional services that lead to an action plan for each student will be a much more necessary and valuable component of any state's overall college readiness and college success strategy.

Ensure Future Educators Have the Skills to Make All Students College Ready

Teacher education redesign has proven to be a particularly vexing problem. High school educators, when challenged on their ability to prepare students successfully for college, almost immediately and perhaps somewhat defensively raise the issue of the quality of teacher education programs. Should not colleges themselves repair or redesign their preparation programs so that the next generation of teachers is better capable of preparing students to succeed in college before college faculty criticize today's high school teachers?

The topic of comprehensive teacher education redesign is beyond the scope of this book. However, several elements can and should be changed in teacher education if tomorrow's teachers are going to be able to help more students become college ready, particularly more students from groups historically underrepresented in college.

In keeping with the four-part model of college readiness and consistent with a parallel recommendation offered earlier for secondary schools, prospective teachers need a solid grounding in the key content of the subject matter they hope to teach—knowledge sufficient not only to teach the content but to develop students' deep understanding of the subject and the cognitive strategies necessary to delve deeply into the subject. Those seeking to enter teaching must be aware of the structure of the discipline and the means by which knowledge is added to the discipline. They must grasp and be able to model the way someone who is expert in the subject area thinks and approaches key problems of the subject.

Unfortunately, much of the emphasis in teacher preservice programs and in-service training offered to practicing teachers is on instructional methods, with no reference to teacher content knowledge mastery. Such trainings either assume that teachers know the content or treat the content as a given. Conversely, when content knowledge is the focus of teacher training, the transmission of the content is often considered an end in itself rather than a means to develop deeper student understandings of the nature of knowledge within the subject area.

Teacher preparation programs face a particular challenge in this regard because the students in those programs receive their content knowledge entirely separately from their education program. Few colleges or universities have well-developed connections between their arts and science schools and their education programs. In many cases, the solution is to offer a version of the content in a course geared specifically toward future educators ("Math for Teachers," "Biology for Teachers"). This practice can result in education students having the least well-developed understanding of a subject area of all students who take the subject. This is certainly not the way to build a teaching cadre prepared to engage students substantively in the fundamental issues of a subject area. If such a course has to be offered, its content should emphasize an understanding of the structure of the subject area, the ways of knowing associated with it, some of the enduring understandings and current controversies in the subject area, and the ways in which experts in the subject area think about the subject and how they add knowledge to the subject. A focus on learning to think like an expert in an area is superior to a watered-down coverage of content topics in survey courses.

This is not to downplay the importance of new teachers being able to employ a range of instructional strategies. Most important for the purpose of college readiness is the ability to develop in students the key cognitive strategies central to college success. Many prospective teachers have some insight into these, having only recently completed their own college education in which they experienced first-hand the expectations of college faculty that they think and reason at high levels of complexity. The preparation program needs to help them make explicit what may be implicit knowledge for them: how to develop in others the habits of thinking and metacognition that they themselves were expected to develop in their own undergraduate programs of study. This involves the ability to construct and implement more complex lessons and assignments, score student work against a set of high external standards, provide feedback to help students revise and resubmit work when need be, use an overall framework such as the key cognitive strategies or other similar model to explain to students the skills they are to develop, and be willing to adapt their instruction to help those who need additional scaffolding to meet the high standards without simply lowering the standard.

Through all of this, these potential future educators should be learning how to weave into their courses expectations that students develop the academic behaviors so important to a successful transition to college. Their courses should expect students to manage time well, keep track of assignments, develop a variety of study skills, set goals, work on complex assignments that require use of all of the aforementioned skills, and persist with challenging tasks. If prospective teachers know how to help students develop these skills, they will be more likely to identify them explicitly as course expectations, which will cause students to place a greater premium on developing and utilizing these skills in a more deliberate fashion.

As noted at several points throughout this book, the U.S. educational system was not set up to make it easy for students to make the transition from high school to college. To the contrary, almost everything about the design of secondary and postsecondary education makes it difficult for students to prepare properly and then move successfully from one learning environment to the other. So much of what must be known to succeed in college is in the form of privileged information that is available to some groups in society much more than to others.

Prospective teachers need to be aware of their potential role as transmitters of this privileged knowledge. What do these future teachers know beyond their own experiences about how to select a college, how to apply and seek financial aid, how to choose a major, and how to interact with college faculty? Being aware that they can be important resources to students can help them think about ways in which to integrate into assignments and class activities the knowledge students need to be prepared to apply to college and make a successful transition.

Many more skills could be listed, but those I have described illustrate the scope of the challenge to get more teachers to a point where they are prepared to help students develop the key knowledge and skills necessary to help more students be college ready. To be fully competent in these areas will require preparation programs that entail longer apprenticeships and more gradual, managed transitions from the college classroom to the school classroom. New teachers need to be sufficiently confident in teaching key cognitive strategies so that they do not abandon the more sophisticated teaching necessary to make students think deeply in favor of simple, manageable tasks and activities such as completing worksheets that may address classroom management issues but are unlikely to be of much use preparing students to go on to postsecondary education.

States can foster this type of program redesign by laying out a set of standards and requirements for the teaching skills that new teachers must demonstrate to be awarded a certificate or license along with the content knowledge they must possess. These types of determinations cannot be made using standardized tests. They depend on faculty in the area of teacher preparation understanding and buying into these important skills areas and then documenting student capabilities (Do they possess sufficient content knowledge? Will they be capable of developing key cognitive strategies in all students?). When prospective teachers fall short in these areas, the preparation program needs to be designed to provide some sort of support to teachers in training who are not yet ready to assume the mantle of practicing teacher and the responsibility to prepare all students to be college ready.

One key strategy that states can encourage is closer partnerships between teacher preparation programs and secondary schools, relationships that go deeper than the schools' hosting student teachers. No one has all the answers for how best to prepare teachers to enable more students to be college ready. High school educators and teacher educators will need to work in partnership to develop new models that ensure mastery of content knowledge and the ability to develop key cognitive strategies in all students. These new models can then inform high school and teacher education redesign simultaneously. Neither group has all the answers, and each needs the other in order to address this challenge.

CONCLUDING OBSERVATIONS

This book has covered a large amount of the landscape on the topic of college and career readiness, but it is nevertheless striking how much more remains to be addressed that was not covered here. For example, statewide data systems must be aligned so that more and better information can flow between secondary and postsecondary systems more seamlessly. The entire issue of technology must be addressed, and with it, the growing gap between the ever-increasing expectations for technological proficiency that postsecondary institutions hold and the vast investment in advanced technologies these institutions have made compared to the rather modest technological expectations and investments present in high schools. The entire issue of parental involvement and participation has barely been touched on here, although in some communities this will be the key to making significant gains in the number of students going on to college and careers. Student motivation is often brought up as a critical factor as well, getting more young people to come to grips with the need to dedicate themselves and focus their energy on challenging tasks in order to be ready for their own futures. New modes of educational delivery, such as online learning and proficiency-based models, may have significant impact on how we prepare students for college and how we judge them ready. All of this is likely to lead to changes in admissions standards, criteria, and processes. Financial aid becomes the single largest issue for many potential first-generation college attendees, and it must be addressed in any attempt to increase the proportion of students going on to college.

I did not omit these topics because they are not important but because I wanted to maintain a focus on dimensions where educators and policymakers can do something about them today, and where they can do a great deal with available resources. A range of new programs will undoubtedly need to be undertaken and new investments made. However, we should not wait until this occurs or take lack of solutions in all necessary areas as a rationale for inaction. My approach in this book has been to suggest actionable steps that can be taken by secondary school teachers and administrators, their postsecondary colleagues, and local and state education policymakers. I want to convey a certain sense of urgency to begin to move forward rapidly on multiple fronts at all levels of education to transform the system into one that is better aligned and more explicitly designed to get many more students to choose to continue their education on to the postsecondary level.

The entire notion of college readiness is evolving at a rapid pace, and its importance as a policy issue increases daily. Efforts by the National Governors Association and the Council of Chief State School Officers to develop common core academic content standards for voluntary adoption by states, in combination with the work of two consortia of states to develop a new generation of assessments designed to capture broader and deeper information on student performance, are motivated in large measure by the goal of transforming the U.S. education system so that it becomes more effective at preparing all students to continue learning beyond high school.

Little doubt remains that secondary education will need to become more focused on equipping a much wider range of students with the knowledge, skills, and abilities to continue learning in formal settings beyond high school. Educators and administrators in secondary schools will be able to draw on updated resources, techniques, and strategies that will help them respond to the challenge. Change will be difficult, but the new American high school will be a dramatically different place that connects much more closely with postsecondary education, a place where essentially all students are taking the necessary steps to be college and career ready.

Afterword

I began this book with an anecdote about my bumpy journey to college and career readiness. I'll close it with another anecdote, this one dramatically different. It's about an individual who was able to do all the right things to be ready for college and career and the forces that had to come together for this to happen. I ask you to draw your own conclusions about how well the system works to enable all students to be ready to pursue the most appropriate postsecondary option available to them.

Genevieve attracted attention as early as first grade. Her verbal abilities made her stand out in class, along with her strong personality, which resulted in teachers' noticing her and paying more attention to her. She did well in primary school, but her parents recognized that the school she was attending was not the best match with her capabilities or personality. They were able to arrange for her to attend another school in this open enrollment district and transport her there every day.

Genevieve was fortunate that this school allowed students to move at their own pace. When she told one of her teachers, "I'm bored," during a math lesson, he recognized that she was not simply being obstinate; rather, she belonged in a more challenging math class, and he was able to move her into such a class. She studied higher-level mathematics in fourth and fifth grades while doing well academically in all other areas. Her verbal abilities and forceful personality were valued here, instead of getting her in trouble, as could easily have been the case in other educational settings.

Near the end of fifth grade, she and her classmates were asked to take a math test. They were not given any explanation of the purpose of the test, only that they could go to recess as soon as they were done. Being a very quick test taker, Genevieve completed the test in record time and headed out to recess, blissfully unaware that the test was going to be used to place her into her sixth-grade mathematics class at the middle school she was slated to attend.

Her score on the test was not stellar, given the conditions of administration. As a result, she was placed in a lower-level mathematic course despite the fact that she had been studying advanced mathematics for two years. Luckily for Genevieve, she had parents who acted on this apparent discrepancy and uncovered the cause of her misplacement. They prevailed on the school to retest her, which resulted in her being moved into the higher-level math class. This change enabled her to be on a track to complete the full range of high school math courses, something she would not have been able to do with her original placement.

During seventh grade, her mother happened to hear about a program called Talent Search while volunteering at the high school that Genevieve's older sisters attended. Sponsored by Johns Hopkins University, the program seeks to identify academically gifted students early based on their SAT scores. Genevieve took the SAT as a seventh grader and did well enough to be identified by Talent Search as academically gifted. This resulted in her name being distributed to a number of mailing lists that leading colleges and universities used to identify potential students. From eighth grade on, she received literature from some of the nation's top universities encouraging her to consider their programs. This attention helped shape her opinion of what was possible for her to achieve if she worked hard, took on academic challenges, and pushed herself. The recognition seemed to give her additional motivation to make the effort necessary to be as ready as possible for college.

In high school, Genevieve took all the right courses, the most challenging ones possible, and benefited from her school's International Baccalaureate program and extensive offering of Advanced Placement courses. She was fortunate to have science and math teachers with master's degrees from prestigious institutions and a love of their subject areas, which helped to inspire her to go deeper in these areas. It didn't hurt that her mother volunteered at the high school in the career center, which provided assistance to students applying to college.

Genevieve made campus visits to many colleges and universities beginning in her sophomore year in high school and attended summer enrichment programs on college campuses. By her junior year, she was very familiar with and comfortable on college campuses. During her senior year, she took two college-level math courses at the university down the street from her high school.

When it came time to apply to college, Genevieve had the help of key adults, including her mother, which enabled her to manage the complexity of applying to a wide range of postsecondary institutions. And although she wrote all her application essays herself and otherwise held up her end of the bargain, the adults in her life solved the many technical and logistical issues so that she could stay focused on her school work and the parts of the application process that were most important.

In the end, Genevieve applied to and was accepted by seven of the top postsecondary programs in the nation. Her strong math and science background gave her a shot at institutions such as the Massachusetts Institute of Technology (MIT). Her personal essay focused on imagination and the role of imagination in learning. She found out after the fact that MIT was looking for students with imagination as a key attribute for that year's entering class. Genevieve had happened to hit on exactly the characteristic that MIT was most interested in cultivating in its students at that time. The stars had aligned. MIT accepted her, and she chose to attend there.

Clearly this is a success story about a student whose ability was recognized and developed by the system. But it's also a commentary on how many things have to go right for even the most talented students to have a shot at institutions where admissions is as much art as science. Consider the number of places where a wrong decision, a poor teacher, a lack of opportunity or support would have made a critical difference in the future of this child. Quality schools, numerous opportunities, parental support, and the ability to avoid key errors and pitfalls all factored into the winning equation.

Although a misstep for Genevieve might have meant only that she attended a different college rather than not attending at all, it's still worth considering what happens to the average student who has none of the advantages or supports that Genevieve had. What happens to students who are verbal and easily bored in class if they are not challenged? Who lack parental support? Who can't match up with a school best suited to their needs? Who have never set foot on a college campus? Who can't get any real indication of how ready they are for college or how they stack up against genuine college readiness indicators? Who can't or won't take the time to complete college applications and struggle to write a cogent essay about themselves and their interests?

Solid evidence is emerging to suggest that many students who graduate with college prep courses and good grades on their transcripts fail to apply to a college that offers the most challenging option available to them. Even the most successful students from low-income high schools systematically underestimate their ability to do postsecondary work and choose institutions at a level below those for which they are eligible to apply. This is a fundamental waste of intellectual capital. Ironically, students who underchallenge themselves with their college choice are less likely to complete college successfully than their peers who do go to the school that offer them the greatest challenge.

How can we level the playing field so that all students truly have the opportunity to be ready to continue learning beyond high school in some sort of educational setting? This challenging goal can be attained only if we commit ourselves fully to creating secondary school environments that are carefully, consciously, and conscientiously designed to align with postsecondary readiness, where students can't make bad decisions, where they are not as dependent on activist parents or specialized opportunities.

I noted in the Preface that Clark Kerr was responsible for California's Master Plan for postsecondary education, which enabled me to get an opportunity to reach my potential. We need to think about something similar now, but this time aimed at the alignment between high school and college—a new plan for rationalizing, simplifying, and making explicit what it is that students need to do to be ready for college and careers, how secondary schools need to be organized to make this happen, and the role that postsecondary institutions need to fulfill to support this goal.

This book provides some guidance and suggestions to schools willing to take the steps necessary to improve the likelihood that all students will have available to them the choice of pursuing a postsecondary education. States, national organizations, and the federal government seem ready to make a real commitment to college and career readiness. Are schools ready to respond?

Appendix A
Two Examples of Tasks That Develop and Assess Key Cognitive Strategies

The two tasks presented in this appendix are drawn from the College-readiness Performance Assessment System (C-PAS), an innovative formative assessment designed to track the development of the Key Cognitive Strategies (KCS), which are thinking skills necessary for college readiness and success. C-PAS is designed to measure the KCS through rich performance tasks that teachers embed within existing curricula and that align with curricular requirements. It is a powerful tool to help guide and inform a school's efforts to prepare every student for post-secondary success. The information generated from C-PAS measures student development of the KCS over time in grades 6–12. This system is designed to help all students, regardless of current academic skill level, develop the thinking skills necessary for future success. The key cognitive strategies are one of the four dimensions of the college readiness model presented in Chapter One (see Figure A.1).

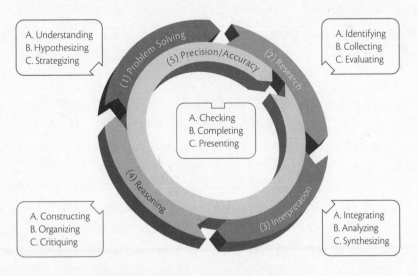

A. Understanding
B. Hypothesizing
C. Strategizing

A. Identifying
B. Collecting
C. Evaluating

(1) Problem Solving
(5) Precision/Accuracy
(2) Research

A. Checking
B. Completing
C. Presenting

(4) Reasoning
(3) Interpretation

A. Constructing
B. Organizing
C. Critiquing

A. Integrating
B. Analyzing
C. Synthesizing

FIGURE A.1 KEY COGNITIVE STRATEGIES MODEL

For more information on the methods and strategies presented in this chapter, go to http://CollegeCareerReady.org.

SAMPLE MATH TASK

OVERVIEW FOR TEACHERS

Description: Students explore income distribution using the Gini coefficient, a measure of inequality that economists and social scientists often use to quantify income and wealth inequality. Students choose two countries, research data on income distribution for the countries, and represent the data graphically and by calculating the Gini coefficient. Students use their analysis to make and support an argument about the relative changes in inequality in the two countries over a period of time.

Final product: A report on the relative changes in inequality in two countries.

Task level: Algebra II

Prior content knowledge: Students should have command of area formulas and know how to compute areas using decomposition or complements. They should be able to use percentages, graphing, and ratios in problem-solving situations.

Preparation

- Read the teacher task information and student task information.

- Make a copy of the Student Task Information and the worksheets for each student. You may decide to distribute all pages at the start of students' work, or provide pages individually as students work through the parts of the task.

- Arrange student access to graph paper, calculators, and a spreadsheet program as tools for creating graphs and determining areas.

- Arrange student access to the Internet to carry out research using the World Income Inequality Database from UNU-WIDER United Nations University World Institute for Development Economics Research, http://www.wider.unu .edu. Alternately, download the database (Excel file) and make the file available to students.

- Become familiar with the UNU-WIDER database. On the home page, choose the Research tab. In the left sidebar, choose Database, and download the database file.

- The database presents decile data directly as income shares. In the problem-solving part of the task, students will do percentage computations with simple distributions in order to understand the decile data.

- Note that the database also includes calculated Gini coefficients, which you can use to quickly identify substantial errors made by students.

- Some of the data in the UNU-WIDER database are more reliable than others for the purposes of social scientists (as described in the "quality" column in the database). This is good to know but should not be significant for the analysis students will do in this project.

Vocabulary

- decile
- economics
- Gini coefficient
- Lorenz curve
- ratio

Time frame: Plan about two weeks for students to solve the problem, write their first draft, and finish their final draft. Schedule class days to complete the research if students do not have access to the Internet out of school. Most of the remainder of the task is generally completed out of class.

Task modifications: If a modification is made to any part of the task, the modification must be requested using the C-PAS online system.

NOTES

Work products listed in the student task information are required and may not be modified. See the student task information for the complete assignment.

Problem Solving

Understanding

- With the class, read the introduction in the student task information.

- Have students work in pairs on the situations given in the Introductory Exercises worksheet. The situations employ artificially simple income distributions for the purpose of familiarizing students with the concepts of equality and inequality, plotting income distributions, and calculating the Gini coefficient. Provide access to graph paper, calculators, and a spreadsheet program as optional tools for determining area.

- As students work, engage the class in discussion of specific strategies and general considerations in finding areas required to compute the Gini coefficient. Some simpler strategies you provide instruction on are:

  - Cutting the shape up into several pieces, each of which has an easier area to compute.

  - Imagining the shape as a difference of two easier shapes and subtracting.

  - Putting the shape on graph paper and approximating its area by counting squares.

  - Students who will be approaching the calculus topic of Riemann sums in the near future can be pointed toward the use of trapezoids in particular.

Hypothesizing

Notice students who are comfortable speculating about income distribution and how it may have changed over time in the countries they choose. To prompt students who are hesitant, you might say, "Record whatever thoughts you have. It will be interesting to see what you think after you've collected data on the countries."

Some students may already realize that their strategies for finding areas are approximations; therefore their calculations will be approximations.

Research
Collecting

In the UNU-WIDER database, students may not find the data they are hoping to find. Prompt them to choose other countries to investigate.

Interpretation
Integrating

- If students have access to computers, they can create their graphs of Lorenz curves using Excel. Distribute the How to Make an Excel Graph of a Lorenz Curve worksheet.

Analyzing

Suggested scaffolding prompts to use as students analyze the data are:

- Does a higher Gini coefficient mean a country has more or less inequality?
- What can you say about how the Gini coefficient is different from the earlier year to the later year?

Reasoning

Constructing

Suggested scaffolding prompts to use as students draft their reports are:

- Were your speculations at the start supported by your research and analysis?
- Why do you think your findings are the way they are?
- Why might the income equality in [country] have improved?
- How is the income inequality different in your two countries?
- Are there problems or issues with the data? Are there aspects of your reasoning where you feel support is lacking? Are there aspects where more information would be useful?
- Are there potential problems with your methods of analysis and calculation?

Precision/Accuracy

Checking, Completing, and Presenting

Final drafts are due. In a single packet for scoring, students turn in all work products listed on the assessment checklist.

EXTENSIONS

There are many directions students might go once they have completed this task. They might pool their data to try to draw more general conclusions. They might also explore deeper questions such as the following, some of which are more mathematical than others. (Some are significant social science questions that are still the topic of active academic research.)

- What happens to the Gini coefficient when all incomes double?
- What happens to the Gini coefficient when two countries unify?

- Would your results be the same if you used only five income bands? Only three? If you used twenty? Or one hundred? Or if each person was split out?

- What are the good and bad features of the Gini coefficient as a measure?

- Are there other measures of inequality you could devise? When is each measure better, more appropriate, or more informative?

- What if incomes are redistributed? What schemes could reduce inequality and still get the support of most of the population? Are these fair?

- Is income growth related to income inequality? How?

- Which is more important, the average income or the inequality of income?

- What income distribution is "right"? (Note that incomes differ for many reasons, including age, education, cost of living, and effort, as well as race, wealth, and historical patterns of advantage or disadvantage.)

SOLUTIONS

Introductory Exercises

Introductory Exercise 1
Perfect Equality
Gini coefficient 0

Decile	Share	Cumulative	Uniform
0	0	0	0
1	10	10	10
2	10	20	20
3	10	30	30
4	10	40	40
5	10	50	50
6	10	60	60
7	10	70	70
8	10	80	80
9	10	90	90
10	10	100	100

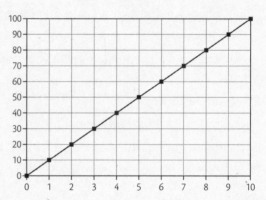

Gini coefficient:

Area between the cumulative distribution and uniform

over

Area between the cumulative distribution and zero

Trapezoid areas (under Lorentz curve)

From 0 to 1	5
From 1 to 2	15
From 2 to 3	25
From 3 to 4	35
From 4 to 5	45
From 5 to 6	55
From 6 to 7	65
From 7 to 8	75
From 8 to 9	85
From 9 to 10	95

Gini coefficient
0

Top-Bottom Decile Ratio
1.0

Introductory Exercise 2
(Near)-Perfect Inequality
Gini coefficient about 1 (0.9 due to deciles)

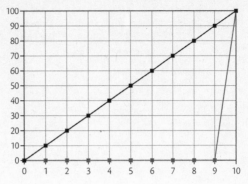

Decile	Share	Cumulative	Uniform
0	0	0	0
1	0	0	10
2	0	0	20
3	0	0	30
4	0	0	40
5	0	0	50
6	0	0	60
7	0	0	70
8	0	0	80
9	0	0	90
10	100	100	100

Gini coefficient:

Area between the cumulative distribution and uniform

over

Area between the cumulative distribution and zero

Trapezoid areas (under Lorentz curve)

From 0 to 1	0
From 1 to 2	0
From 2 to 3	0
From 3 to 4	0
From 4 to 5	0
From 5 to 6	0
From 6 to 7	0
From 7 to 8	0
From 8 to 9	0
From 9 to 10	50

Gini coefficient
0.9

Top-Bottom Decile Ratio
#DIV/0!

Introductory Exercise 3
Some Inequality
Gini coefficient 0.3

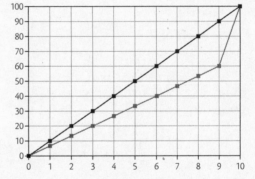

Decile	Share	Cumulative	Uniform
0	0	0	0
1	6.66666667	6.66666667	10
2	6.66666667	13.3333333	20
3	6.66666667	20	30
4	6.66666667	26.6666667	40
5	6.66666667	33.3333333	50
6	6.66666667	40	60
7	6.66666667	46.6666667	70
8	6.66666667	53.3333333	80
9	6.66666667	60	90
10	40	100	100

Gini coefficient:

Area between the cumulative distribution and uniform

over

Area between the cumulative distribution and zero

Trapezoid areas (under Lorentz curve)

From 0 to 1	3.33333333
From 1 to 2	10
From 2 to 3	16.6666667
From 3 to 4	23.3333333
From 4 to 5	30
From 5 to 6	36.6666667
From 6 to 7	43.3333333
From 7 to 8	50
From 8 to 9	56.6666667
From 9 to 10	80

Gini coefficient
0.3

Top-Bottom Decile Ratio
6.0

Introductory Exercise 4
Greater Inequality
Gini coefficient 0.5
Other nine persons' income is 200/9~22.2

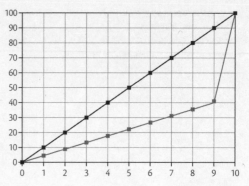

Decile	Share	Cumulative	Uniform
0	0	0	0
1	4.44444444	4.44444444	10
2	4.44444444	8.88888888	20
3	4.44444444	13.3333333	30
4	4.44444444	17.7777778	40
5	4.44444444	22.2222222	50
6	4.44444444	26.6666667	60
7	4.44444444	31.1111111	70
8	4.44444444	35.5555556	80
9	4.44444444	40	90
10	60	100	100

Gini coefficient:
Area between the cumulative distribution and uniform
over
Area between the cumulative distribution and zero

Trapezoid areas (under Lorentz curve)

From 0 to 1	2.22222222	
From 1 to 2	6.66666667	**Gini coefficient**
From 2 to 3	11.1111111	0.5
From 3 to 4	15.5555556	
From 4 to 5	20	**Top-Bottom Decile Ratio**
From 5 to 6	24.4444444	13.5
From 6 to 7	28.8888889	
From 7 to 8	33.3333333	
From 8 to 9	37.7777778	
From 9 to 10	70	

Introductory Exercise 5
Relatively low inequality (top:bottom ~ 2:1)
Gini coefficient 0.132

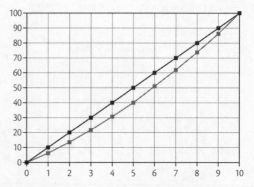

Decile	Share	Cumulative	Uniform
0	0	0	0
1	6.4	6.4	10
2	7.2	13.6	20
3	8	21.6	30
4	8.8	30.4	40
5	9.6	40	50
6	10.4	50.4	60
7	11.2	61.6	70
8	12	73.6	80
9	12.8	86.4	90
10	13.6	100	100

Gini coefficient:
Area between the cumulative distribution and uniform
over
Area between the cumulative distribution and zero

Trapezoid areas (under Lorentz curve)

From 0 to 1	3.2	
From 1 to 2	10	**Gini coefficient**
From 2 to 3	17.6	0.132
From 3 to 4	26	
From 4 to 5	35.2	**Top-Bottom Decile Ratio**
From 5 to 6	45.2	2.1
From 6 to 7	56	
From 7 to 8	67.6	
From 8 to 9	80	
From 9 to 10	93.2	

Sample of Student's Data for One Country at One Time

Sample: United States, 2000
Luxembourg Income Study
March Current Population Survey
from World Income Inequality Database, Revision 2

Decile	Share	Cumulative	Uniform
0	0	0	0
1	1.791	1.791	10
2	3.528	5.319	20
3	4.732	10.051	30
4	5.923	15.974	40
5	7.173	23.147	50
6	8.495	31.642	60
7	10.122	41.764	70
8	12.32	54.084	80
9	15.996	70.08	90
10	29.919	99.999	100

Gini coefficient:
Area between the cumulative distribution and uniform
over
Area between the cumulative distribution and zero

Trapezoid areas (under Lorentz curve)

From 0 to 1	0.8955
From 1 to 2	3.555
From 2 to 3	7.685
From 3 to 4	13.0125
From 4 to 5	19.5605
From 5 to 6	27.3945
From 6 to 7	36.703
From 7 to 8	47.924
From 8 to 9	62.082
From 9 to 10	85.0395

Gini coefficient
0.392297

Top-Bottom Decile Ratio
16.7

Reports

Data students collect will vary.

OVERVIEW FOR STUDENTS

He declared he had kept nothing from the Men, and Share and Share alike with them in every Bit.

BY DANIEL DEFOE, *ROBINSON CRUSOE*

Description: Do modern societies share and share alike? Or is it true that the rich get richer and the poor get poorer? Is the distribution of income different in different countries? Does the distribution change over time? How can the tools of mathematics be used to analyze the equality—or inequality—of distributions of income?

Final product: A report about the relative changes in inequality in two countries over a period of time.

Key cognitive strategies: You will use the following key cognitive strategies as you work. Each key cognitive strategy includes three aspects, described here.

Problem Solving

- Understanding what is being asked
- Hypothesizing about potential answers
- Strategizing about how to address the problem or question

Research

- Identifying what information is needed
- Collecting the information
- Evaluating the quality of the information

Interpretation

- Integrating sources or data and information to prepare for analysis
- Analyzing data or information for patterns or main points
- Synthesizing by making connections and drawing conclusions

Reasoning

- Constructing an argument or proof and supporting it with evidence
- Organizing the argument in a way that makes sense
- Critiquing the argument to improve it

Precision/Accuracy

- Checking work for errors
- Completing all assigned parts of the task
- Presenting information using precise terms and correct layout

The problem: Is the distribution of income different in different countries? Does the distribution change over time? How can the tools of mathematics be used to analyze the equality—or inequality—of distributions of income?

Using data from the United Nations, you will analyze the distributions of income in two countries you choose. You'll start with familiar tools of statistics, graphing, and area, and then use a new tool called the Gini coefficient.

You will make and support an argument about the changes in income inequality in two different countries.

Final product: A report about income inequality in the two countries you research. You will write two drafts and include:

- Your initial thoughts about the income distribution in the two countries

- A record of your research, including data collected from two countries at two points in time and your evaluation of the data

- A table and graph of your data and calculations for each country

- Your interpretation of the data and calculations

- A well-reasoned and supported argument about inequality in the countries you researched and how it changed (or didn't) over time

Directions: Complete the work products assigned. Keep all of your work in a folder that you will hand in with your final product.

Part 1: Problem Solving

In this part of the task, you will think about the problem that has been posed and how you might approach it.

Understanding

Work products: Introductory Exercises worksheet

- Lorenz curves worksheet

- Gini Coefficient worksheet

Suppose we are examining the distribution of income in a village of 10 people. There are some basic steps that will help us analyze the distribution and draw conclusions. Use these steps as reference as you work on the five situations on the Introductory Exercises worksheet.

- Find the total income.

- List all 10 incomes shares in order from least to greatest.

- Express each income share as a percentage of the total.

- Find the cumulative share of income up to and including each person.

- Graph these cumulative income shares against the number of people. Let x equal the cumulative percentage of the population, and y equal the cumulative percentage of income.

- The graphs you made in the exercises are called Lorenz curves. They are one measure of inequality used by economists and others. Complete the Lorenz Curves worksheet (2 pages) to learn more about this mathematical tool.

- The *Gini coefficient* is a way to measure income inequality by turning the Lorenz curve into a number. Work through the steps on the *Gini Coefficient* worksheet to learn about this mathematical tool.

- In your own words, answer these questions:

  - In this task, what are you trying to find out?

  - What is income inequality?

  - How will you see differences among the countries and times you select?

Hypothesizing

Work product: Written description of first ideas

Independent work: Select two countries to study. Explain why you chose these countries. Include any thoughts or best guesses about what you will find out about income inequality in these countries. Justify your response using any knowledge you have of world events and economics.

- Will your results be exact or approximate? Why do you think so?

Strategizing

Work product: Written explanation of planning

Independent work: What steps, in what order, will you carry out to explore this problem?

- Explain in your own words the strategies you will use to collect and analyze your data.

- How could technology help you solve this problem?

Part 2: Research

In this part of the task, you will conduct research to collect data.

Identifying

Work product: Written description of information needed

Independent work: Explain what information you need to answer the questions about these countries.

Collecting

Work products: Collected data and description of procedure used

- To retrieve the decile income data you need, go to the UNU-WIDER database (http://www.wider.unu.edu) and choose the Research tab; then click on Database in the left sidebar. If the specific data you want are not there, find related data (in that database or elsewhere) that are consistent with your initial choices.

Independent work: Describe your data collection procedure so that someone else could follow it exactly. Make sure to cite your source.

Evaluating

Work product: Written evaluation of your data collection

Independent work: How do you know you have collected data relevant to the question you are answering?

- Do you have any concerns about the credibility of your source or the validity of the data? Explain why or why not.

- Did you encounter any problems collecting your data? How are you sure you followed the right data collection procedure to get the data you need?

Part 3: Interpretation

In this part of the task, you will interpret the data you have collected.

Integrating

Work product: Graphs of data

Independent work: After you have collected and organized your data, construct the Lorenz curves for each country and time (a total of four graphs).

Analyzing

Work product: Written analysis based on graphs and calculations

Independent work: Calculate the Gini coefficient for each country and time.

- What do you notice about the income inequality? Do you see any patterns or trends?

Synthesizing

Work product: Written conclusions

Independent work: What are your overall conclusions about the data you collected? What do they tell you about the countries you researched?

 ### Part 4: Reasoning

In this part of the task, you will write your report, clearly communicating the reasoning that supports your findings and conclusions.

Constructing

Work product: Rough draft of report

Independent work: Use the results of your research and analysis to write a thesis statement about the income inequality in the two countries and two times you selected.

- Using your research and analysis, briefly explain and support your thesis. Clearly connect the results of your analysis to your thesis.

- Be sure to explain the tools you used. Someone who has not worked with these tools should be able to understand you.

- Discuss potential weaknesses with your thesis, areas where you feel support is lacking, and areas where more information would be useful.

- Discuss (describe and respond to or defend against) a conflicting point of view or thesis using your research and analysis. Could someone else interpret your data differently?

Organizing

Work product: Rough draft report

Independent work: Label your sections.

- Organize your report in a logical order.
- Use tables and graphs in a way that enhances understanding of your work.
- Identify your final conclusions clearly.

Critiquing

Work product: Rough and final drafts report

- Give your report to a peer or your teacher who will review it and return it to you.

Independent Work: Write your final draft, revising your rough draft using the feedback you have received and your own evaluation.

 ## Part 5: Precision/Accuracy

In this part, you will check your work for errors and make sure you are presenting your work appropriately.

Checking, Completing, Presenting

Work product: Final draft or report

Checking

- Are your calculations correct? How did you check for errors?
- If you used rounding, did you round correctly?

Completing

- Did you show all of your calculations?
- Did you complete all work products in the Assessment Checklist?
- Did you thoroughly edit your work?
- Did you include all needed information?

Presenting

- Are tables or graphs that you included clearly labeled?
- Is your work clear and legible?
- Did you include all necessary units?
- If you used variables or formulas, did you define them?

Assessment Checklist

A completed task includes all of the work products shown below.

KCS	Aspect	Work Product	Due	Complete
	Understanding	Completed Introductory Exercises Worksheet		
	Hypothesizing	Written description of first ideas		
	Strategizing	Written explanation of planning		
	Identifying	Written description of information needed		
	Collecting	Collected data and description of procedure used		
	Evaluating	Written evaluation of your data collection		
	Integrating	Graphs of data		
	Analyzing	Written analysis based on graphs and calculations		
	Synthesizing	Written conclusions		
	Critiquing	Rough draft report		

	Constructing Organizing Critiquing	Final draft report		
	Checking Completing Presenting	Final draft report		

WORKSHEETS

Introductory Exercises

For each situation below, follow the basic steps given previously and then answer the questions. Record your work for each situation on a separate sheet.

Situation 1: Every person earns $50,000.

- What is the average income?

- What does the graph look like?

This is an example of *perfect income equality*.

Situation 2: One person earns $500,000 and the other nine earn nothing.

- What is the average income?

- What does the graph look like?

This is an example of near-perfect income inequality.

Situation 3: Every person earns $50,000, and then one person gets a raise to $300,000.

- What is the new average income?

- How many people actually benefited from this change?

- What does the graph look like?

- Where is it relative to the first and second graphs?

Situation 4: The one person's raise to $300,000 came out of the others' incomes, so that the average income remains $50,000.

- What is the new income of the other nine people?

- What does the graph look like?

- Where is it relative to the first and second graphs?

Situation 5: The ten incomes are (in thousands) 32, 36, 40, 44, 48, 52, 56, 60, 64, and 68.

- What is the average income?

- How does the highest earner's income compare to the lowest earner's income?

- What does the graph look like?

- Where is it relative to the first and second graphs?

Lorenz Curves

You used Lorenz curves to represent the distribution of income in the introductory exercises. Lorenz curves are a way to visualize the distribution of income. You can use this tool to see the distribution of income in an entire country by lumping people into 10 income groups, or *deciles,* and making the same calculations and graphs.

Did you notice that the Lorenz curve is always *between the graphs* in situations 1 and 2: the straight diagonal line for perfect equality and the kinked graph for perfect inequality? Which of these graphs represents the society that is the most unequal? Which represents the society that is most equal? How do you know?

Notice how each part of the graph of the following Lorenz curve is labeled.

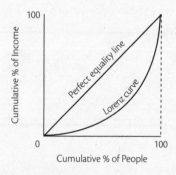

Label the parts of the following graph.

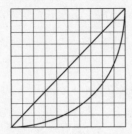

Gini Coefficient

Complete the steps below. Use the graph you labeled on the Lorenz Curves worksheet.

1. Find the area between the perfect equality line and the *x*-axis. Explain the strategy you used to find the area.

2. Approximate the area between the Lorenz curve and the perfect equality line. Be as accurate as possible. Explain the strategy you used to find the area.

3. Divide the area between the Lorenz curve and the perfect equality line by the area between the perfect equality line and the *x*-axis. Round the answer to the nearest hundredth.

This value is called the Gini coefficient. As you have seen, the Gini coefficient is a way to measure income inequality by turning the Lorenz curve into a number.

The Gini coefficient is calculated as a ratio:

$$\frac{\text{Area between the Lorenz curve and the curve for perfect equality}}{\text{Area between the curve for perfect equality and zero (horizontal axis).}}$$

How to Create an Excel Graph of a Lorenz Curve

1. Label column A "Perfect Equality Line." Label column B "Lorenz Curve." The data in column A are always 0, 10, 20, 30, . . . , 100. The data in column B are the cumulative percent of income.

◇	A	B	C
1	Perfect Equality Line	Lorenz Curve	
2	0	0	
3	10	1	
4	20	3	
5	30	6	
6	40	10	
7	50	15	
8	60	22	
9	70	30	
10	80	40	
11	90	60	
12	100	100	
13			
14			
15			

2. Highlight all your data, and then click on the Chart Wizard icon.

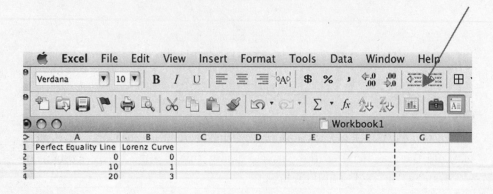

3. For Chart type, select Line. For Chart subtype, select Line with markers displayed at each data point.

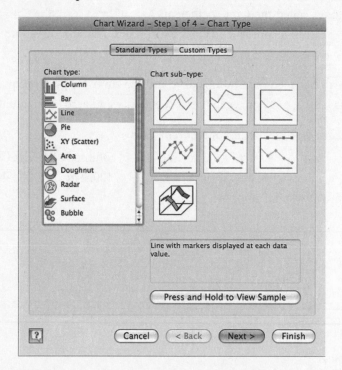

4. Click Next. In the window that appears, click Series at the top.

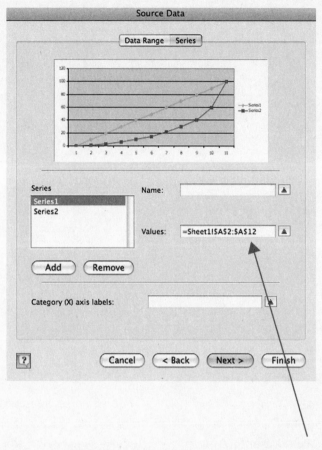

5. Now change the *x*-axis labels. Start by clicking in the Values field.

6. Next, in your data, highlight cells A2-A12. The cells should now have a moving dotted line around them.

7. Return to the chart wizard by clicking the small rectangle shown below.

8. Click Next. In the window that appears, enter labels for your graph as shown in this example.

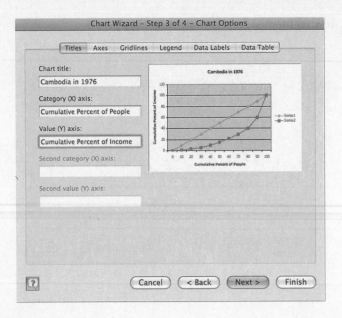

9. Click Finish.

10. You can now copy and paste this graph into your Word document.

SAMPLE ENGLISH TASK

OVERVIEW FOR TEACHERS

Description: Students work from a black-and-white photograph to compose a narrative poem. This task has its origin in the photo poetry of James Masao. Masao mastered the art of transferring visual images into the written word in his photo poems. In "From a Factory Window 1912," Masao describes a young girl at work, on a Sunday, at a weaving loom. Inside the dusty window, a spider captures a fly in its web. Outside the tall windows, two men play a game of Sunday golf.

Final product: Students compose a narrative poem, 10 to 14 lines in length.

Task level: Grade 7

Prior Content Knowledge

- Students should have experience writing short, narrative descriptions; reading for comprehension at the literal and interpretive levels; generating literal and interpretive questions; and creating literary devices such as similes and metaphors.

- To preassess students' readiness for this assessment, you might distribute copies of a narrative, free verse poem that is a favorite of yours. Ask students to highlight the lines they like best. Facilitate a discussion in which students share why they like the lines. Have students discuss the attributes of the poem and how to recognize free verse.

Preparation

- Read the teacher task information and student task information.

- Make a copy of the Student Task Information for each student. You may decide to distribute all pages at the start of students' work, or provide pages individually as students work through the parts of the task.

- Gather works by James Masao to share with students.

  - *From A Three-Cornered World: New and Selected Poems* (University of Washington Press, 1997)

  - *After the Long Train: Poems* (Bieler Press, Minneapolis, 1986)

  - *Crossing the Phantom River* (Graywolf Press, 1978)

  - *Journal of the Sun* (Copper Canyon Press, 1974)

- Collect a selection of black-and-white photographs for students to choose from. Recommended sources are: *Life* magazine (1940–1970); literary arts journals such as *The Sun*; and photographs of the Great Depression.

- Collect black-and-white photographs with human or animal subjects—at least one for each student; copies will be taken home.

- Arrange student access to materials for making a colored drawing, to free verse poetry, and to computers for word processing (optional).

Vocabulary

- free verse

- photo poem

- story truth

Time frame: Plan about three weeks to have students answer all questions, write their drafts, receive feedback, and produce the final drafts of their poems.

Task modifications: If a modification is made to any part of the task, the modification must be requested using the C-PAS online system.

NOTES

Work Products shown in the Student Task Information are required and may not be modified. See the Student Task Information for the complete assignment.

 Problem Solving

Understanding, Hypothesizing, and Strategizing

Engage students in the following activity, explaining that it is an introduction to a task they will be undertaking. Provide these instructions:

- Make a list of the items in your bedroom.

- Flesh out the list with descriptive detail about the items in your room. Describe the color, shape, position in the room, or comparison with something else (simile or metaphor), as though you were describing your room to a blind person.

- Use your list to write a descriptive paragraph written solely in the third person.

- Turn in the description, unsigned.

- Take another student's description, at random, and reproduce in a colored drawing the "picture in words" that you received.

- Turn in the drawing, which will be displayed with others' drawings.

- Look over the drawings and find the one that depicts your room. If the description as written was accurate, exact, and detailed, this should be easy!

- Discuss as a class the elements of descriptive writing that help the reader visualize a person, event, or scene.

With the class, read the Introduction in the student task information. Explain that like journalists and news reporters, students will not only be describing exactly what they have seen in a photograph, but will also be communicating a message. Emphasize that this is an opportunity to both capture the "truth" and be creative.

Read to the class several poems by James Masao. You might read each poem several times.

To further help students understand the task, select an art or historical photograph that captures a moment in the life of its subject. Ask the students to work in groups and list:

- The setting and details of the photograph: What they "know" about the subject of the photograph
- What they do not know about the subject of the photograph
- Questions they would need to ask the subject or the photographer in order to gain a full understanding of the scene and the life of the subject
- Plausible answers to these questions with the goal of lending depth, color, and plot to create a more complete portrait and a story truth

Use the groups' notes to create a class model poem. Focus on:
- Description
- Order of details
- Filling in the narrative
- Condensing narrative detail into the concise wording of free verse

Also discuss with students:
- Similes: a comparison using *like* or *as*
- Metaphor: a comparison without the use of *like* or *as*

Now students write a definition of free verse poetry to confirm their understanding of the topic. Check students' definitions and discuss any significant misunderstandings with the class.

Hypothesizing and Strategizing

Students select from the provided photographs one to use, taking a copy to keep. They review their photographs and begin thinking about what information they will include in their photo poems. They list some preliminary ideas about the kinds of information they will contain.

Students then list questions about their photographs, including questions they will need to answer in order to describe the photo as is, and "stretch" questions, which are questions they will ask themselves in order to further develop the story truth.

Interpretation

Integrating, Analyzing, and Synthesizing

- Students list important details about what they actually see in the photograph. These are details that give the student information about the "story" that is depicted. They organize these details in a way that allows them to write comments about the details during their analysis.

- Students next analyze the photo by describing the meaning of each detail they identified from the photograph to give the reader an impression of what they "know" from the photo. This is the beginning of the story truth. Although students are encouraged to be creative, it should be clear that their descriptions are written in a way that allows a person who is reading them to begin mentally recreating the photograph.

- Students begin to list questions about the things they do not know based on the photograph (*for example,* Does she have a family? Where does she live? What will she do next? Where does she go in the winter?). They can use the "stretch" questions from the Problem Solving section as a starting point for this list.

- Finally, students review all of their details and explanations and write a paragraph that synthesizes their thoughts on what is happening inside and outside of the photograph. They describe the most important details and come to some conclusions about the story truth.

Reasoning

Constructing, Organizing, and Critiquing

Now, students begin constructing the story truth that they will write about in their poems. They will likely first need to review their notes and determine an organizational strategy to use in the poem. *For example:* Do they want to write their poem about the past, present, or future of the character? Would they rather carefully describe the moment in time depicted in the photograph? Do they want to develop their character within the poem?

Students will likely have identified more details than they can describe in a 10- to 14-line poem, so they next make choices about which details to include.

Students draft their poems. Encourage them to write freely and include rich details about the story they are trying to tell. Students should also remember that narrative and poetry forms are different. They should try to capture the style of poetry while still clearly depicting the story truth.

The next step is peer editing. This will work best if both partners have a copy of each other's poems. The student pairs carry out a four-part process:

- Partners take turns reading their own poems aloud.

- Partners share the exact words they like in each other's poems orally or by highlighting the words or phrases that most bring the photo poem to life.

- Partners share their thoughts about the poem—positively and what does not seem complete or clear.

- Partners frame a question of their own that may need to be answered within the poem.

Students revise their poems and re-read them to their partners.

 Precision/Accuracy

Checking, Completing, and Presenting

Final drafts are due. In a single packet for scoring, students turn in all work products indicated on the Assessment Checklist.

After final drafts are turned in, students should have a second copy of the poem in order to complete a class reading of his or her poem. Students arrange their seats in rows or in a circle and listen as each student "performs" his or her poem.

OVERVIEW FOR STUDENTS

Description: What if a photograph could talk? What if you could interview the photograph's subject(s)? How would you introduce your subjects to an audience? How would you describe your subjects? And what questions would you ask them? You might consider the basic W's: who, what, where, when, and why. What else would you want to know about your subject?

Final product: You will compose a "photo poem" from a black-and-white photograph. Your poem will be concise and extremely detailed. If a reader were to draw a depiction of your poem, it would clearly match the photograph.

Key cognitive strategies: You will use the following Key Cognitive Strategies as you work. Each Key Cognitive Strategy includes three aspects, described here.

Problem Solving

- Understanding what is being asked
- Hypothesizing about potential answers
- Strategizing about how to address the question

Interpretation

- Integrating information to prepare for analysis
- Analyzing information to determine key points and meanings
- Synthesizing by making connections and drawing conclusions

Reasoning

- Constructing a line of reasoning and supporting it with evidence
- Organizing the line of reasoning in a way that makes sense
- Critiquing the line of reasoning to improve it

Precision/Accuracy

- Checking work for errors
- Completing all assigned parts of the task
- Presenting the final draft appropriately

Directions: Complete the work products assigned. Keep all of your work products in a folder that you will hand in with your final product.

Part 1: Problem Solving

In this part, you will develop your understanding of photo poetry and think about how you might approach composing a photo poem.

Understanding, Hypothesizing, Strategizing

Work product: Responses to questions.

Your teacher will introduce this task with a short activity and then share a few poems by James Masao. Select a black-and-white photograph that contains at least one human and/or animal subject. Study it, without writing, for five minutes and then write your responses to these questions:

1. What do you think your photo poem will include? What kinds of information will it contain?

2. List some questions that you will need to answer in order to describe the photo as it is.

3. List some stretch questions that you will have to ask yourself to create the story truth.

4. Finally, explain why you selected this photo.

 Part 2: Interpretation

In this part of the task, you will interpret the photograph you chose.

Integrating, Analyzing, Synthesizing

Work product: Responses to questions.

Independent work: To begin creating a story truth, think about the following questions. Record your thoughts.

1. What do you actually see in the photo? List some important details.

2. As a poet, what do you "know" from the photo based on the details you listed, even if it is not visible? This is the beginning of your story truth.

3. Write some questions about the details that you do not know from the photo. *For example:* Does she have a family? Where does she live? What will she do next? Where does she go in the winter? Use your stretch questions from the Problem Solving section as a starting point.

4. Answer the questions you listed with story truth. *For example:* "Sun shines through the branches of a single tree. A young girl wears a torn, white, oversized sweater. Her eyes are large and heavily lashed."

5. What might the photographer actually see outside the frame of the photo? *For example:* "Behind her a sea of cotton plants waves in the hot wind."

6. What might the photographer know about the subject that is not apparent by looking at the photo? *For example:* "The girl's fingers are cut and her palms are raw."

7. What might you, as a poet, know about the events preceding or following the photo? *For example:* "That morning she learned the truth about the scales that weigh the raw cotton."

8. What are your overall thoughts about what is happening inside and outside of the photo? What do all of your observations make you think about the photograph and the subject within it?

 Part 3: Reasoning

In this part of the task, you will compose your photo poem

Critiquing

Work product: Rough draft poem

Independent work: Start to construct your poem. Here are some questions to consider:

- In relation to the photograph, do you want to describe the past, then the present, and move to the proposed future?

- Do you want to tell the story of the character or the main subject caught in this moment?

- Are you going to have your poem move through time or be purely descriptive?

- Do you want to indicate that the character is "stuck" and wants to move on physically or mentally?

- Once you have decided on a direction for your poem, you will need to choose the best evidence from the photo to support your story. You will likely need to "impeach" some evidence that you collected in the Interpretation section so that you only include the best information in your poem. You might also find that some necessary pieces of information are missing from your analysis and that you need to add your own details that fit with the story. *For example:* "The girl has never felt silken cloth, soft woven wool, or the petals of a rose. All she has ever known: coarse muslin, the fluff of raw cotton, and the roots of potatoes."

- In free form, compose your poem without worrying about editing along the way. Let your mind flow with the words of description and the story that you are trying to tell.

- Remember that there is a difference between narrative and poetry form. Try to stick to a 10–14-line poem and use the following questions to guide your review of your draft:
- Have you created a visual portrait in words?
- Is the wording clear, descriptive, and concise, so that a reader could reproduce your poem in a visual drawing?
- Does your poem capture a moment of truth greater than its parts?
- Does your poem begin with a descriptive first line that wins your reader's attention and then stimulates your reader to keep reading?
- Do your descriptions create a clear visual portrait in words?
- Does your last line hint of future actions, ask a probing question, or tie the reader back to the poem's beginning—or all of these?

Critiquing

Work product: Record of peer review

- Now exchange your poem with a partner and follow this four-part review process. Record the feedback you receive.
- Partners take turns reading their own poems aloud.
- Partners share the exact words they like in each other's poems orally or by highlighting the words or phrases that most bring the photo poem to life.
- Partners share positive feedback and also anything that does not seem complete or clear.
- Partners frame a question of their own that may need to be answered within the poem.

Independent work: Make revisions to your poem based on peer feedback. Submit it for teacher review and comment.

Constructing, Organizing, Critiquing

Work product: Final draft poem

Independent work: Complete your final draft poem, revising based upon appropriate feedback and your own evaluations.

Part 4: Precision/Accuracy

Before turning in your poem, check for errors in mechanics and citations. Use the checklist below. Make sure you present your final product appropriately for the assignment. Be ready to submit all of the required work products.

Checking, Completing, Presenting

Work product: Final draft poem
Independent work: Before submitting your poem, use the checklist below.

Checking

- Grammar, punctuation, and spelling errors

Completing

- Completion of all work products on the Assessment Checklist
- Removal of unnecessary information in the final product

Presenting

- Proper formatting
- Precise language use, appropriate to your audience
- Appropriate labeling of all work products
- Correct sentence structure and agreement

Assessment Checklist

A completed task includes all of the work products shown following.

KCS	Aspect	Work Product	Due	Complete
	Understanding Hypothesizing Strategizing	Responses to problem-solving questions 1–4		
	Integrating Analyzing Synthesizing	Responses to interpretation questions 1–8		
	Critiquing	Rough draft poem Recorded feedback		
	Constructing Organizing Critiquing	Final draft poem		
	Checking Completing Presenting	Final draft poem		

Appendix B
Example Items from the School Diagnostic

The College Ready School Diagnostic is designed to yield information on all four dimensions of the college readiness model presented in this book: key cognitive strategies, key content knowledge, academic behaviors, and college knowledge. The diagnostic enables schools to identify the areas in which they already excel and offers approaches for incorporating strategies not yet utilized. Administrators, counselors, teachers, and students in a school complete the diagnostic, yielding a comprehensive profile of college readiness that is used both as a baseline against which improvements can be measured and a framework for recommending specific actions that can be taken to improve the school.

 For more information on the methods and strategies presented in this chapter, go to http://CollegeCareerReady.org.

EXAMPLE ITEMS TAKEN FROM THE SCHOOL DIAGNOSTIC
Administrator and Counselor
Academic Behaviors

- Teachers or staff use a common syllabus format across courses in core content areas.
- Our school: Provides agendas, planners, or electronic calendars to students.

Contextual Skills

- Students visit a college campus as part of an advisory or other school-sponsored activity.

- Our school: Provides parents access to direct assistance when filling out the FAFSA.

Teacher
Academic Behaviors

- Students create to-do lists to prioritize and keep track of tasks.
- Students utilize multiple note taking techniques.

Contextual Skills

- Students receive written or electronic information about financial aid.
- Students submit a college application as a graduation or course requirement.

Key Cognitive Strategies

- Students turn in multiple drafts of major writing assignments.
- Students construct a thesis statement in order to answer a research question.

Key Content Knowledge

- Students have been exposed to: verb tenses and their correct uses.
- Students have been exposed to: the distinction between kinetic and potential energy.

Student
Academic Behaviors

- I use unstructured time during the school day to complete homework.
- I review notes to prepare for tests or exams.

Contextual Skills

- I have visited a college campus.
- I am provided financial aid information on an annual basis.

Key Cognitive Strategies

- I obtain information from a variety of sources to complete assignments.
- I proofread my papers to find and correct grammar and spelling errors.

Key Content Knowledge

- I have been given the opportunity to learn at my school: a variety of strategies for understanding the origins and meanings of new words.

- I have been given the opportunity to learn at my school: the basic shape of a quadratic equation.

Appendix C
Resource List

This appendix lists the types of resources available on the Educational Policy Improvement Center (EPIC) Web site. This is not a definitive list. Additional resources are available at www.CollegeCareerReady.com.

Key Cognitive Strategies Resources

- *Association for Supervision and Curriculum Development (ASCD).* ASCD has worked with a number of education experts to develop professional development programs, online courses, and publications to help educators learn, teach, and lead. Differentiated instruction, understanding by design, and what works in schools are the focus of much of its professional development offerings. http://www.ascd.org.

- *Habits of Mind series.* Edited by Arthur L. Costa and Bena Kallick, the Habits of Mind series was written to help students, adults, and organizations cultivate the habits of mind that will help them solve problems in school and other areas of life. http://www.habits-of-mind.net/.

- *Purdue Online Writing Lab (OWL).* This Web site offers over two hundred free resources for writing and teaching writing, research, grammar and mechanics, style guides, English as a Second Language, and job search and professional writing, including materials specifically designed for instructors and teachers of seventh to twelfth grades. http://owl.english.purdue.edu/.

- *SpringBoard.* College Board's SpringBoard program is a comprehensive instructional program in English/language arts and mathematics that reflects powerful research-based understandings about how people learn. http://professionals.collegeboard.com/k-12/prepare/springboard.

Key Content Knowledge Resources

- *ACT College Readiness Standards.* The ACT College Readiness Standards cover English, mathematics, reading, and science and are designed for use with EXPLORE, PLAN, and ACT student test scores. http://www.act.org/standard/infoserv.html.

- *American Diploma Project K–12 Benchmarks.* The American Diploma Project's K–12 benchmarks articulate the skills students need to have acquired by the end of high school in order to succeed in college and careers. http://www.achieve.org/K-12Benchmarks.

- *College Board Standards for College Success.* These content standards are for middle school and high school English, math, and statistics, leading to preparation for Advanced Placement or college-level work. http://professionals.collegeboard.com/k-12/standards.

- *Core-Plus Mathematics Project.* Core-Plus Mathematics is a four-year math curriculum from the National Science Foundation that features interwoven strands of math subjects and focuses on habits of mind and connections between subjects. http://www.wmich.edu/cpmp/.

- *Math Forum.* A Web site by Drexel University for improving math learning, teaching, and communication. Resources include problems and puzzles, online mentoring, research, team problem solving, collaborations, and professional development. http://mathforum.org/.

- *National Science Education Standards.* These standards are designed to foster scientific inquiry and literacy in students and outline the knowledge and skills students should develop at each grade level. http://www.nap.edu/openbook.php?record_id=4962&page=R1.

- *Principles and Standards for School Mathematics.* The *Principles and Standards* were designed by a commission appointed by the National Council for Teachers of Mathematics to provide guidance for educational decision makers and describe the mathematical understanding, knowledge, and skills that students should acquire from prekindergarten through the twelfth grade. http://www.nctm.org/standards/.

- *Standards for Foreign Language Learning.* These standards describe the best instructional practice and should be used in conjunction with state and local

standards and curricular frameworks. http://www.actfl.org/i4a/pages/index
.cfm?pageid=3324.

- *Texas College and Career Readiness Standards.* The College and Career Readiness Standards in English/language arts, mathematics, science, and social studies were developed by subject matter experts and are designed to prepare high school students for entry-level college course work. http://www .thecb.state.tx.us/collegereadiness/TCRS.cfm.

Academic Behaviors Resources

- *Cornell Study Skills Resources.* Cornell's Learning Strategies Center has several study skills resources available for download, including a template and directions for using the Cornell note-taking system. Also included are resources related to time management, reading and learning from lecture, studying and taking exams, and stress management. http://lsc.sas.cornell.edu/.

- *Study Guides and Strategies.* A Web site with extensive study skills resources, all available for copying, adaptation, and distribution in print format (in noncommercial settings). http://www.studygs.net/.

- *Learning and Study Strategies Inventory (LASSI).* An assessment to measure students' awareness about and use of learning and study strategies related to skill, will, and self-regulation components of strategic learning. http://www .hhpublishing.com/_assessments/LASSI/.

Contextual Skills and Awareness (College Knowledge)

- *American School Counselor Association Standards for School Counseling Programs.* These standards for school counseling programs encompass academic, career, and social goals for students. http://www.schoolcounselor.org/.

- *College.gov.* A Web site produced by the U.S. Department of Education that provides high school students information about going to college, including why to go to college, how to select a school and apply, and how to pay for college. http://www.college.gov/wps/portal.

- *KnowHow2Go.* A college planning Web site provided by the American Council on Education and Lumina Foundation for Education for middle and high school students, and mentors. http://www.knowhow2go.org/.

- *National College Access Program Directory.* A searchable directory of college access programs for students, parents, counselors, and researchers. http://www.collegeaccess.org/accessprogramdirectory/.

Other Resources

- *Advancement Via Individual Determination (AVID).* AVID is a college readiness program currently offered in more than fifteen hundred middle and high schools. Research indicates that it can raise student achievement by creating a culture of high expectations and support for students to meet those expectations. http://www.avidonline.org/.

- *Talent Development High Schools Program.* A comprehensive reform model from the Center for Social Organization of Schools targeted at large high schools. It outlines organizational and management changes, curricular and instructional innovations, and methods for enhancing parent and community involvement. http://web.jhu.edu/CSOS/tdhs/index.html.

- *College Board MyRoad.* A college and career planning resource offering validated personality assessments and suggested careers and majors, tips for postsecondary success, and other resources for college and career planning. https://myroad.collegeboard.com/myroad/navigator.jsp.

- *Naviance.* Specializes in K–12 educational resource products designed to support students in planning and preparing for graduation, college, and career. The Naviance suite includes test preparation, learning inventories, community surveys, and data management tools, among other applications. http://www.naviance.com/.

Index

College Knowledge

What It Really Takes for Students to Succeed and
What We Can Do to Get Them Ready

By: **David T. Conley**

ISBN 978-0-7879-9675-8
Paperback | 384 pp.

"The most comprehensive and detailed overview ever published on how to improve secondary school preparation and success for college. Research based insights, practices, and policies for all audiences trying to better connect secondary schools and colleges. Both K-12 and higher education must work together in fundamentally new ways to implement Conley's vision."
—Michael Kirst, professor of education and business administration, Stanford University

"College Knowledge *should be required reading for all secondary education majors and graduate students who will work with high school students preparing for college. Officials responsible for high school reform in State Departments of Education will also find* College Knowledge *valuable."*
—Teachers College Record

Based on an extensive database of information about high school students in all 50 states, along with interviews from more than 400 university faculty and staff, this book lays out the basic knowledge and skills college-bound students will need in English, math, natural sciences, social sciences, second languages, and the arts. Its guidelines cover important study skills and knowledge in each subject area. Parents and educators will find this book to be an indispensable guide to the fundamental knowledge and habits of mind their college-bound kids need to develop before they leave high school.